THE TYRANNY OF HISTORY

W. J. F. JENNER

THE TYRANNY OF HISTORY

THE ROOTS OF CHINA'S CRISIS

ALLEN LANE
THE PENGUIN PRESS

ALLEN LANE
THE PENGUIN PRESS

Published by the Penguin Group
Penguin Books Ltd, 27 Wrights Lane, London W8 5TZ, England
Penguin Books USA Inc., 375 Hudson Street, New York, New York 10014, USA
Penguin Books Australia Ltd, Ringwood, Victoria, Australia
Penguin Books Canada Ltd, 10 Alcorn Avenue, Toronto, Ontario, Canada M4V 3B2
Penguin Books (NZ) Ltd, 182–190 Wairau Road, Auckland 10, New Zealand

Penguin Books Ltd, Registered Offices: Harmondsworth, Middlesex, England

First published 1992
1 3 5 7 9 10 8 6 4 2

Set in 12/14pt Lasercomp Bembo
Printed in England by
Butler & Tanner Ltd, Frome and London

A CIP catalogue record for this book is available from the British Library

ISBN 0–713–99060–0

CONTENTS

===

Principal Chinese Dynasties

c. 8000 – *c.* 2000 BC)	(Neolithic
c. 2000 – *c.* 1500	Xia
c. 1500 – *c.* 1066	Shang
c. 1066 – 221	Zhou
c. 450 – 221	Warring States
221 – 206	Qin
206 – AD 23	Western Han
25 – 220	Eastern Han
220 – 280	Three Kingdoms
220 – 265	Cao Wei
265 – 316	Western Jin
317 – 420	Eastern Jin
420 – 581	Northern and Southern Dynasties
386 – 534	Northern Wei
581 – 618	Sui
618 – 907	Tang
907 – 960	Five Dynasties
960 – 1127	Northern Song
1127 – 1279	Southern Song
1115 – 1234	Jin (Jurchen)
1279 – 1368	Yuan (Mongol)
1368 – 1644	Ming
1644 – 1912	Qing (Manchu)
1912 – 1949	Republic
1949 –	People's Republic

CHINA
1992

KAZAKHSTAN

KIRGIZIYA

MONGOLIA

Xinjiang
(Turkestan)

Gansu

Qinghai

Tibet

Sichuan

NEPAL

●SHIGATSE
●LHASA

BHUTAN

INDIA

BANGLADESH

Yunnan

BURMA

VIETNAM

Bay
of Bengal

LAOS

THAILAND

SIBERIA

Heilongjiang

Inner Mongolia

Jilin

Yellow River

CHENGDE ●

SHENYANG ●

Liaoning

Sea
of
Japan

PEKING ●

KOREA

Tianjin
Hebei

Ningxia

Shanxi

Shandong

QINGDAO ●

Yellow
Sea

JAPAN

Shaanxi

X'IAN ●

KAIFENG ●

Henan

Anhui

Jiangsu

ZHENJIANG ●

NANJING ●

SHANGHAI ●

Yangzi River

Hubei

SUZHOU ●

HANGZHOU ●

Zhejiang

East
China
Sea

Hunan

Jiangxi

Guizhou

Fujian

N

Guangxi

Guandong

CANTON ●

TAIWAN

HONG KONG ●

500 KMS

400 MILES

South China
Sea

Hainan

Land over 5200 ft.

A Note to the Reader

This book deals briefly with vast issues too urgent to be left till they can be viewed with the wisdom of hindsight. China's general crisis affects not only the Chinese fifth of humanity but everyone else as well, and it needs to be thought about if the developments of the next ten or twenty years are not to take us completely by surprise. In it I offer my views, the subjective opinions of a fifty-year-old middle-class Englishman, as nothing more than speculative generalizations in the hope of enlivening the discussion. Footnotes, with their implied claim that this is a book written within the conventions of the academic game, would have given a misleading impression and have generally been omitted.

It is virtually impossible to think a thought about what we call China that has not been expressed before, when talking either about China or about somewhere else, and I make no claims for originality in what follows. There is no way in which the mental debts of a lifetime can be acknowledged, and I have not tried. Some of the historical issues touched on here will be dealt with less summarily in a much larger book that will follow later.

Although I have been much involved with China and Chinese matters all my adult life, I cannot but have an outsider's view. If I make comparisons with Europe, it is because I am a European, and I have always found comparisons between the two ends of Eurasia a means of seeing both more clearly. It is not because I take Europe as the norm by which to judge China.

In writing a book that takes a bleak view of the present roles of the high cultural values and political traditions of China's tyrannical past I am aware of the risk that my position may be misrepresented as 'anti-Chinese'. This is not a book about what is right with China. In these pages I have not written about all that is attractive and good about people and life in China or attempted to explain the country's irresistible appeal, or paraded my admiration and affection. All these are topics on which I could have written, but they are not relevant to this book's arguments and are therefore omitted. It is because I care about the future of the country and its peoples that I raise uncomfortable issues that have to be considered. It may well be that some of my generalizations are too sweeping, that some of my judgements are one-sided and that I dwell too much on the problems and not enough on encouraging aspects of contemporary China. I certainly do not write from a position of superiority, and, were it relevant, I could say plenty about the shortcomings of my native England or the Australia where I now live.

Nor do I wish to create the impression that the end of ancient tyrannies would be the end of the many living elements in Chinese cultures. While a certain conception of 'China' may well come to an end in the next few decades, the post-imperial Chinese world could, with luck, be an improvement on the present dictatorship. A crisis is a point at which choices have to be made and from which things can get better as well as worse.

Once upon a time, when the United States led the West in armed hostility to China, it seemed right to defend a country that was misrepresented and demonized. In recent years such a position has felt uncomfortable, even condescending. My present opinion is that it is much better to express something of the despair I feel about present predicaments and my hopes about escape from them than it would be to observe a tactful silence. If time proves my pessimism to be unjustified, so much the better.

A warning to readers, a *caveat lector*, is that none of my arguments should be accepted unless it rings true when tested against your experience of China at first or second hand. Even if an argument does seem plausible, it should be treated only as a suggestion, as a possible way of looking at things.

What follows grew from a talk at the University of Adelaide

early in 1989 and from the four Sir Douglas Robb Lectures that the University of Auckland invited me to give later that year. Other parts were first aired at my old department in the University of Leeds and for my present employer, the Australian National University. Here Pam Wesley-Smith has typed and retyped with endless patience, while Geremie Barmé has lent essential encouragement and insights and my wife Kaining has provided the support without which it would never have been completed. My editor, Ravi Mirchandani, has removed many infelicities of expression. None of them should be held in any way responsible for the views that follow.

W. J. F. J.
June 1991

1. TYRANNIES OF HISTORY

The state, people and culture known in English as China are in a profound general crisis that goes much deeper than the problems of a moribund communist dictatorship. It is a general one to which everything from the remorseless increase of population to the influence of an archaic writing system contributes. The very future of China as a unitary state is in question as the only other great nineteenth-century empire, the Russian one, crumbles. The tradition of Chinese high culture that once led the world has long been in terminal decline. What ties all aspects of the crisis together is the past: what has happened in the past and the past as perceived. Today's objective problems, like the subjective ones that make their solution even more difficult than they would be otherwise, were created under two thousand years of bureaucratic absolutism. The history of tyranny is matched by a tyranny of history: perceptions and thought patterns from the past bind living minds.

The siege and massacre of Peking in 1989 and the whole range of policies that have followed them, policies evidently aimed at undoing many of the apparent changes of the last decade, raise more insistently than ever the dreary possibility that China is caught in a prison from which there is no obvious escape, a prison continually improved over thousands of years, a prison of history – a prison of history both as a literary creation and as the accumulated consequences of the past. The essence of this prison is that there is no easy escape from pasts and the ways they are perceived, which restrict the present to a greater extent than most other cultures of the world are restricted by their pasts.

The prison effect is caused by the very triumphs of earlier Chinese cultures, by the richness and magnificence of China's pasts and by the extraordinary achievements of the peoples living in what is now China. China's present and future problems illustrate a phenomenon that can quite often be observed in human society: the more success-ful, complete and self-sufficient any social or cultural system is at one stage of its development, the harder it is to escape from that system. It is central to the thesis of these pages that it is precisely the achievements of the Chinese past that have created the present difficulties. The prison could just as well be described as a palace, a palace as vast and magnificent as any in human history. But palaces can also be prisons, especially if they are surrounded by high, windowless walls with very few gates in them.

Like any other state, China is a figment of the imagination, of many imaginations. There is no inherent necessity determining the borders of the present Chinese state. Those borders are more the product of the relative strengths of empires, Manchu and European, in the late nineteenth and early twentieth centuries than of anything else. What we mean when we say China and Chinese, or the equivalent words in other languages, is rarely closely defined, even when referring to the present. When talking about thousands of years the need to be more precise than we usually are becomes even greater. Is the history of China the history of all and only the people who since the last glaciation have lived in the territories now ruled or claimed by Peking? Such an approach has an obvious appeal to officials who want their multinational empire, which holds most of the territory of the Qing empire in its final form, to be seen as having by inheritance the right to rule all peoples within its frontiers. Or is it the history of the peoples and states that have seen themselves as belonging to a culturally defined set of traditions that can be called Chinese? This set of traditions links culture and politics, characterizing them through a system of writing. The distinction between these two ways of defining the scope of Chinese history is one that is often fudged. Those who claim to take the former approach often in reality adopt the latter one.

It is almost impossible for a Han Chinese historian to treat of struggles between Han Chinese and other ethnic groups without seeing the former as 'us' and the others as 'them'. Few contemporary Chinese would regard the wars between the Han and the Xiongnu (who may have been the ancestors of the Huns) or the Qiang (proto-Tibetans) as Chinese civil conflicts in which 'we' were divided. Endlessly retold stories about how the Song general Yue Fei fought the Jurchen (Jin) and raised the slogan 'Return our rivers and mountains' do not give the impression of an ethnically neutral struggle between rival groups of Chinese. Yet in all three cases the 'aggressors' lived wholly or mainly within the present frontiers of the Chinese empire.

Non-Hans win approval to the extent that they allow themselves to be drawn into the Han tradition. They could easily be assimilated on paper, even when they were not in reality, by the homogenizing device of writing their names in Chinese characters and in a Chinese form. It is very hard to imagine historical writing being published in China that saw Han Chinese expansionism as genocidal, though discrimination against Hans, when it does succeed, is invariably shown as a bad thing. When official mainland historians treat of national clashes in which relatively less privileged non-Hans fight – or fight back – against Hans they nearly always have to show the rebels as opposing not an ethnic group or a culture but an exploiting class. History as it is written in China makes it very hard even to consider the possibility that significant numbers of the subjects of Chinese regimes have refused to think of themselves as Chinese or accept the legitimacy of any Chinese rule over them and their territory.

From Chinese accounts, contemporary or modern, one would never imagine of the Muslim rebellion in Yunnan in the third quarter of the nineteenth century that one of its leaders wrote to Queen Victoria requesting, in language rich in purely Chinese references to uprisings and sage rulers of antiquity, to be allowed to become a subject of hers.★ It is much harder to find indications in

★ I would never have believed this if I had not been shown a photograph of the letter by Mr Joe Ford who found it in, as I remember, India Office archives in London.

Chinese sources of the full diversity, ethnic and other, of the 'China' of any period than it is for a European country, even though the European country will be smaller and, I would guess, less heterogeneous.

This unified history has also been a powerful force for a kind of ethnic assertion. For most of the last 1,700 years of the dynastic period much or all of the Han Chinese lands were under the rule of non-Chinese regimes ruling as tiny minorities over the conquered Hans. For the Han Chinese this was a humiliation right up to the fall of the Manchu dynasty. The Manchus had constantly reminded the Han Chinese of their ethnic subjection by forcing them to wear Manchu instead of Chinese clothes and making men shave the front of their heads as a mark of their slavery. The accumulated shame and resentment of many centuries gave the revolution of 1911 a violently racist aspect, with massacres in the Manchu quarters of some cities. Yet, even while hating the Manchus, the revolutionaries wanted to be their heirs, and not just in the Chinese parts of the empire. The attempts of other subject peoples of the Manchus, such as Mongols and Tibetans, throughout the twentieth century to assert their independence have been as far as possible ignored by official history and, when not ignored, abused. Conquerors such as the Mongols of the thirteenth century and the Manchus of the seventeenth have been turned by historical labelling into Chinese dynasties, so that their empires become Chinese empires and their territories sacred and inviolable. Thus history as cultural invention has helped to keep today's Han Chinese in the trap of imperialism, the imperialism of the mind that finds self-affirmation in the subjection of others.

Nowhere has the homogenizing effect been more successful than in creating the impression that the Han Chinese themselves are a single ethnic group, despite the mutual incomprehensibility of many of their mother tongues and the ancient hostility between such Han Chinese nationalities as the Cantonese and the Hakkas. While the occupation of Tibet and East Turkestan has failed to persuade most Tibetans and Uighurs that they are Chinese, so that they can be kept in the empire only by force, historical myth-making has so far been remarkably effective not just in inventing a single Han Chinese ethnicity but also – and this is a far bigger triumph – in winning acceptance for it.

The ethnic issue is only one example of the extremely effective homogenizing effect of history as it has long been written in China. Chinese high culture generally, and the Chinese written language in particular, have had an amazing power to standardize or to play down quirkiness, unorthodoxy and difference. The culture is not disposed to accept the existence of rival, incompatible views of the world, society and politics; it is much more strongly inclined to judge and classify by a single set of values that is the only possible one.

The main historiographical tradition has been one of impersonally written history compiled by officials through processes that were essentially bureaucratic. The most influential histories were those compiled by central governments, generally dealing with a dynasty or dynasties immediately preceding them, in order to give both the present and the future a standardized, a 'correct', view of the rise and fall of past regimes. These histories would be written not from the unprocessed primary documents of the past regime in question but from the second- and even third-hand compilations, extracts and summaries of original documents compiled daily, and then at longer intervals, by the officials of the earlier regime. These primary compilers and editors were moved by conflicting bureaucratic interests. They wanted to keep an accurate and reliable record for future reference while at the same time minimizing the damage that could be done in future if too much dangerous raw information were left to be found by later investigators.

Chinese governments have, for at least 2,000 years, taken history much too seriously to allow the future to make its own unguided judgements about them. Thus it is that we have a remarkably well-organized published record, covering systematically the last two millennia, that rarely tells an outright lie but passes on the views of earlier bureaucrats as modified by later bureaucrats and deals mainly with matters of concern to the monarchy and to officialdom. Officials naturally find themselves, their rankings and their organizational structures interesting and important. They know the value of keeping reliable records of how problems facing central government have been handled or mishandled in the past. Things that are not seen as relevant to the state are more or less excluded, as is excessive detail about organizational matters, which would be appropriate for the specialists in a particular department of government but not for the generalists advising on the big policy decisions. History became the accumulation of administrative experience, and as the precedents were piled up they amounted to a formidable and effective resource. So it was that an eighteenth-century official handling, say, inner Asia could very easily draw on the essential aspects of policies from one or two thousand years earlier; and a late-nineteenth-century provincial governor faced with the capriciousness of the Yellow River would see it as natural and sensible to consult records of how the river had been handled as far back as the Tang dynasty.

Now, it is obvious enough that there could be enormous advantages to the state in having available such well-organized information about the best part of two thousand years on paper (and for a thousand in print), so that officials and potential officials were extremely well indoctrinated in the concerns of government and could get very quick access to that information. It is so easy for a Chinese or foreign historian today to get to officially processed, pre-digested information, reliable as far as it goes, that one is often tempted to go no further, especially when looking at issues or events earlier than recent centuries, for which other evidence can often be found only with efforts that are rarely worth making unless the question at issue is central to what one is investigating.

This accessibility has its price. Non-Chinese historians today who can view traditional historiography from outside the culture and from the mental world of the end of the twentieth century have to make a deliberate effort to avoid being seduced into accepting its judgements with only minor modifications and its choice of what the issues are. If we outsiders are so easily drawn into this admirably well-invented and restricted past, imagine how hard it must have been for any educated Chinese before the late nineteenth century to break out of this mental world. In addition, consider the way in which the Chinese language, especially its classical written version, disguises time. It is not that distinctions cannot be made between what is and what was but that – by contrast with Indo-European languages – the distinction does not have to be made. In English we have to commit ourselves as to whether someone is alive or dead when saying anything about him or her. It is painful to have to switch tenses when talking about someone close to us who has just died, when 'he is' becomes 'he was'. We cannot talk about the past without underlining its distance and difference from us with every verb. But this does not apply to Chinese, which can describe the situation of today, last year and two thousand years ago in the same linguistic forms. And because the Chinese writing code is not essentially phonetic, and the style for writing history changed little over two millennia, the records of the remote and the recent past look much the same. Even though some place-names and official titles in, for example, a biographical chapter of one of the standard histories of the Han dynasty would be different from those more immediately familiar to a nineteenth-century Chinese reader, there would, I believe, have been much less of a sense of remoteness than a nineteenth-century European would have felt in reading Plutarch or Livy in the original. Educated Chinese were encouraged to measure themselves against the standards of models that we would think of as belonging to the past, but that to them would have felt somehow timeless.

The culture encourages great awareness of historical events but very little sense of historical process over the long duration. The popular images of history, the huge corpus of stories that have been passed on, changed or invented in music drama, story-telling, ballads and other kinds of entertainment – including, for the literate few who can afford them, books – coexist timelessly. Events in operas and stories are nearly always set in an identified reign of an identified dynasty, but there is no essential difference between palaces, court-rooms and battlefields supposedly separated by hundreds or even thousands of years. Within a story or a cycle of stories the passage of time is something of which reader or audience is frequently reminded. A story can cover years, even generations. But in the popular cultures and the high culture of the Chinese before the twentieth century there is little sense of secular development or change, unless as a decline from imagined golden and silver ages of remote, pre-dynastic antiquity. Rather we get a sense of unending sets of variations on a few themes.

The general (but not universal) lack of a sense of change over the long duration, which could also be described as an illusion of timelessness, was strengthened by traditional methods of dating – an ever-repeated sixty-year cycle or a numbered year in a ruler's reign-period – that made it hard for anyone but a highly educated student of history to be aware of the many years that separated events that were more than a few decades apart. Before the introduction of European dating in the twentieth century – a convention still resisted by the rump government of the Republic on Taiwan, which continues to date years since the founding of their state in 1912 – someone who wanted to compare the lengths of the Song and Ming dynasties would have had to do complicated sums. To compare different historical periods as a whole, except in moral terms, was unusual; comparisons between specific variables across dynasties were common and depended on the assumption that the backgrounds to the 'good' or 'bad' emperors, generals or officials were much the same. Of course, there were some exceptional individuals who did have a real sense of long-term historical process, but that was in spite of, rather than because of, the traditional approach.

Another obstacle to a sense of history as a long-term process, other than a decline from ancient excellence that can never be matched, was the general tendency to think of the past as something in front of you, not behind you. This is in part a quirk of Chinese language, which talks of the past as in front of or before you, while the future is behind you. (English, curiously, will place one event before another but won't normally put the past in front of you unless in odd circumstances, as when some painful event appears before one's eyes.) The whole traditional culture encouraged one to face antiquity, to look towards the past, to inherit Confucius's sense of a world in decline from the high standards of the early years of the Zhou dynasty around 1000 BC and to assume that older generally meant better. Hence the pursuit of ancient and supposedly better styles of prose by Han Yu and other Tang-period writers, the attempts by painters of Yuan and Ming times to get back to the essence of how the Song masters had painted and the studied pastiches by calligraphers in the last few hundred years of the lettering of tomb inscriptions of the fifth and sixth centuries or of the lean, strong hand of Yan Zhenqing. Where the West has, in this century at least, called on creators to Make It New, China has tended until very recently to urge people to Make It Old. Although there have been innovations in every area, it is almost as if before the twentieth century they slipped in unnoticed until they had become established. *Ci* song lyrics of the ninth to thirteenth centuries, for example, managed to break away from the limits of traditional poetic rules only because these new forms started off as responses to the need for new words in Chinese to popular tunes from Western Asia. Once these new forms acquired recognition and status they too became set patterns to be fairly rigidly adhered to, even when the tunes for which they had originally been written were more or less forgotten. For *ci* poetry to be really respectable it had first to become archaic.

These are all examples from the arts, but they are symptomatic of a tendency that goes right across the culture: the rule that thou shalt commit no novelty, unless it can be hidden or else disguised as a reversion to something from the past that has since been lost. This backward-looking position (to use the assumptions of English) can be seen as late as the last years of the nineteenth century and the early part of this one, when, for example, Kang Youwei wraps his proposals for drastic reform in the language of reversion to a remote and imaginary past. Not even emperors were safe from comparisons with antiquity: none of them could even hope to rival the mythical Yao and Shun.

Just as in everyday life there is usually a backward-looking approach to family obligations – your duty to your parents to repay their efforts in rearing you takes precedence over your investment in your children, for which they in turn will take care of you – so in the life of the state and the culture there is no easy escape from the power of the past. The dynastic state both drew on this power, as when it imposed the syllabus of mind-numbing orthodoxy on which candidates for the public service were examined, and was itself quite strongly inhibited by it from looking for new ways of handling problems, not absolutely but sufficiently to make even necessary innovation much more difficult than it really needed to be.

The obstacles to thoroughgoing reforms were normally extremely effective except when a new regime was being put together after a period of destruction that made some new approaches essential. One of the most daunting disincentives was the overwhelmingly hostile treatment in bureaucratic histories of attempted innovation in the past. This meant that there were few respectable precedents for drastic change and little guidance in the historical record about how to carry out fundamental reforms with success. The consequence was that when an emperor was persuaded to undertake big changes he and his unorthodox advisers did not know how to go about it, which led to such failures as those of Wang Anshi in the eleventh century and of the 1898 reformers. Even the once revolutionary Communist Party has become the prisoner of its own history and finds it hard to undo some of the wilder measures of its early years in power.

Official history, be it Confucian or communist, naturally tends to perpetuate orthodox views, such as the notions that there can only be one legitimate government in the Chinese world at any one time and that moral judgements are central to historiography, which cannot properly be neutral on essential questions. Whoever controls the compiling of a history wins the right to decide who are the goodies and who the baddies. The legitimacy of governments is always worrying, particularly as almost every dynasty won power by methods that were, by strict Confucian standards, shady: hence the extreme sensitivity to anything that may show the founders of one's own dynasty as gangsters.

China's high culture has been for most of the last two and a half thousand years essentially this-worldly and has not usually had much

official concern for notions about immortal souls or reincarnation –
when Buddhism was powerful these were matters for the common
people in which gentlemen educated in the Confucian texts could
publicly admit only a mild interest. The historical record that would
be written in the future was the only real hope of immortality for
the powerful of the day. To leave a name that would be 'handed
down through ten thousand antiquities' yet to come was a clichéd
expression of the wish to be shown in a good light in future histories.
Just as the record of the past was an essential guide to how to deal
with the problems of today, so the records of one's own time yet
to be compiled, and their distribution of praise and blame, were
something so worrying that they might even influence present
actions. History thus plays a role comparable to that of religious
texts in other cultures. It is also the Last Judgment. The religion of
the Chinese ruling classes is the Chinese state, and it is through
history that the object of devotion is to be understood. The rulers
of dynastic China, like their present-day successors, did not have to
bother about what they would look like on television news or in
the next day's paper; but many of them cared what history would
say about them, just as European monarchs have worried about
whether their souls were heading for heaven or hell after death.
History thus held, and still holds, the present in its pincers. One jaw
is the record of the past; the other is the future record of the present.

These generalizations have been so sweeping that none of them
is quite reliable. We should also pay our respects to the extraordinary
talents of such historians as Sima Qian who, with his father, more
or less invented a form in which to compile a history of the Chinese
world up till the second century BC – a success so great that it
became a straitjacket for the next two millennia – or of Sima Guang,
whose chronicle covering the 1,362 years from 403 BC to AD
959 remains the most convenient and reliable guide to the *histoire
événementielle* of China in those centuries nine hundred years after
it was compiled and infinitely superior to anything dealing annal-
istically with any other part of the world over a period even a
quarter as long. There is not space here to discuss the emergence of
local histories; or the private, unofficial memoirs and histories that

are generally much better as sources of information for the last thousand years of imperial China than the sterile official compilations; or the cheeky way in which Li Zhi in the sixteenth century cocked many a snook at accepted views of the past. But when all the reservations are made and all the respects paid to the high professionalism of the best historians, it is painfully obvious that the historiographical traditions by which China was prepared to encounter the changed world of the nineteenth and twentieth centuries came close to blinding her to what was new. It took half a century for the message to sink in that the British pirates and drug smugglers on the Cantonese coast in the 1830s represented forces far more significant and dangerous than the little local nuisance they might have seemed to be at first. History served the Qing court well in showing how to deal with huge internal challenges to the established order, such as those mounted by Taipings, Nian, Muslims, Hmong ('Miao' to the Chinese) and others in the third quarter of the nineteenth century. They all fitted into ancient and accepted categories. But Europe did not, and it was more or less ignored, by contrast with the eagerness with which Europe gathered intelligence on China from the seventeenth century onwards.

The difficulty in understanding and evaluating cultures that were different from those familiar to Chinese history as it was written was one of the most important reasons why the Qing state was so ineffective in its response to European and American aggression. The evidence was available, but it simply could not be assimilated. By contrast, Japan, which until the 1850s had its doors more thoroughly closed against physical contact, had kept a corner of its mind open, so that it could adapt and become a modern imperialist power itself less than fifty years after its doors had been forced.

History as perceived has continued to exercise tyranny over minds in this century, though many things have changed. While the influence of modern Western approaches in the 1920s and 1930s never broke out of very limited circles – Chinese historians writing in China were relatively more isolated from the outside world than novelists, essayists and poets – two nineteenth-century European approaches did change ways in which the past was seen: archaeology and Marxism. They extended and modified established attitudes to the past instead of replacing them. Just when a few bold spirits were turning the fire of scholarly criticism on many of the accepted records of China's remote antiquity (and, in so doing, developing tendencies that had been developing since the eighteenth and nineteenth centuries) the past could be rehabilitated.

By recovering through excavation material evidence of a past that antedated reliable bureaucratic records Western-style archaeology made it possible scientifically to reclaim for Chinese history an antiquity and culture that rigorous questioning of the traditions handed down in written sources was threatening to shoot to pieces. When so much of the past was under fire, and when China was in danger of losing the comforting thought of many thousands of years of continuous culture, it was good to be able to point to the predecessors of the historically established stages of Chinese development that were being revealed by the spade. Even in the chaotic 1930s a hard-pressed National government found some funds for the archaeologists who were showing at Anyang that the Shang state of the second millennium BC was not just a myth and that its culture had a long local development behind it. By the 1950s the Communist Party government was eagerly using archaeology on a much larger scale not only to demonstrate the antiquity and originality of Chinese culture but also to show that in China also early human society had developed along the lines posited by Engels, on the strength of his reading of the American anthropologist Lewis Morgan, from primitive communism through patriarchy and the growth of private property to slave society. The archaeological evidence seemed to indicate that China fitted into a standard pattern of human development instead of being deviant and therefore inferior. It also pointed to a basically home-grown prehistory and could be used to argue that the essentials of early Chinese cultures had not been borrowed from abroad. These considerations were both so important that, long before the era of mass foreign tourism, large sums of public money were spent on turning sites such as that of the neolithic village at Banpo in the outskirts of Xi'an into huge museums that were virtually shrines.

How far twentieth-century perceptions of China's past have been influenced by Marx is a question not easily answered. To be sure, he has been invoked endlessly since the 1920s, but the approach to history that has been dominant since the 1930s owes more to Engels, Stalin and Mao than to Marx himself. This has meant that in the name of Marx the Stalinist model of the development of human society, from primitive communism through slave society to feudalism, has been imposed uncritically on China's past. We shall look later at the difficulties of tying the label 'feudal' to Chinese society and also at how historians found the sprouts of capitalism, the inevitable next stage of universal human social development, in pre-modern China – but in a form that could not reach fruition after the intervention of Britain and other foreign powers in the nineteenth century distorted the course of Chinese history, so that what followed was to be not full capitalism but instead a 'semi-colonial, semi-feudal' stage of development. Only the industrial proletariat and its vanguard, the Communist Party, could deliver China from that and lead China on to the next stage, socialism, which would eventually give way to the dream world of communism, a utopia so remote that it was not worth thinking seriously about. So the argument ran, and, though full of holes, it gave the Communist Party historical meaning.

This required model for interpreting history seemed exciting in the 1930s to some intellectuals. It offered a way of seeing Chinese history as a process that was getting somewhere; it purported to be both scientific and universal; and it was agreeably offensive both to Chinese political and intellectual authorities and to most foreigners. Simplified Marxism probably did more good than harm in its first decades by challenging traditional approaches, especially as it was in those days still obliged to produce evidence and arguments. But, once backed by the power of the state and the Communist Party, it soon turned this interpretation of history into an orthodoxy that was strictly enforced and took away nearly all possibility for exploring alternative approaches to the past. It co-existed with traditional historiography rather too well, reversing many moral judgements on people and policies of the past within traditional categories but sharing many old methods and concerns.

Maoist history drew on Marx, Engels and Stalin's ghost writer in its rhetoric but remained profoundly traditional underneath. It accepted with very few modifications the tradition of state-centred history, making only a few changes to the concepts of orthodox dynastic succession. While some groups and individuals were reclassified as good or bad instead of the reverse, this did not challenge the basic categorization of the unitary past. After all, reversal of verdicts was a long-established game within the tradition. Li Zhi had played it very well in the sixteenth century, and his works were widely reprinted in the early 1970s to be used in Mao's last attempt to impose his view of China's history, the almost incredible effort to present a tradition that advocated strong state power at the expense of society as a truly revolutionary one. The Mao era strengthened the moralizing approach to the past, changing only a few of the criteria of judgement. And because Mao himself was something of a Chinese history buff who had expressed his own views on some issues, historical discussions that went beyond arguments over goodies and baddies, or over when slave society became feudal, became well-nigh impossible. The exceptions tended to be periods that Mao was not much interested in, such as the third to sixth centuries A D.

Although people previously condemned by history as brigands or mutinous soldiers were now praised as the leaders of supposed peasant uprisings, while emperors and ruling classes were attacked in some respects, Maoism developed and propagated a modified traditional historiography, changing it only enough to enable it to continue and to flourish. Even the myth of progress made it easier to accept tradition: the past's shortcomings could thus be seen as something that a later and more enlightened age was remedying. The Communists took an overwhelmingly positive approach to powerful and expansionist emperors. The fascination with emperors extended even to the wretched nonentity Pu Yi, whose submission to the communists was deeply gratifying long before his story was used to make money for them. How appropriate it was that the rulers of the People's Republic gave such a high priority to the editing and publishing of the main official histories of the past, in attractive, low-priced and accessible editions, and that the symbol of their state was the main gate of the palace of the Ming and Qing autocrats. It is as if the French revolutionaries had taken Versailles as the symbol of their republic.

That these questions are of much more than academic significance is brought home to us by the present fate of a few genuinely critical approaches to China's history that emerged in the 1980s. The amateurishly made but hotly controversial television series *River Elegy* was screened in 1988 to the delight of all those who see China's past as a dead weight from which people need to be freed if China is to have a future. *River Elegy* blamed traditional values for most of China's present ills, taking the Yellow River as a symbol of much that was associated with inner, rural, walled-off China. Even when first shown, the series aroused much hostility from people who were appalled by what they saw as its negation of much of China's past. The end of the Mao era had more or less corresponded with the death of the radical aspects of Mao's traditional approach to history, so that there was now a growing divergence between those who were more conservative than ever about the past and those who wanted an intellectual and emotional break from it.

The division between traditionalists and smashers goes much further than the little world of historians. It can be found among writers and artists and, more important, among the country's rulers. It is, as the cliché has it, no coincidence that the same top people who are conservatives on attitudes to the supposed history of China tend also to be those most vindictive towards critics of the unworkable political, economic and social order left over from the Mao era. One of the messages of those who sent the troops into Peking was that China's imperial past was not to be maligned.

The iconoclastic approach to images of China's past was associated with the 'bourgeois liberalization' and development strategy that implied writing off much of inner China for the time being and trying for fast economic growth in the eastern third of China through a few-holds-barred primitive capitalist strategy with maximum involvement in the world economy. Not the least of the accusations made against Zhao Ziyang after his fall was that he had allowed *River Elegy* to be shown on television and suppressed publication of an article attacking it that saw print only after the People's Liberation Army washed Peking's streets in blood. When it did appear the piece by the pseudonymous Ji Jiayan was as vitriolic in its denunciation of *River Elegy* as Yao Wenyuan had been in his attacks on writers in the 1960s – and Yao had done something without precedent in human history by rising between 1966 and 1976 to the highest levels of power on the strength of unpleasant book reviews. If Yao was reading the *People's Daily* in his cell in 1989 he would have approved of Ji Jiayan's style and recognized the sort of ideological terrorism that in his day could leave its victims in gaol or even dead. The ferocity of the attack shows that *River Elegy* had hit its mark.

Since then critical thinking about China's pasts and the invention of them as history has faced serious difficulties. The defenders of today's imperial dream – a rich, prosperous, socialist and unified China under the effective control of a party centre that can keep at bay all the influences of the outside world as other communist dictatorships crumble and fall, nationalist passions rage and the economically viable parts of China have discovered the temptations of capitalism – need to hold the peoples of China in the grip of their stale vision of history. Although there is no longer any chance that China's present rulers will be able to rebuild the myth of their own historical inevitability, the grip of a much older tyranny of history will take a lot more loosening. China's ills go far deeper than in the particular dictatorship that is now approaching its end.

2. HISTORIES OF TYRANNY

===

Whatever happened to the Chinese state? It certainly has not softly and suddenly vanished away. In our time it has been conspicuously present, doubly so if we count the Communist Party apparatus as an extra state machine. The written history of twentieth-century China appears to be overwhelmingly the history of states falling, rising, contending for power and legitimacy, changing or failing to change. And in recent years we have been reminded over and over again of the power of the state, especially the repressive power that grows from the barrel of a gun.

However far back we go, the written records tell us mainly about regimes, rulers and officials. There can be no civilization on earth that has so long and full a record of state structures and official posts; there can be no other civilization to which the state itself has for so long been so central, not just as a practical necessity but as an institution worth any amount of attention in its own right, an institution that is almost sacred in its unquestionableness. Even at its most radical the Maoist critique of Chinese history never really broke the conventional notion of a succession of legitimate regimes going back some four thousand years to the Xia.

We take the Chinese state, past and present, so much for granted that we have to be deliberately naïve to ask how it got from its remote and obscure origins to the condition it is in now. What have been its essential characteristics over the millennia, and why did it develop in the way that it did? To answer these questions properly on the basis of thorough research would be the task of many lifetimes. For the time being some working hypotheses may perhaps be useful, as long as they are taken as being no more than speculation.

I know of no adequate existing theoretical model. The notion of the 'Asiatic mode of production', Marx's own acknowledgement that his interpretation of history was not universally valid, is of interest only to students of European thought: it tells us nothing about China. Neither does Wittfogel's development of it, the concept of an 'Oriental despotism' founded on the state's control of water: most of the essential characteristics of archaic and dynastic Chinese states were developed in north China, where the agriculture is nearly all unirrigated. There is in the historical literature from China's past and its modern successors a daunting amount of detailed discussion of the particular characteristics of the official apparatus of particular states or of the evolution of a particular organ of government under a succession of dynasties. But it is hard to find an adequate summary of what the state essentially was, how it related to society and how it changed over time.

On the origins of the state in China the evidence is too thin to permit anything more solid than guesswork. There is a fragmentary written tradition about the earliest dynasties and (though it was invented later) about pre-dynastic rulers; there is also archaeological evidence, from wide areas of what are now north and east China, of widening differences in the quality and amount of burial goods during the later Neolithic in the fourth and third millennia BC, to the extent that some sumptuously buried skeletons can be taken to be those of tribal chiefs. On this structure develops the state, becoming fully formed by the thirteenth century BC, when with their mastery of writing, bronze and the weapons system carried by the war chariot the later Shang kings could control most of north China that was not too hilly or too marshy for warfare on wheels. But whether the Shang state was as much like later Chinese regimes as later accounts suggest remains to be established. What does seem to be probable is that by the time the Shang was replaced by the Zhou at some time around 1050 BC one of the characteristics of 'Chinese' states — whether the central one or its many local feudatories — was the elimination of whatever might have remained of tribal assemblies. Perhaps too one of the characteristics of the 'barbarians' was that power was less centralized and absolute among them. One of the essential features of being 'Chinese', in the sense of belonging to the bundle of traditions later celebrated by Confucius and other pundits of the *ru* school of orthodox traditional learning, was to be much less free than one's 'barbarian' neighbours. There are signs that the 'Chinese' actually took pride in their rigid and autocratic political structures. There is certainly an unbroken continuity linking the states of contemporary China with the Shang one of over three thousand years ago.

It has been argued, notably by H. G. Creel, that the bureaucratic state generally thought to have developed between the fifth and third centuries BC was essentially in place long before. Whether or not this early development happened, those centuries saw a huge growth in central power in the rival sovereign states that were struggling for survival. The old order based on hereditary feudal relationships – land or office held in return for service to a liege lord with one's own vassals in time of war – gave way to a world of absolute insecurity, in which any state might be attacked by a combination of any of the others. Faced with absolute threats, states had to be able to mobilize all their human and material resources for total war. The six or seven leading contenders were so well balanced that the struggle for domination lasted for centuries, allowing time for a new kind of state power to gain a degree of direct control over the whole population that is hard to parallel in any major state elsewhere in the world before the eighteenth century.

Although the evidence on the organization of state power in this appropriately named Warring States (Zhan Guo) period is patchy, there is an inescapable force to it. The main players in the game each had a population that was, at a guess, numbered in the millions rather than hundreds of thousands or tens of millions. These states could reportedly field armies big enough to take hundreds of thousands of casualties in a single day's fighting in the third century BC. No doubt some of the figures that found their way into the accepted historical record have been very generously rounded up to include the conscripts transporting grain and supplies to the front, sometimes along especially built walled supply roads running for hundreds of kilometres. Military commands rarely underestimate the losses they have inflicted on their enemies. But even if we discount the figures very heavily, it does look possible that the major powers of the third century BC could each raise armies comparable in size to all the armed forces of the Roman Empire, which was very badly strained to bring four or five legions together (25,000–30,000 men) for a campaign. We do not have to accept the assumption of some Westerners that the Warring States figures are exaggerated by at least ten times just because western Eurasia was incapable of organizing slaughter on such a scale. After all, if we compare the Roman frontiers in Britain and Germany with the Qin and Western Han Great Wall system, the scale of the Chinese defences was so much bigger as to make them different in nature.

It seems reasonable to posit that Warring States regimes and their Qin and Western Han successors could mobilize as unpaid labour and conscript soldiers a proportion of their populations comparable to the proportions that the main participants in the two world wars could mobilize. Within a generation, and after decades of war that would have prostrated a modern Western state, the Qin regime could create a northern-frontier defence system and an empire-wide road network each many thousands of kilometres long; forcibly transfer and resettle hundreds of thousands of households across long distances; demolish unspecified lengths of internal defensive walls between the conquered states; dig canals linking the Xiang and Pearl river systems so as to permit the colonization of the south; construct a tomb system on a huge scale; and put up around the Qin capital a vast complex of full-scale reproductions of 270 palaces of the states conquered by Qin. These were only some of the biggest and most spectacular projects. They would have constituted a formidable list of undertakings by a modern state that had plenty of earth-moving machinery, could wield massive repression and did not care about economic rationality or the rights and well-being of its citizens. I wonder whether even Ceauşescu's Romania could have done it, and I am sure Trajan's Rome could not.

Another astonishing set of evidence of the all-pervasive power of the state in northern China over 2,200 years ago came with the

chance discovery in December 1975, at Shuihudi in Yunmeng
county of Hubei province, of the coffin of a man in his forties. He
had evidently been a minor legal official under the Qin regime until
his death in or shortly after the year 217 BC. What made the find
so valuable was that he had been so devoted to his job that he took
his working reference books to the grave with him: his coffin
contained his bones and 1,155 strips of bamboo, each inscribed with
a column of writing, and a few dozen more that cannot be read any
longer. Fortunately for us, they had not been processed in any way
by historians; and there is no reason to think that they are anything
other than what they seem to be – the conscientious petty official's
reference manuals.

They reveal a world even more closely controlled – in intention
at least – by the state than we imagined before. Consider this excerpt
from the Qin *Field Statutes:*

After timely rainfall, and when millet has begun to ear, an immediate
written report must be made of how many *qing* have received rain and
have millet that is earing, and of fields that have been cleared but have
not yet been put under cultivation. There must also be immediate reports
of the amount of rain and of the number of *qing* benefiting when rain
falls after the crops have started growing. Furthermore, there must be
immediate reports of the number of *qing* affected by drought, storm,
flood, insects and swarms of anything else that harms crops. The counties
near [the regional or national capital] shall send the written reports by fast
runner; distant counties shall transmit them by post.

The implications of this document are worth thinking about, pointing as they do to a regime that was trying at least to keep detailed,
quantified central records of the state of the crops almost field by
field in every county of the empire. Maintaining that sort of control
would be a daunting task for a government equipped with com-
puters and telecommunications. Doing it before the invention of
paper, when all the data had to be gathered and stored on strips of
wood or bamboo, would have been impossible without an enormous bureaucracy. That bureaucracy had to keep records not only
of land, crops and human resources (people is hardly the word to

represent the way Qin saw its subjects) but even of the animals:

Farm oxen will be inspected in the fourth, seventh, tenth and first months. After each year there will be a major review in the first month. For the best [ox] the field constable will be rewarded with a jug of wine and a bundle of dried meat. The labourer will be excused one period of corvée duty, and the head stockman will be rewarded with thirty days. For the worst [ox] the field constable shall be reprimanded and the stockmen penalized with two months [forced labour].

If the oxen are used to work the land, the owner will be given ten strokes for each inch of girth an ox uses.

A state that could keep the detailed local and central records implied by such regulations must have had the administrative machinery needed to maintain huge armies in being while at the same time moving populations around and mounting vast construction projects. The historical records look a lot more credible since the find of the Shuihudi documents. It is now much easier to believe that the bureaucracy reached into every village, conscripting men for forced labour and military service, running a Gulag economy of permanent and temporary state slave labourers, enforcing ideological and administrative unity on the conquered territories, imposing draconian discipline on the officials themselves as well as the general population and doing things with the sort of methodical efficiency that we do not associate with later imperial China. This was all different in kind from anything in western Eurasia before the eighteenth, if not the nineteenth, century.

It is hard to measure the power of a state over its subjects, especially when the evidence as to how far intentions were realized is so sparse, but it does look as though Qin's drive for total control, permitting its subjects to get ahead only through farming and war, came very near its goal. One rough but useful indication of state power is the proportion of each subject's time that is controlled by the state, directly or indirectly, through forced labour, taxation and other means. How much of its subjects' time did the Qin state control? Here we can only guess, but, taking the different kinds of tax, forced labour and military service together, it could be that the

Qin government exercised control over somewhere between a sixth and a quarter of the adult males' working time – not so very different from the proportion of working time taken through taxes by modern states. But in our world high taxation is spent mainly on education and welfare, neither of which was of much concern to Qin.

Such a state developed under the pressure of total insecurity and the endemic threat of destruction by its rivals. To some extent Qin harshness was blunted under the Han regime that followed, but most of the essentials remained. Although central power was never again as absolute as under the Qin, a powerful factor ensured that the state remained strong: the frontier. The Han empire's northern frontier had poor natural defences against neighbours with the mobile striking power of the pastoral Xiongnu, who, when united and inclined to attack, could strike at targets deep in the Han heartlands with mounted armies tens of thousands strong. Such major raids could not be stopped at the frontier. They could be prevented only by diplomacy, bribery and intimidation. The best defence was to bring about divisions among the Xiongnu and their later successors and to back this measure with the certainty of massive retaliation from a Han state with the will and the means to launch co-ordinated attacks across the Gobi barriers to the grasslands in what is now the Mongolian People's Republic, destroying Xiongnu herds and people. Such a defence policy involved immense costs. Standing armies had to be maintained far from crop-growing areas with strong strategic reserves able to cover attacks from any-where along the thousands of kilometres of frontier and to launch massive retaliation.

To maintain such a defence policy required a strong state machine. It had to be able to force peasants into service under frightful conditions on the frontier even if their families were left to go hungry; to keep its own bureaucrats under control; to resist the temptation to use resources in more agreeable ways; and to win the endless struggle with local magnates for the control of those peasants. This was an uphill, even Sisyphean, struggle, but it was essential if any state were to hold north China and thus survive. There might be periods when the threat from the steppe seemed to recede, as under the Eastern Han, but it would always re-emerge, as when other nations, originally from across the frontier, took a terrible revenge early in the fourth century AD for the way they had been treated before then, destroying ethnic Han central power in the north so thoroughly that it was not to be restored for nearly 300 years.

Until the nineteenth century the pressure of the northern frontier continued to make the political unification of north China under a strong state imperative if any stability were to be created. This pressure applied just as much to non-Han as to Han Chinese regimes: the Northern Wei, a Xianbei regime, had to guard their conquests in north China against Rouran pressure from the north in the sixth century, and the Jin barbarians who had driven Song power out of north China in the twelfth century found themselves faced with, and then overwhelmed by, the Mongol menace in the following one.

The power of the early imperial Chinese state cannot all be put down to the dangers threatening from across the frontier, even though those dangers were so much greater than the external threats to the Roman empire before the Huns, Vandals, Goths and the rest of them made life difficult from the late fourth century onwards. There were also internal factors, not the least being the absence of forces and institutions strong and independent enough to challenge the autocratic state's claims to absolute control.

From the ancient world to our own times nearly all autocratic regimes in Europe have had to share their power, at least in appearance, with other institutions. The Roman Empire preserved some of the forms of republican oligarchy. Medieval and early modern states had to contend with Churches, with chartered burghers or with some form or other of assembly or parliament, however limited in its representation. Besides, it was much harder in western Eurasia to assume that any government was the only government in the civilized world. There were always neighbours with comparable civilizations.

In China, however, the Qin had inherited a very old notion –

that there could and should be only one legitimate central government – and taken it a lot further. This view has survived to the present day. The Qin also inherited and passed on the assumption that the subject had no areas of privacy that could be defended against the state if the state chose to intervene. China had no concept of citizenship. There were some very important concepts that were intended to, and often did, inhibit arbitrary state power, concepts to do with what was right and proper. With absolute power went the obligation to ensure that the empire was properly run, even to the extent of holding an emperor or a local ruler personally responsible for natural calamities. Bad regimes could, in the last resort, be overthrown in ways that were accepted as legitimate by the standards of the high culture and of popular cultures too. Officials were seen as having a duty to defend the system's values by protesting at wrong actions by their superiors, up to the emperor himself, even at the risk of their lives. But these safeguards were all aimed at abuses of absolute power, not at the power itself. Neither individuals nor groups could tell the state to mind its own business, though officials could and did warn of the dangers to the state itself of interfering too much in areas not conventionally thought to be the state's business. Property was insecure, though the force of custom strengthened *de facto* property rights in the second millennium of imperial rule.

Many other factors made for the peculiarly high degree of control over society at which the early imperial state aimed, often with success. There was nothing in the political traditions handed down from Shang times by *ru* scholars, and modified by the totalitarian political thinkers of the Warring States and succeeding Han periods, to challenge the legitimacy of the absolute state. After Qin had unified the Chinese cultural world politically no later dynasty would settle for anything less in theory, though most had to in practice.

Once the machinery had been created it was very hard to dismantle it. There were long periods when the power of the central government went into relative decline, as when the Eastern Han dynasty lost control of more and more of the peasants to local magnates in the second century AD. The Chinese world could be divided for centuries on end between rival regimes refusing to acknowledge each other's legitimacy. But through all this the institutions and the political values perpetuated themselves that were ready to restore a stronger state and unified rule over the whole Chinese world as soon as circumstances permitted. The political values that supported unification were based on the assumption that diversity was inherently wrong. Some of those patterns were very ancient, going back to the second millennium BC. The main differences of opinion were about what form of compulsory unification of ideas would work best. In the second half of the first millennium BC Confucians, Legalists, Mohists and others had all sought to impose their own, and in the Western Han period a hybrid of these and other traditions could be put together without too much difficulty. Other concerns of political thinkers were with the best techniques for strengthening the monarchy, with how bureaucrats could best manipulate their rulers and with how rulers could best keep everyone else in their place. The politics of bureaucratic control were to be among the most powerful and poisonous legacies of the period. We saw in 1989 some Warring States political thought in action: the monarch lying low, forcing his subordinates to reveal their own positions, then intervening with ruthlessly applied force to impose his will on a system that seemed to be escaping his control.

Another way of assessing just how powerful the early imperial state was is to look at a much later successor: Qing China in the nineteenth century. It is obvious at first glance that despite a population perhaps seven times as great as the nearly 60,000,000 the Han had on its books, and despite all sorts of technical and other changes, the Qing state was far weaker than the Qin, Han, Cao Wei, Northern Wei, Sui and early Tang regimes. When faced with British drug-runners on the south coast, the Qing government could not get together the couple of hundred thousand troops and sailors who, under an effective unified command, would have been able to push the intruders back into the sea with the military technology available to them. Even if we allow that part of the cause of the Qing's hopeless incompetence in the Opium Wars was their inability to see the nature of the foreign threat, the difficulty they had in coping with internal risings during the third quarter of the nineteenth century points to a very weak state machine. The Qing armies were committed in penny packets, under divided commands, to deal with rebellion after rebellion until the threat to the survival of the state became so serious that exceptional measures were taken that broke all sorts of rules, and large emergency forces were raised on a new basis. And when foreign military and other pressures became heavy again towards the end of the nineteenth century the Qing could not cope. Had they been able to put half of 1 per cent of the population into the armed forces and their logistical support services, and to make or buy rifles and artillery for them, the Manchu empire could have shown its many invaders the door. They could not and did not, and the Qing state fell. But while the Qing was hard put to mobilize one or two in a thousand, the Qin and early Han states could mobilize perhaps ten times as high a proportion of their unfortunate subjects.

This is only one indicator of how the state had weakened. It had more or less lost the ability to conscript people for military or labour service. Taxes, even with all the extra levies to support the corrupt, were a minor burden compared with rent levels of up to half the crop paid by tenant farmers and interest payments for survival loans running at several percentage points each month. Below the level of the county, with its population of several hundred thousand, the state's direct involvement in social and economic life was kept to a minimum, whereas the Qin and Western Han states had tried to run village life, appointing officials right down to the millet-roots level.

This long-term decline in effective state power was not a bad thing from many points of view, and it certainly made a difference. One of the most basic types of control that was virtually abandoned was the ability to conscript unpaid labour that could be used for public works and defence. Another was the allocation of arable land, generation by generation, to every farm family, something that governments tried to do for over a thousand years before the system broke down finally around the end of the Tang dynasty. An excavated wooden document with a date equivalent to 309 BC from the state of Qin, which was published in 1982 (*Wenwu* 1982. 1), contains an order for the reorganization of the field system into a standardized form, and there is plenty of evidence for a number of very ambitious attempts to control the land allocation over the millennium that followed. Of these the *juntian* (equal-field) systems of the fifth to eighth centuries AD are perhaps the best known, can be documented from both processed and primary sources and can even be seen on the ground in field patterns that survive to this day, as Frank Leeming has shown. All these systems required a huge and sustained flow of bureaucratic energy. The interests of the state had to be enforced against local vested interests, from powerful local magnates who ran what were in effect petty kingdoms to peasant families who did not want to lose the land to which they were no longer entitled after the death of some of their members. Despite all the failures dynasty after dynasty managed to reassert the royal claim to control landholding for a thousand years. This called for the sort of bureaucratic tenacity and inevitability that a modern state needs to enforce income tax. So, at least, it would appear.

By the tenth century AD the state had given up this uphill struggle. In one of those unexciting but fundamental changes that alter the nature of human society the Song state recognized existing landholdings and taxed them by area, while also regularly raising levies in cash or kind instead of forced labour. In its second millennium the dynastic state implicitly accepted private landownership, taking only such land as it needed for its own purposes. By the early eighteenth century the Qing government was so confident of its ability to manage on a fixed income that the Kangxi emperor abandoned for ever the possibility of raising extra revenue from the land tax by freezing the land tax rates in perpetuity. Though there were later to be found ways of getting round the limits, the Qing government condemned itself to be short of money throughout the nineteenth century by denying itself the main potential source of it.

We are often told that the monarchies from Song times onwards were increasingly autocratic, and it is clear that even in the seventeenth and eighteenth centuries the Qing government was able to conquer a bigger area of inner Asia than any previous regime ruling China apart from the Mongols. So was the state getting weaker and losing control or gaining in strength?

The dynasties of the second millennium may have given up the effort to maintain some of the controls that those of the first millennium imposed, and the amount of a farmer's time of which the state disposed may have fallen to 5 per cent or less by the nineteenth century, but these dynasties lasted much longer. There was only one change of dynasty in the last 540 years of imperial China, and with all their faults the Ming and Qing achieved remarkable stability apart from two bad periods in the middle of the seventeenth and in the nineteenth centuries.

The state's abandoning of its right to allocate land did not lead to a corresponding growth in great landed magnates. The regimes of the second millennium did not face the challenges from local magnates that had crippled and then destroyed the Eastern Han regime and whose support had been essential to any dynasty that hoped to last in the succeeding centuries. The earlier dynasties' systems of land allocation seem to have been only partly effective in preventing very big landholdings by hereditary aristocrats and others. They had allocated land for dependants and – under some dynasties – even for draft animals. Perhaps the land regulations had been intended mainly to make taxable large holdings that the state was unable to eliminate. In the last thousand years of imperial China the state was actually better at preventing the development of such threats to its power. It disappeared great magnates. It knew how to survive.

It also learned how to prevent things from happening, thanks in part to its use of recorded history. The ability to learn from the mistakes of the past went a long way back. No dynastic regime after the Qin overworked and overpunished its people so harshly. After Wang Mang, an imperial in-law, took the throne from the Western Han regime from AD 9 to 23 the families of empresses were kept under better control. Never again were royal princes allowed the excessive power that at the end of the third century AD

had led to the terrible civil wars that brought down the Western
Jin dynasty and led to nearly three centuries of instability. After the
Tang a powerful Buddhist Church never re-emerged in China,
unlike Tibet and Mongolia. The dominance of the military that had
shaped China from the fourth to the tenth century was ended by
the Song dynasty. The Mongols taught the Manchus how not to
run an alien conquest dynasty. From the Ming the Qing learned
how to cut the gentry down to size, reducing its privileges and
sweeping away nearly all the institutions of manorial serfdom. For
all the supposed autocracy of the Ming and Qing dynasties, the state
became better able to cope with weak, lazy or stupid emperors: the
system learned how to run itself.

Once the public service was staffed mainly by career officials
recruited not for entrepreneurial skills but for the ability to pass
difficult but increasingly trivial exams, as happened from Song times
onwards, the bureaucratic instinct to avoid repeating previous, well-
documented, mistakes had plenty to work on. The secret of preventing things from happening was fragmentation, and this was
something at which the state got better and better, reaching a
culmination under the Qing. We will look later at the fragmentation
of activity that enabled a huge economy, or set of economies, to be
run by an infinitely large number of tiny units and at the fragmentation of the mind that Ming and Qing education brought
about. They were both essential to the regime's survival for nearly
three centuries.

The state system itself was fragmented and divided against itself
so thoroughly that nobody had enough authority to do anything
unusual. Qing political institutions added ethnic divisions to all the
other checks and balances in the political structure they had
inherited, so that the Han Chinese, about a hundred times more
numerous than the Manchu–Mongol ruling coalition, were used
extensively in the system of government without being able to take
it over. A tiny, regular élite bureaucracy – a few tens of thousands –
was divided against itself in every possible way and kept distinct
from the army of clerks, runners and the like who did the actual
work of keeping the government machine working. Military power

was divided up particularly carefully and separated from civil power, with the consequent inefficiencies in putting down rebellion we have noted, but the system also ensured that no commander or coalition of commanders would have the capacity to repeat the rebellion of Wu Sangui, the very powerful general who, with his allies, caused the Manchus a deal of trouble in the south and the west in the 1670s. Fiscal power was also kept deliberately divided so that no part of the bureaucracy could hold the court to ransom. The palace itself was prevented from playing too large a part in political life by much tighter control of the numbers of the court eunuchs, who after Ming times did not become an alternative security apparatus able to dominate the government machine.

It was because China was politically, in Sun Yatsen's words, a dish of loose sand that the imperial system lasted as long as it did. But for it to work it had to be certain. There could be no prospect that things were going to be different in future. The obsession with history and with legitimation from the past helped.

All this made innovation difficult and dangerous, though not impossible. The earlier Manchu emperors brought about some drastic reforms; and the temporary emergency measures to deal with the internal threats of the 1850s to 1870s threw a lot of the principles of fragmentation out of the window, concentrating hitherto unthinkable powers in the hands of commanders who were allowed to raise their own armies in their own home provinces and given the authority to levy the taxes to support them. These changed institutions were hard either to abolish completely or to reintegrate into the system, so they were to contribute to the destabilizing and overthrow of the dynasty at the end of the last century and the beginning of this one. At the same time the fragmentation principle made it difficult to the point of impossibility to change the whole political structure from one aimed at preventing things from happening to one intended to make things happen without thereby destroying it.

It was not for lack of trying. When, after the Boxer movement and the eight-power invasion of 1900, the Manchu ruling house finally accepted that profound changes were essential to cope with international and internal pressures that threatened to destroy its empire, it undermined everything that had kept its system going till then. The reforms of the dynasty's last ten years broke down many barriers. Scholars cramming the classics for the official exams in isolation were turned into volatile, politicized students in modern-style schools in China and abroad, exposed to the spiritual pollution of foreign ideas. New-style armies had enormously increased fire-power as well as officers and sergeants educated in modern ways. The old bans that prevented the gentry within a province from getting together for political purposes gave way to provincial assemblies. The fragmented and fairly harmless late traditional guilds were replaced by pushy chambers of commerce.

The Qing attempt to break out of the prison of the past was a brave one. It failed, but could the transition to a constitutional monarchy based on new institutions adapted from abroad have worked? If the Empress Dowager had lived another few years instead of dying in 1908, might she have maintained her resolve and pushed ahead when the changes were beginning to hurt powerful Manchu vested interests in 1909 and 1910? After all, as the slaughter of Manchus during the revolution of 1911 in Xi'an and other cities showed, the Manchus had a lot to be frightened of. Perhaps a Qing court with an iron nerve and clear vision could have succeeded in giving up enough of their power to keep some, and in changing the very nature of the state. Or perhaps the system was inherently unreformable. The contemporary parallels seem alarmingly relevant, whether we look at the fall of the Qing from the point of view of the Manchu ruling house or from that of their subjects.

The collapse of the Qing state in a matter of weeks late in 1911 ended much more than a dynasty. The whole traditional state fell to pieces, and despite the hopeless inadequacy of the Republic that replaced it the restoration of the dynastic system, as it had developed over the previous two thousand years, was impossible. The outward forms of that tradition of the state were finished. In the eighty years since then no adequate replacement has been found. The military regimes of the early Republic gave way to the military regime of the Guomindang, which was in turn replaced by a new regime that came to power through armed force.

The early Republic had only the form of a Western-style state. It failed the basic test of preserving sovereignty from external threats and was unable to enforce its will in provinces other than those occupied by troops personally loyal to the ruler of the day. Incapable of raising enough taxes to support its minimal existence, it could neither do things nor prevent things from happening. It could only sell out to foreigners.

The Nationalist Republic was rather more effective and able to impose its will in the more modern, Western, industrial and commercial parts of China. It fought off strong challenges from military rivals and had the tenacity not to fold completely in the face of the massive defeats at the hands of the Japanese that continued from 1937 till within months of the Japanese surrender in 1945. But the machinery that enabled it to extract conscripts and taxes was founded on nothing much deeper than its military force. In particular, its rural roots were shallow.

It took the communists to create a state that worked, first in some rural areas, then throughout China. Within a few years of the founding of their People's Republic they had extended their control to every village and had set about reorganizing village life. Every life was touched directly by the state and the Party. They were strong enough to march hundreds of millions of peasants up the hill of collectivism and then down again, and for a quarter of a century virtually all economic activity not confined to the family was under their control.

They reasserted Chinese sovereignty over most of the territories of the Qing empire and stood up to the pressures of the United States, especially on the battlefields of Korea, and the Soviet Union. The Party was able to make its values the national ideology, and for a generation it appeared that the new regime had won control of Chinese minds. It could control and mobilize human resources to transform nature and, by being a government that made things happen, looked as though it would end China's poverty and backwardness and set the People's Republic on the road to wealth and power.

Forty years on things do not seem as positive as the first years of the new order might have led one to expect. The party-state turned out to be so keen on making things happen that it created such catastrophes as the Great Leap Forward famine and the Cultural Revolution. Much of the agricultural growth was eaten up by an increased population, and the spectacular rate of industrial growth proved to be a mixed blessing. By now the problems of the political system are hideously apparent, as the bright young regime that was going to overturn the old world and build a brave new China looks old, shabby, oppressive and irrelevant to China's needs. Like the Qing dynasty in its final years, it seems to be ultimately unreformable: it will allow you a little freedom, but if you try to go further, it shoots you. Indeed, it is apparent that it is in many ways a reinvention of the bureaucratic monarchy.

It now looks as though the problem of what should succeed the Qing dynasty has yet to be solved. The transitional period that began in the decade before 1911 is still continuing. The Communist Party is capable only of offering a return to its own past and to China's earlier autocratic traditions.

The founders of the Communist Party were products of Qing China, educated in its schools and culture and soaked in its values. To them it was only natural that the state should be absolute and that a bureaucratic monarchy was the normal form it should take. When they got beyond the *ad hoc* arrangements of the war decades to build a regular state nobody needed to force them to copy the institutions of Stalin's Russia, which were not hard to adapt to China. What appeared to be an innovatory, revolutionary regime, out to change China and perhaps the world, and for its first twenty years was clearly committed to making things happen, has become a conservative force, willing to make only such changes as are essential to its survival. Once in place, the system became unreformable and unable to adapt.

Attitudes to state power remain heavily influenced by traditional values. The state's power remains absolute and sacrosanct. Though it can often be got round, it cannot be challenged. Politics at the top is played by the rules of palace struggles, which owe more to the political pundit of the third century BC Han Fei than to Marx. All rights are only licences held at the state's pleasure and revocable without notice. The system needs an autocrat at the top, and the autocrat will often maintain control by keeping his underlings so divided against each other that none will dare organize resistance. Conflict within the system cannot be legitimate; neither can any social, political, religious or economic organizations that demand real autonomy from the state be permitted to exist. The state imposes its uniform culture, with only very limited recognition of different cultural identities. It claims to control not only the present but the past and the future as well. Like both the interventionist state of the earlier imperial dynasties and the minimalist one of later dynasties, it needs to keep society weak.

The trouble is that the party-state system, the modern version of the bureaucratic monarchy, no longer works. Mass mobilization, whether for socially divisive struggles or for attempts to remake the natural environment, has been tried too often. The party-state cannot go back to the 1950s and the first flush of enthusiasm. It cannot become even more traditional now that the Pandora's box of dangerous ideas has been opened, but neither can it permit more freedom of discussion without risking being talked out of existence. Continued repression may keep the lid on the cauldron for a while longer, but sooner or later the seething hostility will boil over again.

It almost makes one feel sorry for China's rulers, caught as they are between a played-out past and impossible futures. It is very hard to see the present rulers managing the transition to some political arrangement that can accommodate the conflicting interest groups in China and permit a real political life to develop. Before June 1989 it still was just possible, if one was being extremely optimistic, to see some way of muddling through to a structure in which the Party gradually allowed the people more say in their lives, extended the areas of freedom and somewhat reduced its own role. We know now that this was never on. A government that will besiege and invade its own capital with hundreds of thousands of troops, then do what it did in front of the world's press and broadcasters, is one that sees itself as threatened with imminent collapse.

The bureaucratic monarchy that underlies the Marxist rhetoric is evidently a form of state organization that is very hard to shift. Having looked at its vigorous early phases, we may do well to turn to the role of the emperor in more recent times.

3. Emperors and Bureaucrats

A very old man, living in near total isolation from the country over which he is absolute ruler, spends nearly all his waking time on his bed, drifting between sleep and wakefulness. Unable to feed himself, he petulantly insists that only one person, a young woman, can put the food in his mouth. The span of the attention he can give the current issues on which he has to be consulted is often very short, and what he knows about them is strictly controlled by his staff and limited by his failing mental capacity. What he much prefers is to read and re-read Chinese literature and, above all, Chinese history. In his last year he is going through the *Universal Mirror to Aid Government*, the chronicle of Chinese history from 403 BC to AD 959 that was compiled in the eleventh century and in its standard modern edition runs to 9,612 pages, for the eighteenth time.

Because of his failing eyesight and weakness he can manage only books that are specially printed for him in large type and sewn in the traditional way in thin fascicles with paper (not card) covers that the moribund tyrant can fold back and hold in his hand as he lies on his side, reading himself for hour after hour into the distant past. This is the world he understands and can relate to much more easily than the present, which drifts ever further away and is left to officialdom's devices. He never leaves his closely guarded quarters in the Forbidden City now, and he keeps nearly all visitors out. He prefers to live a grotesque parody of his favourite novel, the eighteenth-century *Hong Lou meng* (*The Dream of the Red Chamber*), in which the teenage hero lives surrounded by young women and girls, all out to please the young master.

Mao Zedong in his eighties can feel comfortable only with young women who are at his beck and call and as dependent on him as any palace serving woman. He rarely meets his political colleagues of the Political Bureau and its Standing Committee, and they are not admitted to the inner sanctum, his bedroom, where he spends most of the day in his white pyjamas or dressing gown. Not even his food can be brought through the heavy steel doors: one of the chosen nurses has to emerge to fetch it when it is delivered in a basket, course by course, and left outside the room.

He rarely sees members of his own family, but can be persuaded, if in the right mood, to let a sister or young girlfriend of one of his nurses pay a call, on condition of absolute secrecy. Back in the early 1960s the Party bosses used to have female companions from the Air Force Political Department's Song and Dance Troupe delivered to dances in the Forbidden City on Wednesdays and Saturdays. The girls, some of them still in their early teens, were expected to partner the leaders on the dance floor and required to make playful conversation to help the great men relax. Some would stay on for a day or two of activities that were not to be discussed by their colleagues in the Song and Dance Troupe.

Palace life is a morbid obsession of Chinese culture. The subject is both repulsive and fascinating, and though the secrets of today's court are kept out of print, no such veil hides those of earlier rulers. Stories about emperors are always popular. When the ghosted autobiography of Pu Yi, the last Manchu emperor, was published in a small edition in 1964 by the publishing house of the Ministry of Public Security it was immensely sought after in Peking. This was at a time when the revolutionary rhetoric of the Communist Party was taken far more seriously than it is now. The book was heavily propagandistic, having been written for Pu Yi by a writer in the employ of the Ministry of Public Security. Because I had been commissioned to translate it into English for Peking's Foreign Languages Press, where I was working at the time, I had a spare copy of this treasure. A class of students of English were so eager to devour it that they took it in turns to read it round the clock, and in a week or two the whole class had finished it.

Since the Mao era many books of gossip about the Qing court and the Manchu royal family have been printed in huge editions and done well for publishers now forced to look for a profit. Recent years have also seen the beginning of a literature about life in China's Kremlin, the Zhongnanhai section of the Forbidden City. Although today's emperor is still protected by taboo, Mao no longer is. And for some time now Mao's heir apparent, Lin Biao, has been an unrestricted target.

Unfortunately there is not much independent confirmation of accounts such as Guo Jinrong's *Mao Zedongde huanghun suiyue* (*Mao Zedong's Twilight Years*), the source for the beginning of this chapter. Published in Hong Kong in 1990, it purports to tell the story of Meng Jinyun, one of the two young women who between them were the only people allowed in Mao's bedroom in the last year or so of his life. Meng had been one of the teenage companions at the palace dances of the middle 1960s and had struck the right balance between flirtatiousness and deference in her little chats with the chairman.

Mao did not forget the girls who took his fancy. Meng came back to see him nine years after the dances were cancelled in the Cultural Revolution. Although she had seen serious political trouble that had landed her in prison and labour camp, Mao took her back immediately, and she stayed with him as one of the three women of the bedchamber. Before long Mao turned against one of the three, who was banished from the presence. For the last year of his life the other two had to be in constant attendance in alternating four-hour shifts. Just how much they controlled him is hard to judge from the published evidence. They certainly had to coax him into allowing himself to be fed and medicated and had some say in interpreting his wishes.

The sharp division between the dying Mao's bedroom and sitting room paralleled that in the imperial palaces between the *gong*, the residential quarters or harem, where the only intact adult male was the emperor, and the *dian*, the throne rooms where the emperor could receive his officials. Chinese palaces were much less open than European ones, where kings and queens lived and died among their

subjects in ways that would have been unthinkable in China. In
Europe even the king's bedroom was the scene of half-public events,
as matters of state were discussed with nobles and officials while he
got up in the morning. Though Louis XIV was, arguably, the most
powerful man in Europe, he affected the style of a nobleman living
among noblemen, superior but not removed from the rest of
them.

Chinese emperors, with the exception of some of the successful
gangsters who by their energy, ruthlessness and ability founded new
dynasties, were much more secretive. The monarch was rarely seen
outside the palace complex, and even in the dawn audience for
officials held in the throne halls the atmosphere was one of ritualized
intimidation calculated to remind officials of their inferiority. Ceremonies were marked by much kneeling and kowtowing, an action
that so shocked ambassadors from eighteenth- and early nineteenth-
century Europe, in which monarchies were still very powerful, that
it was an obstacle to diplomatic relations and gave the English
language one of the few words it has absorbed from Chinese. Before
an official who was called to audience could see the emperor he had
to pass through vast and intimidating courtyard after vast and
intimidating courtyard and gateway after gateway, and all in the
half light before the audience began at dawn. Everything was
designed to overawe; and as the penalties for displeasing the emperor
could be very severe, the wise official did not take a strong position
in the audience on matters that might bring a frown to the dragon
countenance. That a few did is a mark of their personal courage.

Although some emperors took to the field with their armies, or
made progresses through the country with enormous entourages at
vast cost to the local communities that had to provide suitable
temporary palaces in which to receive them, they had few chances
to observe the ordinary lives of their subjects or even to experience
the problems with which their officials had to deal. Yet all power
in the state was ultimately in their hands. In reality officials could
obstruct the imperial will very effectively through standard bureaucratic manoeuvres or by invoking the authority of the past. Only
an exceptional emperor could control his officials. And yet in over

two thousand years the imperial state did not see the emergence of autonomous government institutions that limited or shared, as of right, the monarch's powers. Although the machinery of state could continue to function under a weak-minded, lazy or incompetent emperor, this was achieved essentially by following precedent and by preventing new things from happening, as far as that was possible. When new policy decisions were needed the imperial state was often unable to cope. The accumulation of the recorded experience of government, through history written by officials for officials, made anything other than absolutism unthinkable. For the system to work there had to be an autocrat and a bureaucracy. But the autocrat could not possibly have enough understanding or knowledge of the vast and populous Chinese empire to make informed decisions on most matters.

Emperors who, with the support of only part of the bureaucracy, tried to bring about fundamental changes were nearly always frustrated, either at once or a little later. The Han emperor Wu Di's attempt to strengthen state control over an economy that was encouraged to be more commercial did not long survive his death in 87 BC. The usurper of the Han throne, Wang Mang, might have succeeded in founding a dynasty a hundred years or so later if he had not also tried to make drastic changes that struck at the interests of the great families from whom his senior officials were drawn. So it went on until, for a few months in 1898, the penultimate emperor of the Qing dynasty issued a string of decrees that might have revived China but threatened officials, the military and the Manchu royal house. A palace *coup* had him put away until he died ten years later. Most emperors did not try seriously to rock the ship of state.

The principal exception to the rule of autocratic weakness was the self-made emperor. He founded a dynasty after a period of chaos in which previously existing bureaucracies were weakened and so could to some extent set the rules himself. His ability to control large organizations was proved by the fact that he, rather than his countless rivals, triumphed. Even such emperors could end up as prisoners of their own officials and courtiers. Mao, once one of the most dynamic rulers in Chinese history, and one who so resented officialdom that he kept trying to pull the rug out from under it, most spectacularly in the Cultural Revolution, lived long enough to become a prisoner of the palace and the past.

Mao in his dotage was very obviously incapable of running even his own life, let alone those of his countless subjects. As China moves further into the 1990s gerontocracy rules again. Is China doomed to autocracy, losing a Mao only to succumb to the palsied grip of another autocrat who boasted several years ago that he works for only a quarter of an hour a day? It would be comfortable but unrealistic to regard the Mao and Deng dictatorships as temporary aberrations from normal political life in China. After all, the Qing dynasty fell in 1912, and the rhetoric of democracy has been much heard throughout this century. The Communist Party, like its Guomindang predecessor, is an organizational structure that, while not democratic in any Western sense, does appear to put power into the hands not of an individual but of a ruling group, the Political Bureau with its dozen or two members or the five or six of them on its Standing Committee. The Communist Party machine seems to be an oligarchy rather than a one-man dictatorship.

Events point the other way. Once the communists had established reasonably permanent control of enough territory to run an effective state in north-west China during the Japanese war, they acted like a rebel dynasty in earlier centuries. They had to have their own Son of Heaven, who would hold the system together by imposing his will on its component parts. Mao had remarkable qualities of intellect and personality that equipped him to play the part, and as he was far better acquainted with Chinese than with foreign history and literature, he thought like the founder of a dynasty.

In one of his most revealing poems he compares favourably the personalities of his age – by implication, himself – with the great emperors of the past: Qin Shi Huang, Han Wu Di, the founders of the Tang and Song dynasties and Genghis Khan. The final message of the piece is that none of them combined martial prowess with culture and sheer style in the way he did. This poem was written in 1936, when the Communists controlled only a small and backward corner of China, far from the centres of wealth and power. Yet already he was thinking like an emperor.

To someone as soaked in the history of the Chinese state and in the culture of court politics as Mao there was no conceptual difficulty in adopting the secretive and ruthless techniques by which powerful monarchs kept their ministers under control. Mao was very good at that game, as Deng has been since Mao's death. But that does not explain why Mao and Deng have been allowed to play it. If the monarchical leanings had been Mao's and Deng's alone, the Party might have developed otherwise. But the deeply rooted nature of the culture required an emperor. Whether the example of Stalin's Soviet Union also encouraged that tendency or whether the USSR was taken as a model for many aspects of the structure of the People's Republic precisely because it fitted in with Chinese needs for bureaucratic autocracy, Lenin and the First Qin Emperor both gave their blessing to the Chinese communist dictatorship.

That the Chinese high culture needs an autocrat seems to be well demonstrated by its historical inability to cope without one except during disordered times of transition towards a new autocracy. One of the signs of the weakening of Communist Party power since the late 1980s, especially in the countryside, has been the emergence of a host of rustic emperors, each recruiting his band of followers in villages and promising to establish a new order. True dragon Sons of Heaven are a flourishing breed in the medieval world of the contemporary Chinese countryside. According to figures reported by a Chinese university specialist in the world of secret societies, in one prefecture of Hebei province alone the public security dealt in 1987–8 with eighty-one cases of would-be emperors organizing attempts to win the throne. We shall return later to the fiery river of chiliastic beliefs that has, for the best part of two thousand years, flowed deep beneath the normally placid surface of the Chinese countryside and that in times of trouble has erupted in killing and destruction. This tradition is also a monarchical one. The longer-lasting rebellions always set up their divinely appointed kings or emperors with courts and bureaucracies. Once the Chinese Communist Party had become a primarily peasant organization, from the late 1920s onwards, it could not help inheriting those attitudes. The adapted Shaanxi folksong that became one of its anthems, 'The East is Red', speaks of Mao as a saviour star and compares him with the rising sun of dawn.

The peasant preference for saviours and emperors fitted well with the intellectuals' wish to find a place at court or in the national or local bureaucracies of a new emperor. Rebel emperors who managed to set up some kind of state structure of their own were always able to recruit as advisers, ministers and officials men of education who had been trained for the civil service exams.

For the educated the normal measure of success was always a career in the imperial service, to which all other ways of living were second best. Teaching was only for failures, and there were no great independent secular or religious educational institutions where a scholar could pursue a career independent of the state. Religion offered no acceptable alternative either. For nearly all of the history of Buddhism in China – as opposed to Tibet and Mongolia – Buddhist clerics have had only a marginal position at the higher levels of society and have been kept under the control of the secular bureaucracy. Daoism as an organized religion was never a match for Buddhism. While emperors and officials could believe in these and other religions, notably Islam, the religious life could not lead to the worldly eminence of a bishop in medieval Europe, let alone that of a pope. Emigration was no solution for the literate. Even in periods when rival states contested the dominance of the Chinese world they did not offer fundamentally different career patterns for the ambitious educated, and to leave the Chinese world was to cut oneself off from civilization.

No respectable independent profession was open to the educated that could remotely compare with an official career. Doctors could win a certain distinction, but the best would hope for a civil service post in the Imperial Academy of Medicine. Trade was not a way of life for gentlemen, even when they were discreetly dependent on it for their wealth. In any event, state-sponsored enterprises had great advantages over private businesses, which tended to be very small and precarious. Although some writers, painters and calligraphers could earn a living through their brushes, this nearly always required official connections or patronage or, at the very least, the support of leaders of the local gentry, many of whom would have had links with the official world.

The remarkable disappearance of great hereditary aristocratic families by the tenth century AD was so nearly complete as to remove another potential source of support and patronage for thinkers and writers: great country houses or castles supported by large estates. An aristocracy might have acted as a limit to absolutism and dared to regard a monarch as, at best, one of themselves. The aristocrats of the fourth to the sixth century AD had – in private at least – taken such an attitude to the succession of short-lived dynasties founded by generals that ruled south China for two or three generations before the next warlord took the throne. A thousand years later the Ming dynasty permitted princes of the blood – who were hardly likely to question the regime's right to rule – to live in great magnificence but kept them away from real power.

Their Qing successors allowed the princelings of the Manchu royal house much less licence and came down very hard on any questioning of the legitimacy of their rule by the Han Chinese who made up the vast majority of their subjects. While some former officials of the Ming who gave up active opposition were allowed to retire with dignity, for by the strict Confucian standards that the Manchus also upheld an official could not honourably serve two regimes, very few of the educated dared thereafter to challenge the Qing monarchy until its last years, when it was obviously destroying itself. Indeed, by the time the dynasty fell many educated Han men were unhappy at having to give up what had been forced on their ancestors as a mark of subservience to the alien Manchu conquerors: the shaven front of the head and the remaining hair kept in a long plait.

The chaotic Republic did not last long enough to replace traditional attitudes to authority or to enable alternative institutions to put down roots deep enough to resist the tendency to revert to autocracy. Talk about the development of civil society in contrast to the autocratic state in nineteenth- and twentieth-century urban China has been fashionable among some intellectuals in China and in the little world of Chinese studies in the West in recent years, but it is hard to make a convincing case for anything more than the emergence of elements that might, with time and in circumstances other than those of any China that has yet existed, have developed into the sorts of institution that have replaced communist dictatorships in some central European countries.

The tyranny of Chinese history and the history of Chinese tyranny are monsters that have long fed on each other. Before going any further with this exploration it might be appropriate to turn first to where these millennia of autocracy have led: the political structures of contemporary China that support and require a personal dictatorship. It is also necessary to consider the imperial bureaucracies from which they are descended.

Today's China has many of the trappings of a modern state run by a vast, impersonal officialdom. That is an image that fits in with China's claim, which is stronger than that of any other culture, to have invented and developed the bureaucratic state. China's high culture is so profoundly bureaucratic that to those who hold its values any other kind of polity seems inferior, if not barbaric, by comparison.

What was special about the bureaucracies developed in rival warring states during the fourth and the third century BC was that their members were selected not because of their aristocratic pedigrees but only for their ability to serve the monarch. The theories of statecraft that flourished in these centuries taught a ruler the techniques by which to keep his officials under the most effective control, ensuring, through strict punishments and generous rewards, that they served his interests by carrying out all and only the precise duties assigned to each of them. Officials had no job security. Rulers were taught to be constantly on their guard against their ministers and to use secrecy as a weapon against them. Officials at all levels were controlled by strict administrative regulations that left them with as little autonomy as possible. An infinite quantity of reports and other documents flowed endlessly around the system, even when, before the invention of paper, they were written on cumbersome bundles of wooden or bamboo slips.

The master of using bureaucracy and terror to keep his subjects
under control, the First Qin Emperor, lived in the shadows, not
letting his ministers know much of the time in which of his hundreds
of palaces he was at any moment and not revealing his views on
policy questions until his officials had made their views clear. He
also spent much of his reclusive life reading documents, giving
himself a set weight to get through each day. Although the bulk of
the reports was reduced when paper replaced wood and bamboo,
reading remained the main way in which an emperor could get to
know his country, his officials and his subjects. The notes he scribbled
on a document in red were the means by which most of his
decisions were made known to his officials. The emperor was the
servant as well as the master of his bureaucracy and was able to
stay in control of his paper world only through endless drudgery.
An emperor who tried to spare himself the effort left the
machine to run itself. It was hard even for a diligent one to
avoid manipulation by court officials. Even such scourges of
bureaucrats as Mao and Deng became, in their dotage, further
and further removed from what was going on outside their
palaces.

If the bureaucracy were to be kept under control, it had to be
divided against itself. The memory of how over-powerful officials
from aristocratic families had deposed the ruling houses of the states
of Jin and Qi in the fifth and fourth centuries BC was one that later
monarchs were not allowed to forget, especially after Wang Mang
changed himself from imperial in-law and senior office-holder into
emperor in AD 8. From then on civil officials were nearly always
kept in their place, and the powers of offices were carefully defined
and divided. Strife between alliances and cliques of officials in
different parts of the state structure was made difficult. Although
factionalism was inevitable, and at times very serious, it was regarded
not as healthy but as wicked and punishable. In the Qin model the
power structures were designed to keep the controls in the monarch's
hands alone. From the Han dynasty onwards there was some weakening of the principle that officials had to be totally and uncon-
ditionally obedient to the emperor. Confucius's interpretation of

what an official owed his monarch became part of the schooling of the sons of families eligible for office.

In the decades around 500 BC Confucius had invented an imaginary, idealized version of social and political institutions at the beginning of the Zhou dynasty, half a millennium before his own time. In this model everyone was born into a clearly defined social class or caste and had obligations to match his or her status. At the top was the Zhou monarch, and at the next level were the hereditary rulers of the feudal states into which his territories were divided. These rulers had as their senior ministers men of the leading aristocratic families — often cadet branches of the ruling house — and drew their other officials from a rather larger class of knights. The great majority of the population, women and the 'little people', were excluded from office. In Confucius's unrealistic picture of the golden past people at all levels of society behaved correctly toward superiors and inferiors. With privilege went duties. While officials owed their superiors absolute loyalty, this did not imply absolute obedience. If a superior was doing wrong, his subordinates were expected to urge him to return to the straight and narrow. If a ruler turned out to be beyond saving, the only honourable action for a gentleman — Confucius's term *junzi* blurs the distinction between high birth and good behaviour, as does the English word — was to leave his service and live in retirement.

Although the official who really believed in Confucian values was at times an awkward underling for a ruler to deal with and could successfully avoid carrying out some orders, he was more useful in many ways than the official who had no moral standards and would do anything he could get away with. Confucian officials took their duties seriously, including their loyalty both to the throne and to the whole system of values in which they had been educated and that gave their careers meaning. This meant that they were more dependable than officials who were controlled only by external rewards and punishments, especially in postings where isolation meant that they had to make vital decisions on their own.

One thing the Confucian model did not allow was officials overstepping their authority or formally usurping the monarch's power.

Nor was there room in it for any assembly or senate of senior
officials representing the interests of society against the emperor.
Confucian-minded officials had to serve their monarch and receive
their instructions from him, even if the monarch was incapable
of understanding policy issues or of making decisions, and the
instructions came, in fact, from others. They could protest but
neither could nor would push him aside, and he could not control
China without them.

Bureaucracy has thus been inextricably linked with autocracy
for over two thousand years. It takes an exceptionally able and
persevering emperor to assert his control over bureaucrats expert in
making him reach the decisions they wanted. Officials, for their part,
have preferred an autocrat with the intelligence and determination to
keep rival factions under control but with as few ideas as possible.
Although officials have been able to get by for a while without an
effective monarch or regent over them, as when an emperor was
too lazy or too stupid to play his part, this has never worked for
very long. The crucial role of the monarch has probably been one
of the main reasons why the principle of primogeniture has not
applied to succession to the throne, though seniority counts for so
much else in Chinese high culture. An incompetent monarch could
be a disaster. This has made for the sort of instability towards the
end of a reign with which we have been familiar in recent decades,
but it has normally provided a field of qualified rival candidates
from among whom a reasonably competent or ruthless one
could emerge through bitter struggles normally fought out in
secret.

A bureaucracy with shared values offered the only possible way
by which a dynasty could keep long-term control over the vast
territories and population of the empire. The empire could not be
parcelled out, on a hereditary feudal basis, to princes, dukes and
other grandees without running a very strong risk of being pulled
apart sooner or later. This nearly happened in the civil wars of the
princes of the Han ruling house in the second century BC and
actually happened at the beginning of the fourth century AD, when
royal princes fatally weakened the Western Jin dynasty through

their devastating civil wars, which left the way clear for ethnic risings to destroy the capital and the state.

Nor could an emperor trust his generals. There have been extended periods when regional warlords controlled much of the territory of Chinese states, especially in the north, where large armies had to be stationed to hold the long and vulnerable frontier against powerful northern neighbours, from Manchuria to Turkestan. Although they held imperial commissions, these commanders were often virtually autonomous rulers of their territories able to threaten central authority. This problem was especially serious during the last century and a half of the Tang dynasty. The variant on this pattern in the first half of the twentieth century – warlords all over China – had nothing to do with frontier defence and much to do with foreign money and influence. It also left the dictators of the day with very little power.

For a monarch bureaucrats were much better agents of control. They had played that role well in the fourth and the third century BC. Over the next two thousand years and more they were the central and indispensable parts of all state machines. Unlike feudal vassals, they could be promoted, dismissed or transferred at will. They took their duties seriously for the most part. The education for the exams by which the great majority of officials won their place in the bureaucratic élite was an indoctrination that worked. Officials rarely rebelled, and they were not all venal.

The culture is imbued with bureaucratic values to an extent that goes far beyond anything in the American or even the British tradition, which does not give officials much prestige in society and in which hardly anybody outside the bureaucracy knows or cares about civil service structures and rankings. Civil servants are figures to be feared or laughed at, not respected or liked. A career in the public service – with the exception of the foreign service – is not what doting parents dream of for their children.

In China it is, and long has been, different. Although individual officials are often shown in a bad light in stories and plays – they can be portrayed as weak, stupid, cruel, corrupt and other unpleasant things – the bureaucracy as such has rarely come under attack. Good officials are shown as lofty and admirable. To be an official is seen as highly desirable. For many centuries the main purpose of education beyond basic literacy has been to get into the civil service.

China gave the world not only civil service exams but also the system of numerical gradings for civil service posts. Awareness of bureaucratic rank is widespread; bureaucratic titles are very often used. 'Deputy Section Head Zhao' does not sound like a comical form of address in Chinese. Political upheavals can lead to great changes in bureaucratic structures, or to wholesale dismissals and promotions, but the essence of bureaucracy continues unabated. Today's bright young high-flying official is in all sorts of ways the reincarnation of one of the lucky few who made it through to success in the palace exams and a plum job in the imperial civil service.

Because the regular degree-holding bureaucracy was small in relation to the population as a whole – a few tens of thousands out of hundreds of millions in recent centuries – a diligent emperor could hope to control it by meeting and talking with enough senior officials to have a personal impression of each of them and to be able to assess their judgements of their subordinates. An experienced emperor such as Qianlong in the eighteenth century could thus watch over any of his regular officials at one or two removes and observe his top bureaucrats directly, getting their opinions on each other. The technique continues in our own times. Transcripts of interviews between Mao, Zhou Enlai and other top Party bosses and local officials during the upheavals of the Cultural Revolution are remarkably similar to the recorded conversations between Qianlong and his ministers: in both cases much of the discussion is about individual office-holders and their reliability.

Such inquiries have for many centuries been confirmed or supplemented by more devious techniques, such as using intelligence agencies to spy on officials and report direct to the sovereign. This makes it possible to move swiftly against disaffected bureaucrats before they have time to become organized and dangerous.

The bureaucratic monarchy of the 1980s and 1990s has preserved traditions of both recent centuries and much more distant ones, reversing the secular trend towards a less interventionist state machine content to have nothing happen and returning to the strong state of 2,100 years ago. The Communist Party has given China a much bigger bureaucracy than it has ever had before and has used officialdom to impose great changes on society. But, just as the imperial bureaucracy could be controlled by only one person – the monarch or his regent – so this enormous new state and party machine can be held together only by centralizing ultimate power in one man's hands.

The structures of contemporary Chinese society and state are much more conducive to dictatorship than to democracy. The state structure can be envisaged as a number of pyramids. Some are based on local power, going up from villages through counties and districts to provinces and regions. Within these pyramids party and state officials are under the orders of the higher levels and responsible for enforcing their superiors' wishes on their underlings. Other pyramids are those of specialist systems (*xitong*) based on function, which are under local control only to a certain extent at lower levels. Among them are the pyramids of the military regions and the specialist branches of the armed forces, the industrial pyramids that are controlled by central ministries, the open and the secret security apparatuses, the railway system with its millions of employees, the centrally run university system that comes directly under the State Educational Commission and a number of other systems that are all more or less autonomous structures, partly or wholly controlling their own activities. Only the autocrat can maintain a balance between the systems, and that is best achieved by doing as little as possible.

Within each of these pyramids or systems is a large number of component units that accept control from above within their own system but do not necessarily co-operate horizontally with other units, even those within the same system. It adds up to an overall structure that is profoundly conservative, as all units strive to maintain their own positions within their systems and each system defends its interests against other systems. There is widespread awareness of the dangers of trying to extend the scope of one's unit or system because any participant who attempts such adventures will threaten so many other interest groups that coalitions of forces may exert pressure on higher authority to force the miscreant back into line. Competition is thus a conservative influence.

China now has a feudal structure reminiscent of medieval Europe, in which vassals, the system bosses, hold their fiefs from a lord in return for duties and obligations and control their sub-vassals on a similar basis. The feudalism is more collective than individual, and individuals are virtually locked into the system and the unit to which they belong. It is hard enough for an individual to switch between units and very hard indeed to change systems. It is also extremely difficult for a unit to be transferred from one system to another. Peasants remain legally tied to the land, in the sense that it is almost impossible for them to acquire the right to permanent residence in a city. Even though collective agriculture has been abolished and many tens of millions of peasants now move around China in search of work, the rural population remains ultimately subservient to the local lord of the manor – the township head – and his (rarely her) feudal superiors. Peasants are not free, but since the dissolution of the people's communes the dependency of urban dwellers on the work unit is much greater than theirs, and the unit has powerful sanctions that can be used against its members, including sending them off for years of 'labour re-education' by administrative decision without even the formality of a trial.

The feudalization of China by a revolutionary political party in the second half of the twentieth century was not a continuation of tendencies in late dynastic China but a reversion to a much earlier model. One of the most fundamental characteristics of the changes that took place after the Manchu conquest in the seventeenth century was the near elimination of non-economic forms of dependency in the countryside – in other words, the almost complete disappearance of field serfdom in the Chinese countryside and, with it, the manorial economy that had survived till then in remoter areas. We shall return later to the fragmentation of economic activity in late imperial China. The point here is that countless millions of small and very small entrepreneurs were able, through an army of brokers and middlemen, to interact in local, regional and national economies that were very highly commercialized and functioned without large firms or corporations. Although the Qing state did not stay out of the economy, tried quite hard to influence the price of grain and ran some enterprises of its own both before and after the impact of the West, there was little about Qing economic life that could be described as feudal in a European or a Japanese sense. Nor was there anything comparable with the huge industrial systems of Communist China. Yet it is the Qing order that has been labelled feudal or *fengjian* (a word used to translate 'feudal' and its cognates in other European languages) not only in China where the label was compulsory but also in the writing of some foreigners.

The Qing monarchy and its officials relied on the fragmentation of all possible sources of effective challenges. This method worked well as long as the dynasty was concerned more with preventing than with causing events. When in its last years the dynasty deliberately initiated changes by creating new and strong institutions it thereby brought into being the forces that were to destroy it.

Because the Communists were committed to bringing about great and rapid changes in China they could not revert to the Qing model of keeping all economic and other social bodies tiny and weak. For the state to be respected in the world it had to have large and well-equipped armed forces. Effective armed forces needed weapons and other equipment, which meant much more heavy industry than China had in 1949. Only the state could extract the resources to create such industry. In order to remake the political, social, economic and cultural order in every town and village there had to be a huge and actively interventionist state machine. The Communist Party itself had to create structures of its own that would enable it to lead every other institution from the inside while keeping its own identity as a national body that imposed its will on all the component parts of state and society.

In the early years of the new regime the many systems that were created to do new things grew rapidly, quickly becoming powerful and effective. In the weak and divided country the communists had just won by conquest, these new structures did not usually meet with much organized resistance as they took over the territories and sectors assigned to them. In the absence of existing social insurance or other welfare facilities available to all citizens, the new systems had to provide cradle-to-crematorium support for employees and their families, and where there were no hospitals, schools and housing for the staff the systems had to create them. All these provisions encouraged the dependency of employees and made leaving one's unit and system even more difficult than it would have been otherwise.

While the systems were large social institutions much stronger than any that had been seen in China for over a millennium, they were kept under strict control. Once they had filled the space assigned to them, they could expand only inside it. Central, regional and provincial government and Party bodies kept systems within their assigned boundaries. Manufacturing enterprises, for example, were not free to compete with each other for supplies or markets but had to produce to plan. Thus it was that inefficient producers of inferior goods were protected and the more successful thinly rewarded. As central and local planners asserted their supremacy over the market, enterprises tended to become more and more defensive and conservative, guarding their patch fiercely against intruders and being very cautious about stepping outside their territories.

The structures and mechanisms for keeping potentially dangerous institutions in their place and divided against each other have been many and complicated. Systems have been subject to a certain amount of control through the operation of other systems. The railways, for example, seem to be a world of their own. With their millions of employees, they are treated in some respects as semi-autonomous. By their very nature they reach into all parts of the country. They have their own police, their own publishing houses, writers and hospitals. There is a quarter in the western suburbs of Peking that, though out of sight or sound of trains, is railway territory for block after block, complete with one of the city's biggest theatres. Other railway cantonments can be found all over China. But without the co-operation of other systems the trains could not run; and the railways have not been allowed to use their own transport facilities to turn their factories making rolling stock into unbeatable competitors in other fields, or to capitalize on the value of their real estate, or to set their own fares so as to maximize income. The railways have been kept within the limits assigned them.

Of all the systems the strongest is the military one, which can be regarded as a super-system so powerful that it has to be divided into component systems, each of which could match a civilian system and which hold each other in check. The separate military and political command structures within each military system are very effective controls, which are backed up by less visible security networks that will deal very quickly with an officer who might be indulging in thought crime.

No better demonstration of how effective and cumbersome the division of powers within the armed forces is could be found than the siege and assault of Peking. Very large numbers of troops from different military regions were deployed around the capital, some of them having to be moved from great distances. The hundreds of thousands of soldiers were not needed to deal with the unarmed civilian demonstrators, who could have been dispersed by a combination of political gestures and police methods. What brought the troops to Peking in such huge numbers was the need to ensure that there were units from enough different systems present around Peking to prevent any commander from using the chance to mount a *coup*. In the short term this ploy succeeded but only at the cost of irreparable damage to the regime's standing in its own capital and the world and unknown strains on the loyalty of the armed forces.

The military super-system is what, in the last resort, keeps the regime in place and hence is essential. When all else fails the troops are there to prevent total collapse. In the closing stages of the communists' conquest of China and the first years of the People's Republic the army was given almost unlimited powers in running regional administrations until other systems had been built up. In that era, which now seems remote, the army handed power back to civilians in 1953–4 and turned its attention to military matters. Even more remarkably, after regional army commanders had been forced to impose military control over most sectors of society and the economy during the chaos of 1967 and 1968, in order to prevent a total breakdown of order, they once again withdrew to barracks during the 1970s.

There can be few greater strains on an army's loyalty than to put it into the impossible situations it had to cope with during the gratuitous chaos inflicted on China by Mao's dreams, leave it in charge till it had restored order over warring factions that had been allowed to help themselves to weapons from its arsenals, then withdraw it from most of the positions of extra power and privilege it had gained during those turbulent years. It is remarkable that it came through as loyal and united as it did.

The Cultural Revolution did the army's prestige and popularity great harm, as was apparent from some reactions among civilians to the botched invasion of Vietnam at the beginning of 1979, which cost the Chinese army tens of thousands of dead in a few weeks – about half the fatalities suffered by the United States in its entire Vietnam war. In Peking it was not unusual to hear comments soon after the war that the military had finally got what had long been coming to it. Through the 1980s the army never won back the respect it had enjoyed before the Cultural Revolution, and as its plain uniforms were replaced by ones of ever more Ruritanian splendour the new clothing conveyed a message of a soldiery intended not to defend but to suppress, dressed to be not approachable but intimidating. With the general fading of illusions and pretensions about China as a revolutionary society and the disappearance of serious foreign military threats to national interests, the army has become more openly resentful, even hostile, towards the rest of society, especially the parts of it that seem to be getting rich as the command economy has been loosened up and collective agriculture abolished.

The alienation of the military super-system may not have been consciously planned, but it served the autocracy's interests well. A friendly army that identified itself too closely with the people around it would be much less reliable in a crisis. There is no way of telling how long the military super-system can be held together and remain loyal to a regime whose ability to look after it is limited. Other forces will pull the military apart and encourage the tendency to regional warlordism that has always been an actual or potential threat to effective central power for the last two thousand years.

Keeping the military on a leash has never been easy. For most of the last two thousand years the state has needed armies strong enough to protect the long northern frontier from the threat of very large cavalry forces, while also wanting to keep those same armies under control. Some dynasties failed badly. For most of its existence the Tang dynasty could not assert its authority over its generals, and more dynasties fell to their own generals than to foreign invasions or popular uprisings. It remains one of the greatest and most dangerous tests of a contemporary Chinese government's effectiveness to be able, every five years or thereabouts, to move a few very senior officers between commands in different systems of the military world. These are not the routine transfers of generals in democracies, moves that are of minimal interest outside the services themselves, but changes that put strains on the structures of personal dependency within each of the regional and specialist military systems that have developed in the Chinese Communist Party's armed forces since 1927. The genealogies of Chinese military systems are a subject for specialists in the intelligence business that remains as vitally important to the understanding of China's contemporary politics as do noble and royal kinship structures to medieval European history. Each military system has its ancient patrons at the top of the national power structures, and the balance between them cannot be disturbed without threatening the stability of the state. Ultimately all have to be kept in place by a single autocrat who alone manipulates the mechanisms of control, including the security ones, and ensures that nobody else can know enough to threaten his position.

It might seem that the Communist Party itself ought to be the system that holds all the others together and in their places. It is the only political organization that is represented in every unit and structure throughout China and it proclaims itself to be the leading force in the country. It makes no secret of its self-proclaimed right to rule, has incorporated that claim into the successive constitutions that it has imposed on China and enforces it by any means necessary. Its members, now numbering some 50 million, are everywhere and run everything, including the military and security systems.

Communist Party indoctrination has also played a part comparable with that of the Confucian indoctrination of imperial officials. From the early 1940s, when the Chinese Communist Party found the style of operation that was to bring it to nationwide power, the Party has devoted enormous efforts to inculcating standardized modes of thinking in its members, especially office holders. For about thirty years this was very successful in training officials who would think and act in predictable ways that advanced the Party's interests, until the excesses of the Cultural Revolution made it virtually impossible to believe in the Party's ideology.

Although the Party organizations within every system and unit are all formally subject to the control of the Party centre, the reality is that in the 1990s – as for at least two decades before that – the Party organization within each unit or system tends to be concerned much more with defending the sectional interests of the body within which it is located than with imposing unwelcome wishes of the centre. While appearing to be a force for national unity, the local Party structures strengthen the negative autonomy – the ability to resist externally imposed change – of the fiefs and sub-fiefs that make up the complex structure of China's bureaucratic feudalism.

As for the central Party machinery, its importance is usually exaggerated both by Chinese and by foreign observers. During the late 1960s the notionally all-powerful Political Bureau and its Standing Committee virtually disappeared for a number of years, and most of the Party's central bureaucracy was also paralysed. This did not prevent most of the machinery of state from functioning: the trains continued to run more often than not, and urban populations were still provided with the basic necessities, such as grain and water, even when rival factions were killing each other in local civil wars. Nor did the collapse of the Party centre prevent the rapid deployment of troops to take over many institutions and contain, when Mao permitted, the fighting of civilian 'rebel' organizations.

In the autumn of 1976 Peking's equivalent of the Praetorian

Guard launched an effective military *coup* that put a substantial minority of the Political Bureau behind bars without formal authorization from that body. By the time of the May–June crisis of 1989 the Political Bureau and its Standing Committee were once again virtually sidelined, as a handful of very old men and one very old woman were called out of retirement by Deng Xiaoping, who himself had withdrawn from nearly all formal office, to take over the mishandling of events. A year later the Standing Committee was even weaker: not even the Party's general secretary or the government's premier were effective political bosses in their own right. The long and slow death of Deng Xiaoping, still the emperor, and of the three or four other ancient grand dukes whose seniority and powerful vassals enabled them to resist some of Deng's demands, meant that no other potential autocrat could be allowed to take over the controls at the top of all the systems of Party, state, military and security power. Once that were allowed to happen, Deng and the rest of them might be pushed aside.

Meanwhile the authority of the nominal Party centre continued to slip, and regional Party bosses found room to assert their own authority, sometimes forgetting to pay even the formal kowtows to the centre, as when Shanghai documents in 1990 wrote of uniting round the municipal Party committee and its first secretary, Zhu Rongji, without even mentioning the Central Committee, an omission that would have met with swift punishment not so long ago. It is only a slight exaggeration to say that the rule of China by the Communist Party is already over, for the Party is already too badly weakened and divided to be the national force it once was.

While it is a misconception, encouraged by Party propaganda, to think of the Communist Party as a powerful unity that runs the country through the co-ordinated efforts of its members, the countless Party committees and other Party organizations in every unit of every system in China still matter very much, not so much for ideological reasons as because they are where authority resides. Within the unit little real power is given to non-members, so that the Party card remains a ticket to promotion for the ambitious. Although it would not be fair to suggest that all Party members are careerists, observation indicates that nearly all careerists either are or would be Party members. (There have been signs in the last couple of years that some ambitious people taking a longer view of their self-interest have not been trying for a Party card: another symptom of Party decline.)

It would be more realistic to see the Party as the collective identity of China's ruling class. It is much too big to be the equivalent of the civil service of the last thousand years of imperial history, a group to be numbered in tens of thousands. A better comparison is with the millions of men who, until the beginning of the twentieth century, combined wealth, education and power in various proportions and were conventionally given such labels as *shenshi* or gentry. The disappearance of the Qing state examination system and of the imperial bureaucracy changed the institutional basis of the gentry. They could no longer be representatives of the dynastic state's value system through their certified mastery of its scriptural texts, but they quickly changed themselves into the dominant civilian groups in Republican China. The overwhelming majority of the Communist Party's members will be able to adapt themselves to whatever follows the end of Communist China: they need the Party only as long as it is the club that everyone who would be somebody has to join. Many of the institutions the Party now appears to run will prove much more durable than the Party itself, as the collapse of the Soviet Union shows.

The omnipresent and ceaselessly self-promoting Party is thus not really necessary. During the 1980s the ostensible reasons for the existence of rural Party organizations – socialist agriculture and officially sponsored struggles against private ownership – disappeared, as did much of the Party-controlled village-level bureaucracy that ran the institutions of collective agriculture: the teams, production brigades and people's communes. While peasants still face many problems in coping with a market economy, they seem on the whole to be doing better than they did under the leadership of the vanguard of the proletariat.

Although urban Party officials are trying hard to cling to their positions and have proved to be much more tenacious than their country cousins, it remains much easier to imagine a China without the Communist Party than a China without the quasi-feudal pyramids of power that have developed over the last forty years, or without the work units that run their staffs' lives, or without the social values that promoted and were encouraged by units, systems and their patterns of dependency. It is also hard to see any third option to set beside a personal dictatorship (whether or not disguised as Communist Party rule) or break-up and disorder.

The changes of the second half of the twentieth century appear more as somersaults within traditional categories than as a smashing of the walls inherited from the past. As I attempt to show elsewhere, the communists' creation of a strong state trying to run the whole economy was a reversion to patterns of the first millennium of dynastic history, patterns that to Mao were closer, more familiar and more acceptable than the Russian models on which many institutions of the People's Republic were formally based. Only a very strong and very cunning autocrat could bend the state to its will, and the political culture was very receptive to autocracy. Yet in the early 1990s, as in the 1970s, the fate of China could lie in the weak hands of a very old man. China cannot manage without an emperor, and it cannot join the modern world with one. In this, as in so many other respects, present tyranny is also the tyranny of a past that has not only created the conditions for today's ills but has also made their alleviation difficult within the usually accepted conventions about a unitary China.

4. POPULATION, ECONOMIES AND GROWTH WITHOUT DEVELOPMENT

═══

If the history of states were all there was to the study of China's pasts, there would not be much left for later historians to do except bring the story up to date. Nearly all one needs to know about the state itself is there in Chinese histories and compilations. All researchers have to do is to look up the material and present it from the angle that seems most interesting.

Things change completely if we try to look beyond the state or at states' relations with societies. As we have seen, because over the millennia Chinese official historians have been so little interested in the daily lives of ordinary people they have given us very little systematically organized information on a subject that has, to them, not been worth writing about. There are some exceptions, there is a lot of information to be sifted out from the many tens of thousands of books that survive from before the nineteenth century. But the effort is so great that few scholars combine the skills, the patience and the will to do it. It is much easier to stay with the state.

Even in our own times few Chinese historians have had much interest in open-minded explorations of social and economic history. (Some studies of economic history are really only studies of state fiscal history.) There was not much to be gained by investigating subjects on which Mao had made his own views very clear. You were not going to tell the world that the Chairman had got it all wrong on so-called peasant rebellions or question the usefulness of the term 'feudal' to characterize the structures of rural society over the last three hundred years – though rural economic relationships were essentially those of a free market, with land, labour, grain and money being commercially bought, rented or lent. All you could safely do was gather evidence to support the Party line. When some remarkable individuals did venture into what unregenerate bourgeois observers would regard as real history they published their findings with as little fuss as possible. Readers had to work out for themselves the implications of studies that silently punctured the myth of feudalism, a myth all the more essential to the Communist Party as it was the theoretical target of their rural struggles from the late 1920s onwards. Just when historians were starting to open up some of the key issues in the 1980s the shutters came rattling down again.

If ordinary people have been a dangerous subject for history in modern China, for the historians of imperial times ordinary people and their lives were of central interest only when things went unusually wrong or unusually right. A local history might note two-headed babies, or a peasant lad from a very poor family teaching himself to read and learn by heart the classics and pass official exams, or some act of great merit by Confucian standards, such as a young widow preferring poverty or death to remarriage, thus bringing glory on the county or prefecture. Famine would be noted in local and, if bad enough, in national records: it required official action, even if only some remission of tax obligations. Rebellion beyond the scale of the local banditry that was endemic in some poor and out-of-the-way parts of the country was always of interest to the authorities. Indeed, some of the few peasants who actually have their names preserved in the official record are disrupters of order.

Otherwise the peasants are nearly invisible or, at most, seen as part of the landscape, as when they appear as details in a painting, sleeping on the back of a water buffalo, working in the fields or otherwise illustrating the urban official's sentimentalized image of village life. They tend to be seen in broad categories, such as *min* (people) or its modern version *renmin*.* Good *min* – *liang min* in the

---

* 'People' is the conventional translation, but it really means 'commoners' or 'subjects'.

past, *renmin* or *guangda qunzhong* (broad masses) in our time —
know their place. They perform the obligations the state requires
of them, pay their taxes, lead proper family lives, do not get
involved in subversive organizations or shelter troublemakers,
turn out when required to be anonymous crowds of labourers
on public works, and do not bother the local authorities with
fights or serious quarrels. Their women are even more invisible, if
that were possible, in the historical records than the men, as the
state endorsed and supported their subordination to patriarchal
social values that seem in some cases to have denied them even a
name of their own. That difference has been reduced in recent
decades, though women are still at a disadvantage in all sorts of
ways.

One characteristic of the commoners, be they the *min* of dynastic
China or the *renmin* of the People's Republic, is that if they are not
good commoners, they become non-people by official standards.
Imperial China had its untouchables, and so too did Mao's China.
The flag of the People's Republic was designed in 1949 with one
big yellow star symbolizing the Party and four little ones to sym-
bolize the four notional classes that constituted the 'people'. Within
a decade one of those classes, the 'national bourgeoisie', was dropped
from the 'people' and another, the petty bourgeoisie, was treated as
a left-over from the past that should be tidied away as soon as
possible. So the flag had to be left deliberately unexplained for a
generation until further twists in the political story brought the
bourgeoisie and petty bourgeoisie back into the 'people' in the
1980s.

There is thus a mythical 'people' standing between us and the
actual peoples and societies of the past. Only occasionally does the
veil come down, as in Susan Naquin's remarkable study of a rural
sect that mounted an attack on the imperial palace in Peking in
1813. The court was so alarmed by this incursion that the origins
and course of the rising were very thoroughly investigated, and the
records of interrogations were put on file and left there in what
appear to be fairly raw form. A little world of small-time rural
sectarians comes back to life. This is very unusual. On the whole

we know very little about the ways in which the many peoples of China lived, thought, worked and ate. Only some very rough outlines emerge from the mist. If all this reads like a long-winded excuse for the absence of a reasonably clear picture of how China's societies and economies have been formed through time, it is. But it is essential to draw attention to the very fuzziness of any generalizing about this vital subject.

For the subject is a vital one. The crisis of the Chinese state is only part of a much wider and deeper crisis that the past has bequeathed to the present. If modern China had inherited fewer people to the arable acre, other ways of organizing economic and social activity, other attitudes and values, the rulers of today's China might have seen options open to them other than bowing off the stage and leaving things to fall apart immediately or sending in the tanks.

 If we slip into the comfortable habit of thinking of Chinese society or the Chinese economy in the singular, we mislead ourselves. Even when referring to recent decades it is only partly justifiable to talk about one Chinese economy and Chinese society. There are many local economies and societies.

Even the numbers involved can only be guessed at. Long-term econometric history cannot really be written yet, though whether that is a loss of anything but illusions of certainty I am inclined to doubt. The data on numbers of people to which we have ready access are treacherous indicators of actual population. Various regimes gathered figures of taxpayers and performers of forced labour. When these figures fluctuate wildly, as at times they do, it looks as though in a generation or two most of the population has disappeared, when all that has really happened is that the state has lost the struggle with other interests for control of the peasants, and most of them have dropped off the state's tax records. A population figure that stays more or less stable for a century or two in the course of a single dynasty suggests that it stands for a conventional tax quota. Leo Orleans noted that in the early decades of the People's Republic different government departments worked on estimates of the population that were well over 100 million apart. The 1982 census was probably the first to come within 5 per cent of the actual numbers.

Similar problems apply to the figures for cultivated land. Unless we know that we are dealing with actually surveyed land – and surveys are more likely to understate than overstate – the figures are almost certainly notional. Despite satellite photography the actual amount of land under cultivation remains only roughly knowable even now, and the areas on record for the past are only a reflection of the effectiveness of the state machine at different periods. Global figures for food production have no absolute value at all, and estimates of past crop yield per hectare rarely represent anything more than fantasy divided by invention. Attempts to quantify the Chinese past, except in certain carefully limited investigations, are essentially guesswork. This caveat having been entered, let us make up an outline of the population history of China.

For nearly all of the last 600,000 years people were few and far between: hunters and gatherers need space. The first known population explosion followed the transition, around 6000 BC, to agriculture as the means of gaining food that determined the way of life in parts of north and east China. As agriculture gradually changed from slash-and-burn to more intensive cultivation, which is indicated by the more permanent settlements of the later Neolithic and by the evidence of greater social division of labour, population densities presumably increased.

Neolithic farming technology was displaced by iron tools only somewhere around 500 BC, when several hundred years of rapid population growth began that probably multiplied the population several times over. We can see the evidence for this in the much bigger areas enclosed by city walls and the much larger numbers of people in reports of state activities.

The earliest official figures to survive show nearly 60 million on the government's books in the first century BC. This is much more likely to be below the actual population of what is now China than above it. Nobody goes out of his or her way to be liable for tax. Besides, Han power did not extend to most of what is now the far west or the north-east, and most of the higher land of central and southern China would have belonged to peoples who were not Chinese or on the Han dynasty's population registers. The world of highland South-East Asian cultures extended as far north as the Yellow River Valley. So we might invent a total population for the present Chinese empire of around the 70 million mark. This was a level that was to be fairly stable for many centuries and was not to be doubled for well over a thousand years. As this period saw the steady spread of Chinese control outwards and upwards from the main river valleys of central and southern China, it is likely that the increased numbers include the descendants of some peoples who had not been on the Han dynasty's records. To invent a round number, we could suggest a hypothetical population of somewhere around 100 million for Song China in AD 1000.

The next five hundred years see an increase by about half – all these figures are only guesses and subject to enormous error – so that by AD 1500 a notional figure of around 150 million would be conventionally acceptable. We are thus looking at an increase of 100–150 per cent over the previous 1,600 years, a snail's pace, and one many times slower than that of either the previous few centuries or the succeeding ones. It was a population in balance with the environment, which could continue feeding itself off the same land indefinitely.

This stability breaks down in the late seventeenth and the eighteenth century, when it is generally accepted that another increase took place that at least doubled the figure within 120 years – which is probably best explained by the Manchu abolition of manorial serfdom, the reduction of gentry privileges that inhibited the free small-peasant economy and the introduction of maize. This population explosion meant that the Qing empire entered the nineteenth century with between 300 million and 400 million subjects, a growth that took place without the help of significant industrialization or of antibiotics. It took another 150 years for the population to reach the 600 million mark around 1950. The growth rate was checked by Malthusian horrors: nineteenth- and twentieth-century experience has justified the title of a book written by the famine-relief specialist Walter H. Mallory in the 1920s: *China, Land of Famine.*

It may have seemed for a time that the people of China had broken out of this overpopulation/famine trap after 1949. But a decade later they were undergoing what may well have been the biggest famine in human history. And now, a little more than forty years after the brave new start of 1949, there are nearly twice as many people – some say already twice as many.

So we can see, or invent, a pattern of doublings of population over very different spans of time. We can speculate that there were at least two doublings between 500 and 100 BC. The next doubling took perhaps a thousand years or even more. After more centuries of slow growth a fourth doubling happened in the eighteenth century, a fifth over the next 150 years and a sixth in the fifty years since 1949. A seventh does not bear thinking about.

As it is, population growth in the countryside has been slowed but not brought under control. Because there are hardly any public-welfare provisions for peasants and very few peasants can afford to put enough aside for the time when they will no longer be able to do heavy manual labour, each couple has to have at least one son to support them in their old age. As all the land that may be sustainably cultivated was cleared, claimed and planted long ago, the high numbers can be fed only by using more chemicals, clearing marginal upland or semi-arid land that should be left under its natural vegetation, and using up millions of years of underground water reserves, which are being depleted very fast in many of the drier parts of China. According to official figures published in the mid-1980s, there were about 900 square metres of arable land per head. Population growth brings it down by at least 15 square metres a year. Each acre now has to feed four people and will have to feed five by the end of the century. Alternatively, China will depend increasingly on imported grain.

While the third of the Chinese population living in or near the coast and the big cities may well be able to make a go of it in the world economy, the prospects for the other 700 million or 800 million are gloomy. Established forest is rapidly disappearing, and in the areas where most people live there are too few trees left. Despite decades of well-publicized attempts to plant trees to hold back the sand, the deserts are still advancing inexorably. More intensive cultivation of the arable land, more frequent cropping and heavier doses of chemicals have had the results that can be expected, and soil erosion is getting worse. The cities are filthy. Even if we leave the possible consequences of global warming out of our calculations, the relationship between humanity and the natural environment must deteriorate. While some may blame Mao for not slowing down rural population growth except during the famines that followed his Great Leap Forward, it is unlikely that anything short of further major catastrophes or a deliberate refusal to bring in public-health measures could have done much about it. Throughout this period the production of food has just kept ahead of the production of people, and the nuclear family has survived at the expense of its members and the natural environment. This is a trap from which there is no acceptable escape, but it will not affect the whole country equally. Two centuries of coping suggest that most people will get by somehow, but the prospects are grim, especially for inland and upland China.

The underlying ecological problem makes much of the optimism about the prospects for the Chinese economy seem shallow. Economists, as we all know, are hard-headed realists, and when they tell us of the Chinese economic miracle in the 1980s lay observers must not express doubts. Most peasants are richer for the abolition of collective agriculture, increased state-procurement prices, the restoration of private marketing and the encouragement of small business. But for several years now reported grain production has been stuck at around 400 million tonnes. By the time it broke through that barrier in 1990 to reach a claimed 435 million tonnes population growth had accounted for nearly all the extra food. Where peasants do not have access to good markets for their produce or their labour they face hunger. The resources are not available to provide adequate transport and communications for the richest parts of China, let alone the vast inland and mountainous areas.

If official figures are to be believed, China has industrialized at spectacular speed these last forty years. The success of China's rulers in keeping urban wages down has been even more spectacular.

According to official statistics the average state factory wage increased in real terms by only 8.5 per cent in the quarter century from 1952 and actually decreased by over 16 per cent in the twenty years from 1957, the first year in which all of industry was socialized. Yet during those same periods industrial output per worker increased by 260 per cent and 60 per cent respectively. In those years China created an industrial system with some rather interesting characteristics that made it very highly resistant to reform. Each part of the system was protected from foreign competition and from more efficient producers in China. Sales were guaranteed at prices high enough to yield profits sufficient to supply most of the state's revenue and also to provide for so much further investment that the poor returns on it did not matter. Nor did it matter that this growing industrial system tended to produce inefficiently ever more goods that a free market would have rejected. It ensured employment for tens of millions and kept the state provided for, both locally and nationally. As there was no universal welfare system, these industrial organizations had to provide everything for their staff and their families. Dismissals were virtually impossible, and staff numbers tended to increase.

The incentive to update products or to reach international standards was minimal, market share could not be significantly increased by any enterprise, and inefficiency was not penalized. Thus is was that even in the 1980s coal-burning locomotives were still being produced, and in almost every area Chinese industry was at least twenty years behind the modern world. One is reminded of the statistical triumphs of the East German economy and how delusive they proved to be. The reforms of the last few years have only marginally changed the situation, and that often for the worse by allowing foreign competition to devastate some sectors, such as cameras and motor vehicles. The great dinosaur industries cannot be closed without unleashing mass disorder and the resistance of local and central power apparatuses. The rapidly growing non-state economies of coastal regions are still at a primitive stage of capitalist development. The state still treats them with suspicion and hostility. Caught between the command economy and the market economy,

China is now suffering the worst features of both. Fundamental reform is impossible without inviting total chaos. Yet this appalling crisis is the result of earlier great successes, technical, economic and social, which both stimulated and limited each other and connected with population changes in sometimes surprising ways.

Approaching China's pasts as a European makes one constantly aware that Chinese societies have been remarkably weak in relation to the centralized, bureaucratic states that have been running them for at least 2,500 years, although for very long periods economic activity in China dwarfed that of Eurasia's backward far west. Nowhere is that clearer than in the amazing two or three centuries that began around AD 1000, when one might have expected Song China's merchants and manufacturers, whose activities in the commercial parts of the economy became so much greater in scale than anything China had seen before, to demand a political voice. But the burghers never even asked for charters; firms never found the institutional form that would have enabled them to survive for many generations; urban subjects never became citizens.

Whether the development of economic forms and performance in China over the last 10,000 years has been a success story or not depends very much on when, where and at what we choose to look and with what other parts of the world comparisons are made. In one way things have got steadily worse since the early Neolithic: survival has called for ever longer hours of work over the millennia. Slash-and-burn farming required much less work than its increasingly labour-intensive successors. If we go back to north and east China about 7,000 years ago there is plenty of evidence of fairly permanent settlements – permanent because the decisive form of food production was the growing of millet in the north and rice in the east. The many Neolithic cultures of what is now China can stand comparison with other pre-metallic agricultural societies elsewhere in the world. Metallurgy seems to have come a little late by comparison with western Eurasia and south Asia. A few years ago it appeared that mainland South-East Asia was also ahead of what is now China in bronze-working, but that now seems much less likely. Nor were bronze's effects on production revolutionary at first. While we can talk of Bronze Age agriculture in western Eurasia, there are not many signs that bronze was used for food production in China. The supreme skills of the Shang bronze-casters, deployed in the manufacture of the extraordinary ritual vessels, weapons, ornaments and such small tools as knives, were rarely used in the making of farm tools.

Agriculture remained essentially pre-metallic until around the fifth century BC, when a metallurgical breakthrough propelled China, within a few generations, through technical changes that took millennia in western Eurasia. The art of pumping enough oxygen into a furnace to liquefy iron ore, so that iron farm tools could be cast cheaply in moulds, was one that Europe did not acquire till the fifteenth century AD or thereabouts. So while western Eurasia gradually switched from a bronze-using agriculture to one using a few expensive wrought-iron tools, Chinese farmers' productivity soared when they were able to replace implements of wood, stone, shell and bone with cast-iron tools. Cast-iron tools were so cheap that iron spades are not infrequently found abandoned in pits dug from the fourth century BC onwards, whereas very few abandoned bronze digging implements have been unearthed. By enormously increasing the food surplus that each peasant household could produce, iron tools transformed the material basis of life in the more advanced parts of China around the middle and lower Yellow and Yangtse river systems.

Cities grew rapidly. The relationship of peasant and master changed, as both land and labour became commodities and the traditional subordination of serf to hereditary local lord gave way to economic relationships or direct control by the state. As the economies of the Yellow and Yangtse river regions grew, state power grew with them. Successful merchants and manufacturers made fortunes; the currencies of different states circulated widely. Technologies made rapid progress. From being, in material terms, a somewhat laggard member of the world's leading civilizations between 3000 and 500 BC, during the next few centuries China was among the leaders, or ahead of the field, in almost every area of practical technology, whether productive or destructive. The human equivalents of the life-sized toy soldiers guarding the First Qin Emperor's tomb were much better-armed than their Roman counterparts, and the Han peasant was probably ahead of the Roman field slave at growing grain. All this happened during the first great population leap of recorded Chinese history.

It could be argued that by two thousand years ago China had most of the technology of survival, especially of wet and dry farming, with which it entered the nineteenth century and, by AD 1400,nearly all its pre-modern technology of any kind. There is no need here to describe once more the flow of technical creativity from China and its neighbours that Joseph Needham has mapped. With a very sweeping generalization we can say that Europe did not catch up till the eighteenth century at the earliest. Even at the beginning of that century French missionaries were paying China the compliment of engaging in industrial espionage at the porcelain centre of Jingdezhen, where the technical standards, division of labour and scale of operation were all far beyond what Europe could achieve. Indeed, if we look at the pattern of trade between China and Europe as recently as the early nineteenth century, we find that it is rather typical of trade between advanced industrial powers and certain Third World countries: advanced China exports manufactures (especially porcelain and silk) and other high-value luxuries (tea) for which backward trading partners, such as Britain, pay mainly in hard currency they cannot spare (silver) and in narcotics (opium).

In many fields China goes about as far as it is possible to go without modern science and technology. But the obstacles to Chinese invention become ever greater. In printing, for example, the early technique of text reproduction by carving a whole two-page spread in reverse relief on a block of wood was not generally superseded by movable type even though movable type was available. This may be explained by the vast number of characters needed to print Chinese.

The transition to mechanical printing presses was not made until the West introduced printing by machine to China in the nineteenth century. It was never necessary to invent that sort of complicated machinery while cheap labour was available to ink a block and apply each sheet to it by hand. The more sophisticated technology developed during the first 1,600 years of the Christian era coincided with a much slower rate of population growth than those of the centuries either before or after. Generally we find signs that machinery was used less in nineteenth-century China than in the fourteenth century. There was probably a lower ratio of animal power to human power in production and transport. Thanks to the population explosion of the eighteenth century, labour became so cheap that it became less worthwhile to invest in expensive animals and machines.

A parallel consequence in agriculture was that the higher population entailed more competition to rent land or borrow grain. As the price of unimproved land rose there was less financial incentive to invest in improving land. Instead of economic development we find both increasing commercialization without adequate capitalization where communications were good and the cancerous growth of rack-renting and high-interest loans. The debt industry became one of China's biggest, so that when in the 1940s and early 1950s the communists wanted to win peasant support, their attack on big lenders was one of their most popular policies. Unfortunately, usury was only a symptom of underlying scarcities, not their cause. It is inevitable in such circumstances and is, of course, flourishing today.

Until recently discussions of the economic and social history of China almost invariably implied that at any one time there was one economy and one society. More recently there has been a tendency to divide China into a number of large economic regions, to be discussed separately. More realistic, perhaps, would be to see hundreds of thousands of basic village communities each standing in a slightly different relationship to local, regional and national structures of political, economic and cultural power. Some communities with distinct relative advantages and good communications belonged primarily to inter-regional or national trading systems, selling their products to distant provinces and eating grain imported from other regions. At the other extreme would be impoverished village communities, isolated by appalling communications and transport, that produced little to interest the commerce even of their own county and had next to no purchasing power either.

These contrasts are very clear in the first half of the twentieth century, when it is almost impossible to make any generalizations about Han Chinese villages and their economic life. It seems unlikely that the contrasts would have been less visible in earlier centuries. So although the extent of commercialization in parts of Song and Yuan China of the tenth to fourteenth centuries is still amazing, and seemed to the contemporary Venetian commentator Marco Polo almost beyond belief, other regions of the country were surely only marginally involved in the cash economy.

Village societies are particularly hard to discuss because of their invisibility compared with cities. Although city air in China did not make one free, it made one more noticeable. People wrote books about urban life, so we know quite a lot more about the great cities of dynastic China in both the first and the second millennium of imperial rule than about the villages that made them possible. Detailed accounts of life in actual villages before this century are few and far between, though there is a tradition of excellent agricultural handbooks going back to Han times. Even archaeologists show very little interest in village sites later than 500 BC. The study of earlier villages probably has to begin by drawing on the great wealth of detailed studies of actual villages in this century by Chinese and foreign social scientists and other observers.

We must be on our guard against basing any assumptions about rural life in the distant past on twentieth-century experience. It may well be, for example, that the relative stability in population for the first 1,600 years of the Christian era was connected with a greater role than in recent centuries for kinship structures above the level of the nuclear family, whether we call them clans, lineages or extended families. In the previous period states had an interest in promoting population growth for the sake of military power and so encouraged nuclear families. From about 1680 the Manchu government brought in a series of measures designed to curb the power of the local gentry, which had in some parts of China, especially where communications were not so good, been running local manorial economies based on master–serf, rather than purely commercial, relationships. Nearly all gentry privileges were reduced or removed by the Manchus, which led to the almost universal emancipation of serfs, who were then free to set up as settlers with periods of tax exemption while they either cleared new land or brought back under cultivation land abandoned during the troubles of the mid-seventeenth century. Qing rule made it much harder for local magnates to bring serfs back under control other than as tenants, wage labourers or debtors.

In most of China the virtual ending of serfdom, combined with swipes at the gentry, reduced the role of extended family institutions. (Some obvious exceptions are frontier areas, such as Guangdong, Guangxi and Fujian.) With the arrival of food crops from the Americas, especially maize and sweet potatoes (not to mention such other delights as tomatoes, peppers, and tobacco), all was set for the growth of population as new land could be cultivated and as the nuclear family broke away from clan controls to a greater or lesser extent.

Extended families working as economic units had probably had a stabilizing influence on population growth. They could make some kind of provision for the old age of members, and they may also have had an interest in preventing too many people from having to be supported by limited amounts of land. In the patrilineal nuclear family, however, there is the inescapable need to breed sons for one's old age. Without wanting to make too much of this single factor, I would venture a guess that mum, dad and the kids are the main reason why China has experienced growth without development in the last three hundred years. The dominance of the unstable and fissiparous unit, the nuclear family, made for a more fragmented society and helped to inhibit the emergence of large and powerful economic units.

Another aspect of rural life that has to be addressed is the label 'feudal' that was tied to it by would-be Marxists earlier in this century. Quite simply, 'feudal', in its assigned Chinese equivalent *fengjian*, was used because in Engels' scheme it was what came between slave society (as in ancient Rome) and capitalism, and as for one or two thousand years China had been out of the one but not yet fully into the other, it *had* to be 'feudal'. There could be no other conceivable reason for the label. Liege-lord and vassal relationships are hard to find in Han Chinese societies in the thousand years before 1949, though they were used to control rulers of non-Han subject peoples. The later bureaucratic monarchy was much too jealous of its powers to permit the existence of local magnates enjoying the legal status of Japanese or European nobles. When *de facto* barons emerged it was only during a temporary weakening of state power, as in the middle of the seventeenth, nineteenth or twentieth centuries, and the state removed them as soon as it could. Even manorial economies reminiscent of feudal France or England had virtually disappeared by the end of the seventeenth century, after the early Qing dynasty reforms.

How, then, should late traditional China be simply characterized (if such a thing is worth even trying), given the great variety of local arrangements?

On the one hand, economic life was almost entirely characterized by commodities: land, labour and products were all marketable. The value of everything could be expressed in money. Peasants were tied neither to the land nor to a master. The total amount of commercial activity was enormous and grew, especially as population increased. Patient researchers have shown startling increases in the number and frequency of markets in various localities over recent centuries. Since Song times at least, Chinese towns and cities have been intensely commercialized. It was the market economy of the great Song cities that gave the world the commercial culture of the restaurant, show business and the printed novel. While in early imperial China gourmet food and entertainment had been the privileges mainly of royalty and the great families that could afford to support armies of dependants, the lower Yangtse cities of the Song and later dynasties made them available to anyone who could pay.

The market economy also created long-distance trading in commodities as bulky and basic as grain. Earlier dynasties had required peasants to pay taxes in grain and cloth, part of which was delivered to the capital to be used as payment in kind to soldiers and officials;

the Song rulers raised money taxes and let the lure of the market bring grain to the capital, to be bought by public employees with their money wages. The increasing monetarization of economic life continued into this century.

That is one aspect of the secular growth of commercialism in China in the last thousand years. On the other hand, the highly commercialized parts of China fell short of being capitalist, if by capitalism we mean economic structures in which capital acquires an autonomous existence of its own and an enterprise or firm can be distinguished from its owners. Later dynastic China had an enormous number of small entrepreneurs brought together on a short-term basis in an infinite number of small transactions through an army of intermediaries, brokers and guarantors. Each entrepreneur was weak and vulnerable unless he operated as part of a network.

Just as the principle of approximately equal division of property between sons in each generation ensured that landholdings would get ever smaller until they shrank to the one-acre family farm, so it was almost impossible to build up over many generations a business that could be secured against a future family quarrel and the consequent splitting up of assets. Although the farm, the shop, the boat or the cart would be run strictly as a business, there could be no realistic expectation that it would last. Nor were there the large sums of venture capital to permit the emergence of really powerful firms able to dominate a market on a national scale.

We thus need a word to describe economic structures that were commercial and commodity-dominated but were not marked by large accumulations of capital in the hands of individuals or firms. Capital could normally be built up only over a number of decades or, at most, a lifetime or two. There was nothing resembling the limited-liability company or its predecessors, the great trading corporations of early modern Europe, though the total size of economic activity in China was probably not surpassed by Europe until the nineteenth century. All the same, the networks created and maintained across the Chinese world, including the Chinese diaspora, could and did permit complicated trading and credit arrangements and predisposed Chinese business people to doing well under other systems of commercial law and institutional structures, as in South-East Asia under European colonization.

Manufacturing too was formidably well organized on the basis of a very high degree of specialization and division of labour both in the manufacturing centres and across local, regional and national markets. But we do not find big, permanent enterprises other than state-owned ones. The porcelain metropolis of Jingdezhen may have had hundreds of thousands of inhabitants; the story that some pieces passed through seventy or more pairs of hands in the manufacturing process may be only somewhat exaggerated, and Jingdezhen could adapt its production to the demands of Chinese and world markets. Yet manufacture at Jindezhen and the national and international marketing of its products was fragmented and done without big capitalists and big firms.

Fragmentation was not incompatible with size and sophistication. The traditional economy was very good at keeping out foreign involvement right into the twentieth century. But this fragmentation made for political weakness. It enabled established techniques to be refined but inhibited more fundamental innovations.

Although the commercial and manufacturing structures that the twentieth century inherited from the past were not intrinsically incapable of adaptation to other ways of organizing economic activity or to technological change, such transformations needed changes in political structures and values that did not come about in mainland China. Both the Nationalists, when on the mainland, and the Communists were happy only with state-controlled big business. It took colonial rule in parts of the Chinese world to create other arrangements that resulted in the prosperity of Hong Kong, Singapore and Taiwan, less because of the wisdom of the colonial rulers than because the Chinese state was excluded.

The history of farming in the Chinese world is one of the development of techniques that, by pre-modern world standards, were extremely effective at maintaining fertility for millennia, until in the last two or three centuries methods that had worked extraordinarily well before this were abused, increasing total output at the cost of the quality of each life. Put very crudely, the story of agriculture in China over the past ten thousand years can be seen as a triumphant conquest of nature as people have wrested more and more food from the limited amount of arable land. Another view would see a steady decline in the quality of life as ever more intensive cultivation has forced people to work harder and harder just to stay alive.

China of the twentieth century inherited economic systems that were overdeveloped rather than underdeveloped. Their problem is that they had adapted too well to the restraints placed on them by bureaucratic autocracy and the cultural values that inhibited the emergence of anything comparable with the limited liability company or the law of entail. These systems both encouraged and could cope with the ever-growing pressure of population on resources. No regime in the first half of the twentieth century was strong enough to bring about fundamental changes except around the foreign coastal enclaves; and no regime ever got over the Confucian-educated official's prejudice that private enterprise was selfish and antisocial. Compared with Europe, America and Japan, China seemed doomed to backwardness.

The Communist Party tried to break out of the poverty and backwardness inherited from history by undoing a thousand years of small-scale private enterprise. The rush to socialism that led to the Great Leap and famine was a heroic and criminal failure. Whether decollectivization will succeed for most of China remains to be seen. What that has achieved so far is growth without development in agriculture and a distorted development in industry.

5. WALLS

This is a chapter about enclosures, walls and boxes. Walls on the ground and walls in the mind. Enclosures within which all can be controlled and safely structured. Outside is otherness and danger. Between the safety inside and the uncontrollable outside are few windows through which to look in or out. The best enclosing walls are solid, high and unbroken, except for gateways that can be guarded. If the wall can have a moat round it, so much the better.

The walls are not only a thing of the past. Though most city walls have been torn down, the walled compound is still the standard way in which to organize a group of buildings. Even in 1990, when the state prettified much of Peking for the Asian Games, new walls were built to enclose areas that were hitherto unwalled and therefore untidy, if not actually dangerous.

As in some other parts of the world, a wall was an essential feature of cities in ancient and medieval China, and it remained a standard one until the twentieth century. Chinese city walls tended to be much more substantial than European ones. The walls of York, for example, are delicate by comparison with the massive structures that still surrounded inner Peking in the early 1960s and have since been used to fill in the moat and create the space for a road, just as General Wade levelled most of Hadrian's Wall and its ditch into a military road during the Scottish wars of the eighteenth century.

Wall-building was a serious undertaking. The walls were the most solid and permanent part of a city, and north China still has many prominent remains of the walls of ancient cities that have left little else by way of visible structures. Apart from city walls and the

Great Wall system there are hardly any buildings more than a few hundred years old anywhere in China. Parts of the 7-kilometre wall built about 1600 BC to defend the Shang city at Zhengzhou still stand up to 3 metres above the ground; and as the base of the wall was some 10.5 metres wide, we can only guess how many million days of labour were needed to move and pound hundreds of thousands of cubic metres of stamped earth in layers only one or two centimetres thick, one upon another. Yet it is still not clear which Shang rulers made this massively enclosed city their capital or for how long.

Another mighty set of city walls was built nearly three thousand years later when in 1369 the founder of the Ming dynasty decided to do something for his small home town of Linhao (modern Fengyang in Anhui). He designated this small country town the Middle Capital and mobilized labour to construct a city wall 7,760 by 7,170 metres in length. Inside that was a forbidden city with walls 8 kilometres long. The walls of the palace compound were a modest 890 by 960 metres. In 1375 construction stopped, and in 1382 the dismantling of the palace buildings began. The walls had been built before the city they were to contain, and the city was never created. Although walls were not usually so pointless, it was characteristic of a new capital city that its walls came first.

The standard pattern of a capital city in ancient and early medieval China included not just a principal wall but also an outer wall (*guo*) some distance beyond it that enclosed a much bigger area. Within the inner and outer walls were other enclosures: palaces, government departments and other official institutions, residential wards, markets and temples. Each would have its own walls and its gates staffed by gatekeepers. At night all the walled enclosures would be shut, and only the army patrolled the streets. The walls were more essential features of the residential wards than the houses inside.

The walled enclosures were eyeless. Even a palace was barely visible from outside. The tourist's view south from Coal Hill down the main axis of Peking's palace complex is one that only its denizens would have been allowed to see in Ming and Qing times. When the whole complex was a functioning palace system ordinary people were walled out not just from Coal Hill but also from Bei Hai Lake beside it and the bridge dividing that lake from the part of the former Forbidden City that still houses China's rulers, the Zhong-nanhai area. Little more could be seen from outside than the dull red wall, with its yellow-glazed coping tiles, the heavily guarded gates with their towers and very solid doors and the tops of roofs. Behind the walls was mystery and power, from which endless rumours but little hard information would emerge. Whereas most palaces of Europe were high, conspicuous buildings with many windows that dominated through visibility, China's palaces were an enclosed and hidden innerness.

Especially in north China each city house was enclosed, if it could be, by a wall, with its rooms looking inward on to courtyards or, if the house was grand enough, on to a garden. Within the enclos-ing wall was an intimacy that left little private space and made secrets very difficult to keep. The distinction between the inside world of the home and the outside world of the city was nearly absolute.

Not everything in the Chinese city was enclosed. In the later Middle Ages trade broke out of the walled markets, where it had previously been confined under government supervision, and into the public streets. Shops, inns and other commercial establishments lined main streets, turning their faces towards them. Customers could drink their tea or wine while watching the world go by, repairing upstairs in better places to the more exclusive rooms from which they had a better view of what was going on and were less overlooked. One can still get a feel of what these commercial cities must have been like by wandering through the older parts of Suzhou or Shaoxing or jostling along the crowded Dashala outside Qianmen in Peking, a shopping street in the Han Chinese section of the city when the north was reserved for Manchus. But even in Suzhou the best houses were hidden away behind inconspicuous entrances until they opened out into gardens beyond gardens, with walls as games, framing views through gaps in them, leading one round by longer ways to make a small area seem greater, enlarging through division; and the city itself was hemmed in by its wall.

Only in the twentieth century have city walls gone, removed out of greed for the land they occupied or from fear that walled cities might resist the rulers of the day. Instead of the city wall there has been a return to the walled compound. Offices, factories, schools and housing projects are walled or fenced off and gatekeepers put in place to monitor the movements of all who come or go. Even where there is not an enclosure there are eyes appointed to see who calls in at a block of flats. As life in China's cities becomes more insecure, the walls grow higher. I know a compound in Peking that had a wall built around the back and sides when it was first put up in the 1950s. During the Cultural Revolution the wall grew many feet higher, like many others in the city. More recently still, the main entrance has been given an extra line of security with a high metal fence in front of it and a requirement (not always enforced) to prove your identity before entering the compound. As with other aspects of the contemporary Chinese state, the pattern that has been restored is that of the earlier rather than the later dynasties.

It is not only physically that the work unit is usually walled off. Mentally too it is separated from its environment. Within the enclosures of the work place and its housing compounds you belong; here you work, live and will quite possibly die. Your chances of moving out of your unit's enclosures are not very good, and if you are a city-dweller, you are very unlikely to own or rent a home of your own in a place of your choice. In China there is no option of not knowing your neighbours by sight or name, of leaving the job behind you at the end of the working day, of drawing a line between your working and your private self. Within the enclosure all belong together, willy-nilly. You had better get on with your colleagues because you may have to work and live among them for the rest of your life, even if you still bear deep hatreds dating from the Cultural Revolution, when members of rival factions killed and maimed each other in the compound.

The unit tries to protect its collective privacy against the outside world. Its leaders have a strong interest in keeping other units out of its territory; even the police do not usually detain a member of a unit before obtaining its consent. It does not share information

willingly with other units or encourage its members to establish
their own networks of contacts across unit barriers. Behind its wall
the unit keeps the vital personal dossiers on all its employees and
runs its own internal security. These methods of control and
repression can also be used in troubled times to protect members of
the unit from outside threats, as was apparent in Peking after the
June 1989 shootings, when many units were curiously incapable of
carrying out the municipal authorities' instructions to identify those
who had taken part in the protest movement.

Although most city walls have now gone – the few surviving
walled cities now have scarcity value in the tourist market – cities
can still be partly or wholly sealed off. Access by public transport
can be denied to some or all travellers and an open city quietly
closed, as has happened from time to time when Peking has been
made very hard to reach from the provinces, or Lhasa has become
fairly inaccessible after one of its periodic nationalist demonstrations.
Temporary residents and undesirables can be run out of town or
put out of sight for a while, as when Peking was purged for the
1990 Asian Games. An invisible wall makes it next to impossible to
move into a city as a permanent resident: the normal rate at which
new residence permits are granted is about two a year for each
10,000 of the existing population.

Sealing off large parts of China from foreigners has both ancient
and modern precedents. By earlier standards, China has been
remarkably open since the middle 1980s. The normal pattern of
behaviour of the Chinese state was to keep foreigners out whenever
it can and, when obliged to let them in as visitors or residents, to
restrict their movements as far as possible. The state's fear of foreigners and foreign contacts goes deep and is a more serious form of
xenophobia than can usually be found among the common people.

The Chinese are as liable as other nations to let themselves be
stirred up against conspicuously different-looking outsiders in times
of crisis. Yet when the pressure is not on, the country is not a bad
one in which to live for foreigners who adapt themselves to local
ways. To be sure, attitudes to Africans can be appalling, but China
is relatively free from the virulent racial exclusivity of Japan. What

counts in China is not so much the colour of your skin as the way you behave. Foreigners who do not threaten can be accepted. A Westerner living in China is in much less danger of attack than a Chinese in Sydney.

The state has found it much harder to accommodate aliens. They may want to find out about China, to acquire China's secrets, to make their home countries richer or stronger at China's expense, to threaten the beliefs and values of China, to lure local businesses into trading with them in ways that the Chinese state does not control. Formerly the best way to deal with foreigners who had to be let in was to minimize their contact with Chinese people. Diplomatic embassies normally had to take the form of tribute-bearing missions and were escorted closely while inside China. Even traders some-times had to be treated as tribute-bringers and deals disguised as the exchange of gifts. The privilege of a visit to the capital was not very often granted to a foreign or tributary state.

In sixth-century Luoyang foreigners were kept in two groups of four enclosures, separated from the rest of the city by the River Luo. One group of enclosures was hostels for temporary visitors; the other was wards for permanent residents. The arrangements were very reminiscent of the huge Gostinitsa Druzhba (Friendship Hostel) built in the western outskirts of Peking in the 1950s for Soviet specialists and used from the 1960s for housing foreign 'experts' from many other countries under armed guard. If China had to have these aliens around it was best to put most of them into a large, enclosed and well-guarded compound from which nearly all Chinese could be excluded.

Another way of managing traders was to confine them to des-ignated points at the frontier. Thus eighteenth-century Europeans were allowed to spend only a few months each year in China. They were kept to a small island beside Canton from which they were barely allowed to move and where they were not allowed to bring their women or stay for longer than the annual trading season. A wall divided the tiny Portuguese settlement of Macão from the civilized world.

In the nineteenth century the Western barbarians used superior

military and naval force to break out of their confinement and win
the privilege of moving and settling all over China. Where they
had previously been kept in their enclosures, they now set up
their own enclaves in trading cities and ports, tiny colonies and
concessions that could be at the same time politically detached from
China and economically in it. To complete the circle the settlements
would be fenced and barricaded from the inside in times of trouble.
To this day the border of Hong Kong's New Territories is more
effectively sealed from the British-controlled side than from the
Chinese one.

In peaceful times the colonial settlements offered a more open
pattern of urban life. Compare the old walled city of Kowloon, still
looking inward though the wall no longer stands, with the outward-
looking colonial buildings that, wherever possible, face Hong
Kong's magnificent scenery, or old-fashioned Shandong towns with
the turn-of-the-century German architecture of Qingdao, where
Wilhelm II tried to create a model colony on the shores of the
Yellow Sea and left some handsome buildings in the Dahlem style
to suggest what Germany might have done with a few more decades
of control. Both of these colonial cities grew around their harbours,
and both were dangerous breaches in the Chinese empire's self-
isolation.

None of the great cities of imperial China was open to the world
in the way Hong Kong and Qingdao were. Nanjing grew beside
the Yangtse as a capital city for eight dynasties – beside the Yangtse
but not on it. The city was walled off from the great river that was
its life and the reason for its existence. It preferred to develop
between a lesser stream, the Qinhuai River, to its south and west,
and the Purple Gold Mountains and Xuanwu Lake to the north and
east. It is almost as if the Yangtse were not there. Hangzhou hides
from the sea and the Qiantang River flowing into it, preferring to
face safe, pretty little West Lake and the hills behind it. The old
walled city of Shanghai stood slightly back from the same Huangpu
waterfront that European invaders turned into one of the world's
great ports.

Avoiding the boundless and uncontrollable outside world was

something to which the state gave so high a priority that it went to the vast expense of digging and maintaining the Grand Canal to connect the rich rice-growing lower Yangtse region with the capital in the north, even when for nearly five hundred years that capital was Peking. Although summer typhoons, winter gales and fogs, the rocky Shandong coastline and the heavily silted waters of the river estuaries presented formidable problems to mariners, sea transport from south to north was not beyond the technical capacity of China's shipbuilders and sailors, both among the world's best. The rice could have been carried north in big ships, and China would have had the merchant marine and naval power to open up trade overseas. Instead dynasty after dynasty opted for the safe but labour-intensive inland waterway that kept the sailors under control and moved water transport far away from the ocean.

The ocean was dangerous and frightening for later dynastic regimes. Traders who left China's shores to deal with foreigners, perhaps even to live overseas, were no longer completely under the state's control. If Chinese and foreign traders had been free to come and go as they pleased, they would have been living examples of alternatives to absolutism. The traders themselves were not averse to going to Japan or the southern seas to make their fortunes. Chinese merchants were established widely in South-East Asia long before the nineteenth-century colonial powers forced the Qing government to allow them to recruit and export bonded labourers for the Americas, South Africa and South-East Asia. It took courage to leave, not least because the illegal emigrant might not be allowed back, and the Qing government offered no protection to its renegade subjects overseas. Almost anyone trading overseas was in breach of Ming and Qing law, which drove merchants towards piracy. Banning overseas trade except through narrow and tightly controlled government channels justified itself by forcing merchants outside the law and into the world of organized crime. This official hostility to private foreign trade did nothing to open the minds of the educated classes to non-Chinese ways of looking at the world. It was much more sensible to turn your back on the unknown and uncontrollable and to stay safely within the walls of the mind.

When foreign aggression forced the opening of Chinese markets to foreign trade, and then to foreign investment, from 1842 onwards all Chinese governments were deeply disturbed by the loss of their power to exclude the alien. The more a regime was under foreign influence or control, the more virulent was its underlying resentment and hostility. The Guomindang government of Chiang Kaishek, for example, was viscerally at its most anti-American during the 1940s, when its very survival depended on United States support. Its failure to assert the state's right to exclude the 'big noses' did much more damage to its legitimacy in the eyes of those who regarded themselves as China's élite than did its murderous brutality towards the common people.

The new Communist regime of 1949 could, and very soon did, exclude Westerners and close down their missions, schools, hospitals and businesses. To young and old fogies this was one of the strongest reasons for accepting the new rulers' right to power. A government that could boot out those living affronts to a civilization's confidence in its own superiority was a real one, especially when it could stop the United States and its allies in Korea, thus avenging the humiliations of a hundred years and more.

Although the communists showed very early that they could seal off the country from the barbarians who came from the sea, it took a decade to deal with what had, for most of the previous two thousand years, been the main external threat: neighbours along the northern land frontier. Their success in throwing off Soviet hegemony in the early 1960s and in holding out despite economic catastrophe was a triumph for the principle of Chinese sovereignty, and it resulted in twenty years of borders better sealed than they had been since the early nineteenth century. At a high price national independence that came as close to being absolute as is possible in the modern world. There were very few foreigners in the country, and they remained only on sufferance, confined to their enclosures and denied access to most of China except by special permission. By the late 1960s a good proportion of the few foreigners left in China were confined to prison cells. Foreign companies traded under controls as tight as those of the eighteenth century, and though China had clients overseas, it was beholden to no foreign patrons. It sought no foreign investment and few loans and did not depend on foreign trade. It could and did snap its fingers at the rest of the world and enjoy the fear it aroused in Washington and Moscow.

In some ways the modern Chinese state has distanced itself from its dynastic predecessors' notions of the world order. In particular, it has embraced the European idea of a multitude of formally equal states, each enjoying absolute legal sovereignty within its frontiers and obliged to respect the sovereignty of other states. Compared with the United States and the Soviet Union, it has been relatively meticulous in observing the rights of other states, though not the legitimacy of Western colonial rule in Africa and Asia. It is scrupulous in treating San Marino or the tiniest Pacific island statelet with all the formal courtesies. Despite the impression that has been created of Chinese intervention around the world, especially in the Mao era, there has not been much of it other than in support of anti-colonial struggles or at the invitation of governments recognized by China. Except briefly in 1967, when China's Foreign Ministry was seized by radicals, Peking's international behaviour has generally been very correct.

No doubt some memories of the pre-European era, when most states that dealt with Peking went through the form of acknowledging Chinese suzerainty by presenting gifts as tribute, linger on. Britain, after all, has never quite come to terms with the independence of the American colonies and still hankers after lost empires. But in abandoning its predecessors' claims to be the natural rulers of the world the Chinese government has since 1949 insisted on enforcing its absolute sovereignty within what it regards as China's borders. It has been harshly enforced even on peoples who, given the choice, might have preferred not to be incorporated into the Chinese state – Uighurs, Tibetans and others. Sovereignty has also provided the ultimate answer to foreign complaints about abuses of human rights: the Chinese state can do what it likes within its borders. The independence of the Chinese state is not at all the same thing as the freedom of its people. Sovereignty has been another kind of wall.

The price of this walled independence has been poverty and backwardness. It was a price that Mao was willing to make his people pay and that some of them were willing to accept. There was a certain satisfaction in seeing foreigners confined to living in designated compounds and put on display from time to time as representatives of their peoples coming to pay homage at court in Peking like tribute missions in earlier eras. Government officials who enjoyed little freedom, low pay and poor living conditions were compensated to some extent by being given restricted information about what was happening in China that was not available to the outside world. Educated Chinese continued to watch the outside world closely. Within the Party and state machine knowledge of international affairs, though structured by propaganda considerations, was very good. China liked its wall and liked looking over it as well. This, at least, was progress.

No other state in human history has ever put as much effort into walling itself off physically from the outside world as did a number of Chinese dynasties. Defence systems along the northern frontier called for such massive resources that they determined, and perhaps distorted, the nature of the early imperial state in north China, as was argued in chapter 2. Nobody knows how much frontier wall was built in north China between the sixth century BC and the sixteenth century AD, but estimates range up to 50,000 kilometres in all, the main line of defence under those dynasties that maintained a wall system being around 6,000 kilometres long.

Against large mounted armies mobile enough to choose where to strike, a wall was an expensive and negative defensive system, offering no means of destroying enemy power. More effective were diplomacy – keeping the northerners divided against each other through bribery and other means – and a strategy of mounting large expeditions from strong forward bases across the deserts to wipe out the herds and flocks of the pastoral peoples in their safe grasslands to the north of the desert barriers. The walls were more effective in restricting peaceful contacts between the Han Chinese and their

northern neighbours. The happy accidents that have preserved
working documents from watchtowers on the Han-dynasty wall in
the dry sands of the north-west reveal that two thousand years ago
the Chinese state kept a very close watch on the movements of its
subjects in the frontier region. It is evident that nobody was allowed
through the wall either way without an official permit.

As Owen Lattimore observed half a century ago, one of the main
purposes of frontier systems, including the walls, was to keep the
Chinese in. To allow subjects to leave and return freely would have
been to accept great dangers for an absolutist state. It was bad
enough to grant some traders from distant countries temporary or
permanent residence, but they were at least foreigners, and allow-
ances could be made for their customs and religions without really
jeopardizing the state's values. If a Chinese went abroad and acquired
wrong ideas, that could be much more threatening. The deep-
rooted notion that a Chinese born abroad is not really Chinese still
has life in it.

Permitting Chinese students to travel overseas and foreign teachers and ideas to enter China at the end of the nineteenth and the
beginning of the twentieth century was a failure to guard the walls
of the mind that proved fatal to the Qing dynasty. That the various
military regimes of 1912 to 1949 were unable to close the minds of
the educated was to be one of the causes of their successive downfalls.
And because the minds of the educated were only partly opened in
those decades they were to be led into a much more effective tyranny
than the pre-1949 Guomindang could manage.

Nothing in the policies of the Deng years has been more dangerous than the attempt to half-open frontiers and minds. The Mao era
brought the frontiers under very effective control and imposed a
degree of uniformity in expression that helped to create the conditions for standardized thinking. It provided a unified political
language and standard models of analysis and argumentation in
which all who were educated or held any position of responsibility
had constantly to exercise. Mao-think was a crude but often effective
way of approaching virtually anything. It taught people to analyse
any situation in terms of conflicts and contradictions, to accept

change and transformations and to place issues in a wider context. The performances called for by Mao-think involved a lot of words – someone who lived through that era is much more likely to be able to talk in public for a couple of hours on any subject than a Westerner. Mao-think encouraged no critical analysis of what words really meant and was concerned not with truth but with enforcing the world view of the country's rulers. It taught people how to reach correct conclusions by correct argumentation based on unquestionable premisses. It strengthened the sense of Chinese solidarity against the world. Maoism functioned best within its own walls.

Maoist argumentation was nothing to do with resolving differences between rival views presented on a basis of formal equality. His techniques were those of verbally beating a rival into submission, relying not so much on logic as on authority. This was a profoundly Chinese style of argumentation, for all the borrowed jargon of Stalin's Marxism. By insisting that its premisses be accepted – and all the state's machinery of repression was there to ensure that the premisses were not challenged – and by denying doubters the right to use evidence to challenge its assertions, it was irresistible. Maoism needed and inculcated short memories, as the premisses had to be changed from time to time. Yet for all its underlying crudity and the absurdity of some of its basic ideas, it could be subtle and flexible in details and constantly adjusted to changing needs.

When, from 1978 onwards, Deng and his associates tried to reinvent Maoism and encourage a limited amount of critical thinking they were attempting the impossible. It was politically convenient to use Mao's dictum 'Practice is the sole criterion of truth' as a justification for dumping some of Mao's views and policies that evidently did not work. It was ingenious to try to redefine Mao-think as only those things Mao had thought, said and written that Deng approved of in the 1980s. In order to justify the abandonment of collective agriculture and a host of other Maoist measures, the leadership had to prompt and sanction some criticism of past idiocies. Holes had to be knocked through the mental wall.

The problem was, and is, that people cannot be at the same time

encouraged to ask approved questions about hitherto unquestionable
principles and expected to stop where official permission ends. Walls
with gaps do not make very effective enclosures. You cannot say
that Mao was wrong sometimes, even disastrously wrong, and still
retain Mao as the symbol of your regime's infallibility. 'Long live
the invincible thought of Mao Zedong' is an awkward slogan to
post outside the front entrance of the rulers' Zhongnanhai compound when they are also exposing Mao's failures and 'mistakes' –
as mass murders are euphemistically termed. A dictatorship cannot
set about demolishing many of the key institutions of state-run
socialism, especially in the countryside, tell its people about the
material achievements of capitalism and try to introduce some
market disciplines into the economy while preserving just those parts
of a totalitarian ideology that still suit it. As Chinese propagandists
pointed out in an internal document early in 1990, where the Soviet
Union and its client regimes in Eastern Europe started going wrong
was in debunking Stalin. The ideology of a communist dictatorship,
like that of the Catholic Church, must be enforced as a whole and
defended by authority or it will fall to pieces.

Yet the regime needs an enclosed ideology in order to justify its
existence. If the economic successes of the 1980s were achieved
mainly in those sectors where socialism was more or less abandoned,
and the Party is not building socialism but dismantling it, what
need is there for it to go on ruling? For a time the formidable
machinery of repression may prevent some of the most awkward
questions from being asked in public, but this will be only a
temporary palliative. The old enclosures for the mind cannot be
rebuilt.

From the late 1980s there have been attempts to fall back into
more easily defended positions. One such position has been patriotism. Nationalism was always one of the strongest claims the
Communists made on the loyalty of educated Chinese who found
China's humiliations at the hands of foreign powers in the century
before 1949 intolerable. The trouble is that a government making
far more concessions to foreign interests than any previous Chinese
government ever has except when looking down the barrels of

foreign guns finds it hard to play the nationalist game very convincingly.

Appeals to the young to revive China and to rebuild the Great Wall on the ground and in the head may not work when it seems to many of those young people that the best way to start reviving China would be to get rid of the ancients and demolish the enclosures of the mind.

If patriotism turns out to be much harder to defend than at first sight it seemed to be, or if its other defenders decide that it would be stronger with the Party bosses outside, then a last stand could be made in the extensive ruins of tradition. Here at least the Communist autocracy has a good claim to be the true heir of earlier dynasties, as is argued throughout these pages. In the last few years the gerontocrats have become much less selective about which aspects of the Chinese past they lay claim to and are also much less concerned to present themselves as the successors to supposedly revolutionary or progressive traditions. The walls may be crumbling, but there are plenty of them, and they give a comforting sense of security.

Much that a younger and more confident Communist Party would have ridiculed as 'feudal' and backward is now officially approved of for its Chineseness. Once the line would have been drawn between the more plausible aspects of *qi gong* – the control and use of breath and other vital forces in the body – and the martial arts and their wilder claims to give supernatural powers; now the nonsense is gloried in. A regime that once tried hard to consign Buddhism to the museum, keeping only a handful of monasteries going because of their usefulness in foreign relations, now has to treat its monks with a certain respect. The former mixed attitude to emperors who were good at strengthening the state has now become one of much less unqualified approval. In the 1950s emperors were often referred to by their personal names instead of such posthumous titles as Wu Di or Gao Zu or the names given to their reigns, such as Kangxi or Qianlong. (It was a tiresome innovation, as because they were tabooed the personal names are very little-known and in the past were not used, but it was a gesture against the mystique surrounding the throne.) By the 1980s such disrespect was out. Emperors were strongly back in favour, and much less was being said about rebellious peasants.

The aged Party chiefs who had been fiery revolutionaries in the 1920s and 1930s, storming the strongholds of feudalism and imperialism (to use the jargon of the era), were, in the confusion and anomie of the late 1980s and early 1990s, desperate to shore up the crumbling ruins of the Glorious Chinese Past and make them the redoubts in which to withstand the onslaughts of the modern outside world. Most offensive to these defenders of the lost certainties were the enemies within: the alarming minority among writers and thinkers who regard most of China's traditions as so deadly that the only thing to do is to get rid of them as fast as possible. The fury with which such partial rejections of China's past as the 1988 television series *River Elegy* were attacked by conservative commentators is a sign of the terror caused to China's rulers by critical thought about tradition. If the last mental stronghold falls, it will leave the regime ideologically naked. It had failed by the 1970s to make a go of Maoism. In the 1980s it had its chance to patch together a modernizing ideology, but that had fallen apart by 1988. All that is left to it is the comfort of the past: pride in the ineffable superiority of Chineseness; in Confucius, Lao Zi and the rest of them; in the world's most subtle and complicated writing system; in a literature that is inexhaustible; in those high moral standards that, when all is said and done, mark the difference between civilized people and barbarians; in the world's longest continuous recorded tradition of autocracy; in the Great Wall and everything it stands for. It is the comfort of the grave.

Death too has had its enclosures, its Chinese boxes, its walls within walls, for those with the power to do things properly. The compulsory cremation enforced widely in recent decades is one of those revolutionary changes that goes against the grain of the culture, however practical and sensible it may seem to the outsider. A preference for being well boxed and decently buried will reassert itself over the government crematorium whenever the opportunity presents itself. Even though officials know that their ashes will be stored in a state cinerarium, in a container that will be kept in an enclosure appropriate to their rank, it is not the same as the satisfaction of having at home a set of well-lacquered hardwood coffin planks and an auspiciously sited family graveyard.

In the past the best way to be buried was in coffins within coffins in an underground palace within an above-ground palace compound. The Ming emperors sealed off a valley some 40 kilometres square to be their burial ground, and in so doing they were both following precedents going back to the earliest dynasties and setting one for their Qing successors, who appropriated an even bigger area in the Malan valley in Zunhua county, Hebei, to be the repository for their remains and a source of rich pickings for twentieth-century grave robbers.

As archaeologists have not yet seen the huge burial chamber in which the well-rotted body of the First Qin Emperor was placed in 210 BC, we do not yet know if it was as magnificent as its description by the historian Sima Qian. Apparently it was filled with the palaces, officials – in effigy, one hopes – and the marvels and treasures of his life, and into it he was accompanied by all his palace women who had not borne him a son. In a model of the empire rivers of mercury flowed into the sea, thanks to ingenious devices, and crossbows were put in place to shoot any intruder. The craftsmen who set up this underground treasurehouse were all buried alive in the tunnel leading into it. Above the grave was an artificial hill that still rises 43 metres high on a base 350 metres square. Further out was an enclosing wall 1,300 by 578 metres and, beyond that, an outer wall 2,513 by 974 metres. Outside this were the pits in which this antique Hitler had his life-sized model Waffen-SS units buried to guard him in death. The whole enterprise had been worked on by forced labourers – up to 700,000 of them – for over thirty years. For a culture that did not believe in bodily resurrection, this was a formidable effort of exclusion, a non-display of magnificence hidden away behind many layers of very solid screens.

The Qin emperor's body would not have been in a pleasant condition when buried: he had died on the east coast, and, to keep his death secret, it had been carried in a closed carriage with a cartload of stinking salt fish next to it to disguise the stench as it decomposed in the summer heat. Once back in the capital, there would have been coffins within coffins to contain the remains, as is indicated by a tomb from some forty years later at Mawangdui in Hunan.

As Mawangdui is now in the city of Changsha, the outer enclosures for the Han tombs there can no longer be traced, but the underground arrangements of Tomb No. 1, which happen to be very well preserved, are impressive. The good condition of the grave goods, including food and textiles, and of the body itself — a woman in her fifties whose flesh was still elastic when excavated — are astonishing. The coffins have not rotted and can still be seen in the provincial museum. She had six of them, one inside another, three inner coffins and three outer ones, topped by yet another layer of timber. The whole wooden structure was about 6.7 by 4.9 metres and 2.9 metres high, the size of a large room. The outer structures, rough-hewn from massive timbers, have a powerful presence now that they are on display above ground: so much wood to contain one tiny corpse.

The Countess of Dai belonged to a family that was several rungs down the ladder of nobility from the Han imperial house. The senior males of the family were the hereditary chief ministers of the ruling princes of Changsha, holding marquisates in their own right. If a middle-ranking member of the aristocracy could be so solidly and multiply enclosed in her Chinese boxes, it does seem plausible to assume that an emperor or empress would have been even better wrapped and packed.

By the time the Wanli emperor was put under ground in 1620, in one of the last of the Ming dynastic tombs, grave architecture had gone much further. Instead of the log cabins of the outermost coffins, he and the two empresses interred with him had a stone-built suite of large vaults under a mound more modest than that of the Qin tyrant. Above ground was a walled compound on an imperial scale, in which stood large buildings comparable in size and style with the ceremonial buildings in Peking's main palace

complex. It was all kept hidden away from common people inside
its closed valley.

It was much more extravagant and stylish than the expression of
confused thinking that is the structure in which the purported
remains of Mao Zedong are displayed in the centre of Peking. They
are both guarded and on public view. Being situated on the main
axis of Peking's palace complex, the tomb is in the wrong place by
traditional standards. Its design is both grandiose and characterless,
in keeping with the monstrous Great Hall of the People and the
Museum of Chinese History that flank it. Like them, it belongs
neither to China nor to the modern world. It makes the Lenin
blockhouse in Moscow seem dignified by comparison and would,
with the other two buildings, have fitted into the post-war Berlin
that Albert Speer was designing for Hitler. The regime that built
the mausoleum had neither the confidence to be a proper old-
fashioned dynasty that knew how to dispose of an emperor's corpse
by enclosing it many times over and hiding it nor the belief in its
own proclaimed values that would have had the body incinerated
and the ashes scattered. To have put the corpse on view to the
curious who file past has had unavoidable associations with the
public display and humiliation of the remains of executed criminals.
Mao could have been buried as an emperor or burned as a revolutionary. Instead he has been used as a peep show, allowing his
former subjects a kind of revenge. It will be interesting to see
whether China's current gerontocrats have their mortal coils
interred, cremated or stuffed when their time comes.

Economic reform is not intended to lead to the liberalization of
human rights. The openings in walls were never supposed to be
many. For all the changes of the last half century, the state has
wanted its subjects kept in their boxes. Most of China's inhabitants
remain quite well enclosed, and now there are new devices to keep
them in their boxes, such as standard national identity cards that
enable the police to find out very quickly whether people have
strayed too far from their approved places of work and residence.
The First Qin Emperor would have liked the technology but would

have been shocked to learn that it was not being used to give the authorities even greater control over the people. For there is now a large and growing minority that cannot or will not stay put, a floating population of tens of millions who leave their home villages to find work where they can and do not fit into the regular system of controls. Yet, dangerous though the 'blind flow' of job-seekers is to social and political control, economic pressures mean that it cannot be shut off. Some of the state's boxes are losing their lids.

No other form of enclosure is more universal than that of the family, and no other social institution has been as durable and as permanent. After looking at all these other kinds of walls it is time to consider the institution that is both the basic unit of social organization and the state's most effective ally in preventing the emergence of responsible, autonomous individuals and of a civil society that could take on the totalitarian monarchy.

6. FAMILY CIRCLES

═══

The centrality of families in Chinese cultures is one of the things that are often taken less seriously than they should be simply because they are so obvious. There are, after all, enough of them, and the patrilineal family has been one of the things that have defined Chinese cultures over the last 4,000 to 5,000 years.

The evidence of archaeology and of texts recording the traditions of the remote past that were written in the first millennium BC points to ways of life between 6,000 and 8,000 years ago in the earliest settled villages in the areas drained by the Yellow, Huai and Liao rivers that were notably different from those of the more recent past. People lived in small houses, grouped together in small communities of up to a few hundred members, protected by nothing more formidable than a ditch to keep large animals out. We do not know much about living arrangements inside the little semi-subterranean houses with their thatched roofs, but in death the adult members of the community were generally buried in a common cemetery, each with a similar small collection of simple, useful and beautiful pots and other utensils, for the most part not separated into patrilineal descent lines.

Undifferentiated simplicity could not last. By 4,000 years ago male domination is all too obvious from the archaeological evidence: wives buried in submissive postures beside their husbands, wide differences in the amount and quality of grave goods buried with the dead, villages surrounded by walls designed to keep people out, weapons of war and much greater social division of labour.

The patrilineal family is not the sort of institution that just happens or can be maintained without constant enforcement, especially in the forms it has taken in Chinese cultures. The type of family on which Chinese high cultures have been built is one defined by a very finely graded structure of authority and obligations intended to defend and perpetuate male power, patrilineal descent, the power of age and the interests of the family unit put before those of the individual or of the larger society. For this family system to have worked so effectively and for so long it has had to be very well maintained, defended and enforced through law, custom and language.

The essential and distinctive features of the family in Chinese cultures have been that it is a patrilineal descent system in which the central and essential relationships are not those between husbands and wives but those between parents, especially fathers, and children, especially sons. It is an authoritarian structure in which authority is determined by seniority, sex and the closeness of the patrilineal relationship. In each line of descent the older outranks the younger, and in each generation males usually outrank females. Everyone is identified by the surname of the family of birth. This is kept by daughters after marriage, which almost always entails leaving the family of birth and joining the husband's family. The family is nearly always identified with a place from which its forefathers came, and this identification is inherited by later generations even if they have never been there in their lives. When filling in forms Chinese still have to state their place of patrilineal origin, while Westerners are asked where they, as individuals, were born.

A way of looking at the character for ancestor, *zu*, that is not necessarily fanciful is to see in the two elements that compose it a left-hand one meaning 'sacred' and a right-hand one that was originally a drawing of an erect phallus and, even in its modern, squared-off form, still preserves the shape. This is a graphic expression of absolute male dominance in the ancient traditions of high culture as passed on by Confucius.

It would be hard to exaggerate the extent to which the traditional high culture allows women significance only as daughters, sisters, wives and mothers of men. Women can exist and act respectably only by those standards within their patrilineal family of birth or marriage. In real life this has only ever been possible for the rich, but even popular cultures have had in them so strong an element of patriarchal familism that women have had to be very tough and resilient if they were to avoid being squashed. The revolutionary rhetoric of the last eighty years has not yet changed a principle that applied when the Qing still ruled: the only way a woman can reach the highest level of political power is through marriage. Indeed, the Empress Dowager Ci Xi used her long widowhood to win for herself far more control over the country at the beginning of the twentieth century than any other of the wives or widows who have come close to the top since then.

Although women are still usually more restricted by the family than men are, families provide a clearer and firmer identity for men and boys than they do for women and girls. A daughter may be loved by her parents, but she is essentially superfluous to the needs of her family of origin, as she costs nearly as much as a boy to raise but will have to be married off into another family to serve her husband's parents. (For a woman not to be married is a major disaster for her and a disgrace for her parents.) After marriage a young woman is under the authority of her mother-in-law, and once she has borne and reared a son or two she has a reasonably secure place in the new family. As in her old age she will depend on sons and on daughters-in-law, she has to perpetuate the tradition of valuing her sons, who will probably stay with her, more than her daughters, who will not. From her middle years onwards the relationship with her daughter-in-law is both difficult and critical. The younger woman is a threat who may weaken her control of her son; but the daughter-in-law is also essential for her own survival and for producing grandsons. What makes the mother-in-law/daughter-in-law relationship even more difficult is that there is none of the shared experience of the son's childhood that binds adult son and mother. In addition, the chances are that today's mother-in-law was given a bad time a generation ago and now sees the chance to get her own back by practising the sort of tyranny she once endured.

In European traditions one is identified essentially by one's personal name or names. In the rites of passage for birth, marriage and death of the older Christian churches it is the Christian name or names that count. In pre-Christian Europe too the personal name was the essential label. In much of Europe the surname is a fairly recent invention, and it has yet to displace entirely the older convention of a personal name followed by a patronymic that served Scandinavians and Russians well enough until recent times. Surnames were something of an aristocratic privilege, and even among the nobility and gentry were less widely used than Christian names. The Christian name is the label for the soul, the name that one will bear for eternity, even to the Last Judgment.

Not so in China. Personal names are much less frequently used in China than in European cultures, and surnames go much further back. Although in China, as in Europe, there was a time when surnames were a privilege and the 'hundred surnames' meant the upper classes, not the common people as now, that era ended well over two thousand years ago. Surnames have been particularly useful for states that try to keep centralized records of all their subjects.

It is the surname that has been essential in the China of the last two millennia. It is the only name that you take with you unchanged through life. Superior people may have a number of different personal names, and polite substitutes for personal names, in their lives. Some ordinary folk may have nothing more than a number – Zhang Three or Li Four – or a nickname. At one time women, when they married, were known to their new families, the families they perpetuated with their own bodies, by their paternal surname and sometimes by that surname only. To change one's personal name is not very important; to change one's surname is traumatic. You can swear to the truth of a statement on your surname. Such an oath sworn on your personal name would be much weaker. It is not as if the great majority of people have surnames that are in any way remarkable. Nearly all Chinese have common or very common surnames, just as in a European country most people have a common or very common personal name. But the Chinese surname remains the essential badge of one's identity.

Within the family one has an identity that is, in the literal sense, relative. You define yourself within your own generation by seniority and are taught from a very early age to be aware of the subtle gradations of seniority and closeness of kinship within the patrilineal descent line. Chinese culture requires a degree of awareness of relationship structures that is much more analytical than any comparable consciousness imparted by European cultures and their descendants. Written Chinese and the many spoken Chinese languages make distinctions that can be made in English only with great clumsiness. (This is in sharp contrast to the general tendency of Chinese languages to permit much greater imprecision than can English.)

In Chinese it is impossible to say 'my brother' or 'my sister' because there is no common relationship that older and younger brothers, or older and younger sisters, have with you. That is why different words are needed for older brother (*gege*) and younger brother (*didi*), for older sister (*jiejie*) and younger sister (*meimei*). Older brothers and sisters have authority over you; you have authority over younger brothers and sisters. Only uncivilized peoples use the same word for a younger and an older sister.

The English word 'uncle' confuses even more categories. Leaving aside the honorary uncleship conferred on family friends or on aunts' husbands, the English word fails to discriminate between your father's elder brother (*bobo*), your father's younger brother (*shushu*), and your mother's brother (*jiujiu*). In the modern urban West these are not distinctions that matter: all three kinds of uncle are just as closely related to you. In China they are not.

Your father's elder brother is a figure of authority who outranks your own father by seniority in the patrilineal line. Your father's younger brother, however, is felt to be less intimidating because he is junior to your father. That is why children are taught to address young men as *shushu*: it is friendly and at the same time mildly respectful without in any way threatening a father's authority. You expect a *shushu* to be friendly and protective. Both a *bobo* and a *shushu* are family.

Your mother's brothers are not members of your family and do not have any direct authority over you. For that reason it does not really matter to you whether they are older or younger than their sister, your mother. The same word, *jiujiu*, will do for all of them. It may be that there is warmth and affection between you and your *jiujiu*, but they belong to another line of patrilineal descent, and you are joined to them by much weaker links of obligation than those binding you to your *bobo* or *shushu*. Their family is, or should be, a close ally of your family, but it is not part of it.

The failure of English and many other European languages to have a different word for each of these three different kinds of uncle is a sign of underdeveloped or lost awareness of the importance of family. For Chinese cultures family is not just the 'us' to which all but the most unfortunate belong. It is also the centre of a web of claims and obligations very carefully graded according to degrees of closeness and seniority. From childhood you learn to distinguish between older and younger members of each generation. Just as you have a seniority ranking in your generation, you know the seniority rankings of all your sisters and brothers and cousins and uncles and aunts. You know which are part of your family and which ones belong to other families.

The modern Western sense that your family means a number of overlapping circles in all of which you belong and none of which is exclusive – a sense that in recent decades has become even more elastic as divorce and remarriage link ever more nuclear families – is alien to Chinese traditions, by which you can belong to one family only. When a woman leaves her family of birth to join her family of marriage she ceases to be a member of the former and becomes a member of the latter, even while still being an outsider with a different surname. A man when he marries does not become part of his wife's family. It is because family demands are so great, and because the family is your refuge from the world, that there cannot be vagueness or ambiguity about where you belong. Members of the family are bound together not only by common descent; they are also held in closed circles of debts and obligations that have to be honoured if one is to hold one's head high in the world.

Few cultures place as much emphasis on the absolute nature of debts and the absolute need to repay them as do China's. When as a child you become more aware of the world you are taught that your parents have run up a huge credit balance with you by investing much time, effort and wealth in creating you and bringing you up. This is a debt that has to be repaid to them as your creditors in this life if you are to be a real human being. If you are a good son, you will do this by keeping your parents in dignity and comfort in their old age and by burying and mourning them properly after their death.

As a daughter you will almost certainly never have the comfort of being able to pay this debt off. Your destiny is to marry out of the home and join a new family, where you will have to help your husband do his duty by his parents. This puts a burden of guilt on daughters that they rarely shake off completely and that encourages them to feel inadequate for the rest of their lives. When in their turn they become mothers it encourages them to place a similar burden on the shoulders of their children.

As a son you are constantly reminded of your duty to be filial and obedient. You are your parents' investment, and they have every right to expect you to pay interest (*chu xi*), which is what good sons do. A bad son is one who, like most daughters, does not pay interest and should therefore feel guilty of not repaying a debt.

The closed circles of obligation that bind children to their parents mean that young men start adult life carrying the moral equivalent of a huge mortgage debt on which they will have to continue repaying interest and capital until they make the final payment by giving both parents a proper burial and mourning them well. While this debt is being paid off a new burden of debt is being placed on the shoulders of the next generation. As children get older they become more and more aware of the load they must carry, which strengthens the tendency in Chinese cultures for growing up to be a process of losing freedom and autonomy. Babies and toddlers are outrageously indulged, especially if they are boys, but as they get older their lives become drabber. The price of being taken seriously by adults as one grows up is the curbing of one's spontaneity.

The family in which so little room is allowed for personal choice has to be strong in enforcing conformism and suppressing initiative. It is a backward-looking institution that faces the past even when investing in the future and does all it can to ensure that the children will put their parents' and other seniors' interests before their own. Of course, these pressures are not always successful, but they work well enough to make Chinese cultures conservative and to cramp individual initiative and independence. The family teaches you to find patrons and attach yourself to them as a quasi-filial dependant if you want to get ahead.

You are discouraged from such naïve forms of behaviour as saying what you think or feel without first considering whether your frankness may damage a relationship that could be useful to you. Only bad children put their own interests and feelings first. A good and clever child is one who learns well by rote, who can reproduce book knowledge or practical skills as accurately as possible, who says the right thing and who understands how to handle the complexities of relationships and obligations. These skills are essential in setting up one's own network of quasi-familial relationships and obligations in the wider world. Parents must teach their children the essential arts of *shigu*, or worldly wisdom. *Shigu* begins with the assumption that everyone outside the immediate family is potentially dangerous. You must be very careful about having any unnecessary dealings with outsiders and do nothing to antagonize them. To this end it is best to be courteous and affable and to find ways of winning the favour of those who are in a position to do you a good or bad turn. Never speak without thinking or show your anger, except to those under you. Do all you can to behave as is expected of you, and never express an opinion if there is any chance that it may harm you. The social skills taught in the family school of *shigu* can best be seen in the extraordinary skill with which the Chinese bureaucracy exercises its discreet charm over Westerners who may be useful or dangerous, drawing them into feeling that they have a unique rapport with their Chinese hosts and are under some kind of indefinable obligation not to cause them embarrassment or difficulty. Westerners imagine that they are being treated as insiders when, in fact, the techniques used on them are precisely those used on outsiders to avert dangers or bring benefits to the family.

Chinese upbringing puts little emphasis on raising sons and daughters to find their own ways in life or on encouraging mental independence. A good son is one who for three years after his father's death follows his father's ways of doing things, as Confucius put it (*Analects*, 1.11). It is unusual to find parents who do not direct their children's futures but instead encourage their offspring to discover what they want to do with their lives and help them to go their own way. The traditional view of child as investment still makes itself felt as the investors exercise their time-honoured right to control their own capital. It takes some catastrophic interruption of the normal pattern, such as the Cultural Revolution's excitements followed by the sending of nearly all school-leavers to the countryside for an indefinite stay in the late 1960s and early 1970s, to give young people the chance to find their own course in life. This particular series of upheavals gave China its first modern generation: those youngsters in the cities who were between fifteen and twenty-one or so in 1966 and are now in their forties. Although their formal education suffered badly because of the disruptions, they were away from school and from home, the two main sources of standardized thinking. In conditions that were often harsh by comparison with their relatively pampered urban lives, and with many of their parents in trouble, they had to think and act for themselves, even though few of them had had any preparation for systematic reflection. Had they stayed at home and in school, the pressure to conform to the declared values of the culture would have been much greater and the prospects of something being saved from the debris of Communist Party rule would have been even dimmer.

Familistic values go a lot further back in Chinese cultures than the time of Confucius and are spread much more widely than knowledge of the texts regarded as classics by Confucius and his late followers. Even in dynastic times most Chinese were not the followers of Confucius that the small educated minority purported to be. Nevertheless, the attitudes to family expressed in the *Analects*, the most plausible record of what Confucius said, and in the classics that set out codes of correct behaviour (*li*) in daily life and on ritual occasions such as those associated with death, reveal dominant attitudes in the past, attitudes that are not yet entirely dead.

Correct behaviour was based on understanding and implementing the principle that obligations were graded by carefully distinguished degrees of closeness and relative patrilineal seniority. They were also determined by the social status of a family, especially in the centuries up to the time of Confucius. (In the dynastic millennia this aspect of correct behaviour became less important.)

No aspect of correct behaviour is taken more seriously in the Confucian tradition than the treatment of the dead, especially mourning. Although Buddhist and Daoist rituals were introduced into the funeral procedures, the essential elements belong to a line of development that goes back at least three thousand years. Burials, as we saw in the previous chapter, became on the whole simpler over time. The demands of mourning remained high, especially for those family members towards whom one's mourning obligations came into the highest category. Mourning requirements were grouped into bands, and the classification of relationships that determined them were also used in the criminal codes of a number of dynasties to measure the severity of certain offences: the higher the category of mourning one owed a particular relative, the more seriously an offence against him or her would be regarded by the courts, which had the maintenance and defence of correct family relationships as one of their main functions.

The highest band of mourning was that of a son or unmarried daughter for a father or mother. For an official this included twenty-seven months at home, withdrawn from public life, and this strict requirement was followed right up to the end of the nineteenth century. A wife had to share in her husband's mourning for his parents to the same degree; her mourning for her own parents was two bands lower, at the same level as that of an adopted son for his original parents. The adopted son, like the wife, had transferred his principal obligations to his new family, and it would have been quite wrong of either of them to grieve for their own parents as much as for their acquired parents in the new family. A husband's obligation to mourn for his wife's parents was in the lowest band. Mourning expressed not the emotional loss of the bereaved, but the degree of obligation to the dead person.

Although much of the system of mourning required in the Confucian tradition has now been forgotten, along with many of the old rules of correct behaviour, the underlying attitudes have not gone. The principle of graded obligation was central to the family system as understood by Confucius. To Confucius there was no duty of equal consideration for all fellow humans. That would have been barbarism and would have threatened civilization itself. When, in the century after Confucius, the rival teacher Mo Di (who died around the year 391 BC) advocated a social order in which distinctions were swept away and urged people to treat all others as if they were members of their own family – his undifferentiated caring that is sometimes translated as 'universal love' – this principle was treated as a dangerous heresy by Confucians. Although the followers of Mo Di were well organized into a curiously modern centralist political party (one that was modern even to the extent of splitting after the founder's death into rival factions, each with its own *Führer*) and fought with words and weapons for their beliefs, they did not have the staying power of the Confucians and faded away within two to three hundred years. Confucian differentiation, by contrast, lasted as many millennia as Mohism's centuries.

The strength of familism enabled it to ride out the potentially damaging storm of Buddhism. Even at the height of Buddhist fervour in the sixth century AD, when millions of households put themselves under the protection of monasteries in order to escape from state demands for taxes and labour, inscriptions in the cave temples at Longmen record votive statues being carved in order to win posthumous blessings for dead parents and other ancestors – the Confucian virtue of filial piety reasserting itself even in the practice of a religion that in its earlier, unsinified, forms had been an escape from such worldly distractions as home and family. The monastic life that is so central to Indian and South-East Asian Buddhism never really established itself as an essential feature of Chinese culture. The monk or nun was someone who had 'left home' and was therefore to be regarded with suspicion and even contempt. Writers of commercial fiction in the sixteenth and seventeenth centuries could count on their readers' sympathy by showing Buddhist monks in a bad light (carrying on with the women of the households where they collected alms, for example).

It would be hard to match in China the mixture of pride and regret with which a European Catholic peasant family will provide the Church with a son or daughter as a priest, monk or nun, sacrificing future grandchildren for the sake of spiritual consolations and social standing. The Buddhist monk in China cut himself off from his family almost completely. He had to abandon his surname, a much more drastic step than it was for his European counterpart. Few families will take pride or comfort from a son or daughter disappearing into a Buddhist monastery or nunnery. Apart from the losses involved – even a daughter might have brought in a bride price to offset a part of the cost of her upbringing – there has not usually been enough respect for the monastic life to make it seem a desirable sacrifice. As Lu Xun pointed out, Daoist clergy were much better liked than their Buddhist counterparts. This was perhaps because Daoists did not necessarily have to be celibate and were not so far from the family.

Nothing was allowed to challenge the patrilineal family and its principles of authority granted by seniority. That the legal codes of successive dynasties recognized and defended the family was nothing remarkable: the codes of all states do in their various ways. What was distinctive about the legal position of the family in dynastic China was the defence of the rights of seniors over juniors, not only those of parents over children but also those of elder brothers over younger siblings or paternal uncles over nephews. For a younger brother to strike an elder one was a serious criminal offence, even when the elder brother was doing something as outrageous as forcing his attentions on the younger brother's wife. An elder brother could, after his father's death, legitimately sell his sister as wife or concubine to another family. If he sold his own wife or concubine, pretending that she was his sister, he was in serious trouble – a hundred strokes of the heavy bamboo according to the

Qing code. A marriage engagement arranged for himself by a man away from home on government or private business was not binding if older members of his own family, including an uncle or an elder sister, had arranged another marriage for him in his absence. Provided that the marriage he had fixed for himself in ignorance of what his family had arranged had not yet taken place, the agreement made by his senior in the family outweighed any agreement he may have made by himself.

Violence against seniors was very seriously punished, while a very lenient view was taken of violence against a junior member of the family. An illustration of this was the textbook case of one Jiang whose disobedience provoked his father to want to beat him. Unfortunately the father tripped over the root of a tree while hurling himself on his errant son, smashed his head against the tree and was killed outright. For this the son was sentenced to strangulation.

The family's training in awareness of obligations that must be met in this life can teach an approach to living, both inside and outside the family, that is highly calculating. Those brought up this way are not encouraged to do anything for anyone else unless it is to repay a debt or to store up some credit for the future. If you see an accident in the street, you are much more likely to crowd round to look and comment than, by helping, to get involved in what is not your business. You are not encouraged to defend your privacy and autonomy within the family – your letters are for any member of the family who can read, and you will be thought selfish and unnatural if you try to keep your acquisitions to yourself. The boundary you have to defend is not the one around your private self but the one around the family unit.

Whatever your individual efforts may achieve, they will not enable you to escape the constraints of the family. Thousands of years of the family being forced to accept collective responsibility for the misdeeds of any one of its members have left a deep impression. Although in law the principle of collective responsibility no longer applies unless other family members were involved in committing or concealing an offence, the reality is that the immediate family of an offender is still treated as sharing the guilt.

Even outside the family some vital relationships are based on the family model. A teacher becomes a quasi-parent to whom one must submit totally and who in turn is expected to be a patron. Teachers who give bad reports on students who have been dutiful to them but academically incompetent will not be seen as behaving acceptably. As recently as the nineteenth century your employer was recognized in law and custom as being a kind of father, with similar authority over you, including the right to use violence, and a similar duty to protect you and look after your interests. Much of this has been inherited by the modern work unit. In both dynastic and contemporary China the place of work can also function as a substitute family, whether it be the small business that in Ming and Qing China, as in earlier centuries in Europe, treated apprentices and hired hands as part of the household, or the modern large work unit that is more like the extended lineage structure found in those parts of south China where clans remain powerful.

Quasi-families would even be set up in brothels, where young girls sold into prostitution had to treat the bawd who bought them as if she were their mother – and would in turn, twenty years later, buy themselves a young girl to be their old-age pension. This type of quasi-family, which can be observed in eighth-century Chang'an and twentieth-century Taiwan, was unusual only in that it was essentially matrilinear. In using the young as investments for her own future the bawd was treating them not all that differently from the way in which parents have used their sons over many centuries. In medieval and modern equivalents of the European cliché of the whore with the heart of gold the Confucian hooker never neglects her duty to her mother by purchase and would never run away with a man while leaving her to starve. If she does marry, a good bride price must be paid to ensure that the older woman can live in comfort.

Because the distinction between family or quasi-family and non-family is so strong, the ties of obligation that hold families and units together do not extend to the outside world unless one has run up or is owed debts of obligation outside the closed family or unit. In normal times there is only a weak sense of civic duty. Unless you can see a member of the police or of a vigilante group waiting to pounce you do not feel particularly obliged to obey traffic regulations. The general interest in such rules being obeyed by all road users seems too weak to outweigh the personal inconvenience of having to make a hand signal before turning when riding a bicycle along a busy street.

The calculation of obligations owed to you and by you leaves little room for spontaneous acts of generosity to strangers or for becoming involved in affairs of the community or the nation except at times of great crisis. What you do for relations or colleagues is either the payment of a debt or storing yourself up some credit that may be drawn on later. Although there are stirring occasions when people throw the abacus away, forget about calculations of debt and plunge into a struggle for the general good – as during the war against Japan or in resisting the siege and invasion of Peking in 1989 – in normal times the Mohist principle of undiscriminating care, like the bourgeois one of meeting such civil obligations as paying evadable tax because it is not worth living in a country where everyone cheats, will not win much support. That goes against the grain of the civilization. Of course, humanity can and does override calculation, and there is no shortage of good, kind and unselfish people in China. My argument is that this is despite, not because of, family values.

Another aspect of the closed circle of obligations and the awareness of debts that are inculcated by family training is that revenge becomes a duty, another debt that has to be repaid. The indigenous religious traditions of China have never offered a way out of this duty by entrusting the settling of scores to an all-powerful, all-judging deity after death. The posthumous rewards and punishments of Buddhist mythology cannot be left to settle one's scores for one. Revenge has to be taken in this life, just as financial debts have to be met before the new year if one is to look the world in the eye. If debts are not settled, they haunt later generations until they are cleared. Forgiveness is not a virtue, though once you have defeated your enemies you may show generosity and not demand full payment of what is owed you – their humiliation can sometimes be enough. The expectation of vengeance means that every political struggle leaves a mountain of unsettled scores behind, and it makes it impossible to forget the past because the children and grand-children of earlier victims are treated as though they are themselves bound to be one's enemies too, a defensive attitude that has an uncomfortable way of being self-fulfilling. It also encourages an extra degree of ferocity in political conflicts: if your beaten enemies cannot be turned around by your generosity to them in defeat, they and their political or biological descendants will always be dangerous to you and your descendants unless you either destroy them or leave them so badly weakened that they will never be able to get their own back. The trouble with such an approach to vengeance is that it is never-ending: each debt settled opens a new account. Although this process can be controlled within the family or quasi-family for the sake of an overriding common interest in preserving a body on which all its members depend, it is one of the factors inhibiting the emergence of the sort of 'civil society' that optimists claim to find in contemporary China. Revenge cultures, such as those that predominate in China, are held together only by an autocracy that can and will come down hard on its subjects. And even when this repression is effective the hostility seethes beneath the surface, waiting for a moment of weakness to find expression.

One of the great myths of Chinese social history is the myth of the powerful clan or lineage that bound its component nuclear families into a whole. Like all the best myths, it has a basis in reality. In parts of rural China, notably in Guangdong and Fujian, the lineage solidarity of earlier centuries has survived the disruptions of land reform, collectivization and decollectivization to hold some villages together by the ties of shared patrilineal descent and a common surname. It remains possible to call the clan bloods out to do battle with a rival village dominated by another surname; and kinship ties extending to distant cities and even foreign countries can be used to bring business and investment to the village. Some ancestral temples that had been put to other uses during the decades of socialism are now, it is said, reverting to their original functions. Now that there is no people's commune to provide last-resort welfare, the clan will sometimes look after its poorer members.

Such clan institutions as charitable foundations to provide for the education of boys or for the maintenance of ancestral temples and sacrifices have received a lot of publicity over the last millennium. Confucian-educated gentlemen and propagandists approved strongly of such bodies and of their role in teaching correct values by disciplining members who offended against patriarchal morality, by encouraging members to fulfil the obligations appropriate to their position in the extended family and by compiling and printing genealogical records. It was a corrective to the natural tendency of Chinese families to split into their component nuclear households and concentrate on the small family more than on the extended one. It all looked very good to ideologues keen to demonstrate that even under the later imperial dynasties the values and prescriptions of the ancient classics on the correct behaviour of the Zhou aristocracy of a long-gone age were still relevant to a world in which social classes were much less clearly differentiated. The Ming and Qing states' enthusiastic promotion of such institutions suggests to the sceptical observer that so far from being widespread in society, they were, in fact, exceptional – good for publicity purposes, like the Israeli *kibbutz* or the English country house, but nothing to do with the life of the great majority.

Chinese extended families are unstable, fissiparous institutions that rarely manage to contain two or more married brothers under the same roof. Law and custom prevented the creation of great estates or other properties passed on intact, through entail, to one heir in each generation who was obliged to hand it on complete to his heir in turn. Instead property had to be divided more or less evenly between the sons in each generation unless all the sons continued to live in one big household. The richer a man was, the greater the number of wives and concubines he could afford, and the more sons he would probably have. More sons meant more chances of one of them insisting on dividing up the property, especially after their father's death. This made it very hard for any family to remain wealthy for more than three generations. Nor could a family be very poor for generations: below a certain level of poverty a family's sons could not afford to marry.

So strong were the forces pulling the extended family apart that for a couple's adult sons to manage to coexist in a single household was an achievement worth celebrating. Even when a very rich family did manage to hold together, its component nuclear families would often have their own separate kitchens and would eat together only on special occasions. This can be seen in an extreme, and no doubt exaggerated, form in the fanciful depiction of an early eighteenth-century extended family in the novel *Hong lou meng*. Although there was much coming and going between the many little households in the Great Prospect Garden, and they were all economically dependent on the larger family, the social structure in the garden is of a number of closely interrelated nuclear families tied to each other by kinship and economic necessity. Chinese house architecture encouraged this kind of separation. The Chinese great house is not at all like the single, large, multi-storeyed building that is the typical great house or palace of Europe and its former colonies, a structure built for permanence that might be altered or extended but could be expected to stand for hundreds of years, passed on in trust to one heir in each generation, a building big enough to accommodate many relations and dependants. The great Chinese house was many small, single-storeyed buildings grouped around courtyards that could be closed off from each other. The desirability of keeping the extended patrilineal family together – which was in no historical period economically possible for more than the tiniest of minorities – took second place to the Confucian principle of segregating women as far as possible (normally not far at all) from adult males other than their own husbands, fathers and sons. But though the component small families were separated from each other within the outer wall, they stood together against the world as a great family.

More generally in Chinese societies, links with other nuclear families through common patrilineal descent or marriage alliances have served to reduce the isolation and weakness of the nuclear family. Even though collective clan or lineage institutions have not been as strong in most of China during recent centuries as in

Guangdong and Fujian, the networks of kinship and quasi-kinship (such as those of classmates or of colleagues) create possibilities for the exchange of favours and the establishment of relationships stronger than those between strangers. China has yet to make general the kind of attitude to work responsibilities that would cause a shop assistant to feel bad about putting aside scarce and desirable stock for sale to relations. The family principle that obligations to others are graded according to closeness of kinship and relative seniority, and not owed equally to all one's fellow beings or fellow citizens, remains a powerful one. So too does the sense that it is foolish to help people towards whom you have no duties and who will not incur an obligation to you in return.

One of the prime virtues of Chinese high culture since antiquity, one that seems to have been important in popular cultures too, cannot be translated by a single word in modern vernacular English. The difficulty is a significant one. Render *xiao* 'filial piety', as has conventionally been done in writing on China since the nineteenth century, and you will need to explain to most readers that the latinate English term means being dutiful and obedient to one's parents. In modern English-speaking moralities daughters and sons are generally seen as having rather narrower obligations to their parents than in Chinese traditions. We do not acknowledge an adult's duty to obey parental orders. Indeed, one of the main meanings of reaching your majority is that it ends the obligation to do as your parents tell you. Not so in China, where the backward-looking duty of *xiao* never releases sons and unmarried daughters from obedience to their fathers. (Mothers had authority only as representatives of their husbands while their husbands lived. When widowed, they were supposed to obey their eldest sons.)

Obedience to one's father is no longer enforced by law, as it was less than a century ago, but the feeling that parents ought to be obeyed remains strong. This extends to other senior people in positions of quasi-paternal authority. There never comes a time when the 'child' is allowed to grow up and the parent is made to give up power. Thus it is that even when ancient tyrants retire from their formal positions of authority they can continue to exact obedience. Within the quasi-familial structures at the top of the Party machine the highest bosses have over their immediate underlings a personal authority that is unchallengeable, as it is protected by the deepest ethical feelings. The price of filial piety is a high one.

The endless changes of the last century have reinforced the lesson of many thousands of years: the only institution on which one can ultimately depend is the family. The patrilineal nuclear family has been one of the few winners from both the Communist Party's revolutionary phase and the wreck of the revolution. It has changed in a few respects but is essentially unscathed. The social and economic transformations of the 1940s and 1950s altered the relationships between households, even within extended kinship groupings or lineages, so that the families that had once been the dominant ones in a village or county were turned into untouchables, while the poor and middling families went up the social ladder.

Committed as they were by their ideology to struggle between classes, the Communists had, during twenty years of rural struggle before 1949, developed through trial and error formulae for dividing rural society into classes. These formulae were not copied from Russia and were flexible enough to deal with the vastly divergent conditions that existed in the Chinese countryside. The Communist Party gave communities a fairly standardized distribution of families of different classes, with only a small minority of 'landlords' and 'rich peasants', and involved as many people in each village as possible in making the classifications. They remixed power and property in such a way as to get new concepts of rural class accepted and – which was much more remarkable – to make people think of themselves as belonging to the classes to which they had been assigned. One reason why the new categories were accepted was perhaps that nuclear families were not usually split between classes.

It is hard to find in pre-Communist sources any indication of people having much sense of social class in the countryside except for an awareness of an undifferentiated 'us' – the poor, the common people – whose interests were opposed to 'them' – local rich families, extortionate officials, outsiders of one kind or another. There is much more to point to a strong sense of identity with people from the same place, especially if they bore the same surname and were related through the paternal line, against outsiders or with fellow villagers against other villages. In later dynastic China the state recognized few social classes: degree-holding gentry and their households, peasants (including everyone from many landlords to the landless labourers), artisans, merchants and a residual underclass of slaves and other minorities – what was left of the *jianmin* ('mean people') of Tang times – whose sons were formally ineligible to sit the civil service exams. Such a classification, determined not by wealth and property but by social function, was very old and could be further simplified into a division between the gentry and the rest. Other Qing distinctions were based on ethnicity: Manchus, Mongols and naturalized Han Chinese Banner households as the privileged minorities; the Han who made up the overwhelming majority; other minorities and colonial peoples such as Muslims, Hmong and others. The long-term tendency had been for the state to make fewer distinctions of class or caste and to attach less importance to them. The obsessive concern with aristocratic status found in north China in the fifth to seventh centuries AD that led to the state grading families' social rankings would have made no sense to eighteenth-century opinion. By then even titles of nobility were honours with no real substance to them and could be inherited only at a lower grade in each generation.

Where the Qing dynasty had largely ignored economic criteria in its categorization of society, the middle of the twentieth century saw an elaborate set of class divisions with quasi-legal status imposed on country and town. The striking similarity is that both dynastic and communist autocracies did their categorizing by nuclear families, not by individuals, and that the classifications were hereditary. Thus is was that, long after the disappearance in the middle 1950s of private ownership of land, of other means of production and of private business, the children and even grandchildren of those who had been classified in relation to property in the years around the founding of the People's Republic inherited that status. People also inherit the political status of a father or grandfather, irrespective of socio-economic classification. Thus if one member of a family was labelled a 'rightist' in 1957 for some indiscreet comment during the Hundred Flowers campaign, the whole family would be categorized as a rightist's family unless they broke all ties with the principal victim through such means as divorce.

Advantages can be inherited too. The poorer a family was in 1949, the better, for the next thirty years at least. A father killed on the Communist side in the civil war left a good legacy to his children: to be descendants of a revolutionary martyr. The privileges of the children and grandchildren of China's present rulers are nothing unusual by the standards of other poor and backward countries, though they would have been thought of as excessive in the China of forty years ago. Now the gilded youth are preparing their families' bolt-holes overseas against the day when it becomes necessary to get out. Once upon a time it would have been almost unthinkable for top Communist officials and their families to have bank accounts and property overseas. Now the only questions are where and how much. The regime may not look like a permanent fixture, especially since the collapse of so many other Communist Party regimes, but families go on.

For better for worse, for richer for poorer, in sickness and in health, in the last resort the family is all there is. Like it or not, you go up, go down, or stay where you are with the family. It was always that way, and there is no sign that it will be otherwise for as long as the present cultures last.

When attacking families they regarded as enemies and borrowing tactics used against hostile armies, such as encouraging internal rebellions and defections, the Communists never took on the nuclear family as such. Even in the exhilaration of the beginning of the Great Leap, when some villages were setting up communal kitchens and even tearing down their separate houses to build new blocks and terraces, families stayed together. Their property has been taken, redistributed, collectivized, decollectivized. Members of millions of families have been forced to live apart by being sent to jobs in different places, by penal exile and by the rigidities of the *hukou* system of residence permits that make it hard for someone who has become an urban resident to be joined by family members, but the family unit is defended and enforced by law and custom, just as it always has been.

Fitful campaigns by the communists have changed the legal position of women to one of full formal equality, to the extent that the current PRC Constitution and Marriage Law place on sons and daughters an equal obligation to support their parents, something that society will take a long time to accept. Equal pay has long been the rule in the state sector; though, as in other parts of the world, jobs that are seen as women's work tend to be worse-paid than ones men usually do. In the cities it is normal for women to have full-time, regular jobs and for employers to provide such support as child-care facilities to make it possible for them to continue working once they have families of their own. Women may own property in their own right, and in questions of divorce, which is allowed but strongly discouraged by the state, the woman's wishes normally prevail. A wife no longer has to accept new wives joining the household. These changes add up to quite a lot, though less than equality in real life. Families have been modified but not transformed. Women occupy some positions near the top, but rarely at the pinnacle, of power structures.

The state and organized society remain bitterly opposed to anything that threatens the stability and continuity of the patrilineal stem family. Sexual freedom was never officially condoned, and people may still be punished for pre-marital or extra-marital sex. In many communities a young woman who goes out regularly with a man is virtually committed to marrying him or else being disgraced. Especially for a woman, not marrying is a very hard choice to carry through, and a woman who divorces will be treated with suspicion and even contempt that is only somewhat reduced by her remarriage. Women remain the victims of domestic violence, from which they receive even less effective legal protection than in Western countries and which is accepted as normal. Stories about mothers-in-law assaulting daughters-in-law, or making their sons beat their brides into submission, are disturbingly frequent.

Attacks on the family by anarchists and other radical intellectuals in the first quarter of the twentieth century had some influence on the Communist Party in its early years. Mao wrote in 1927 of triangular sexual relationships that were very common in the villages of Hunan in a tone that carried no hint of disapproval. Once the Communists had some territory under their control they reverted to more traditional values. Attacking the family would have doomed their cause, even their survival, in the villages. A woman's right to a divorce, for example, was and is suspended if her husband is a serving soldier. Mao's 1927 observations on rural sex were dropped from his *Selected Works* in the 1950s.

The power of tradition has asserted itself in the way that the household has been protected by law and custom and even in the very common tendency, when talking about villages and other rural communities, to measure their population by the number of households rather than the number of individuals. Under collective agriculture work-points were earned by individuals but credited to the family. Since the abolition of the people's communes the household has remained the unit that contracts for land or other resources and has been more vital than ever as a source of support for the sick and old now that the rudimentary rural welfare benefits of the Mao era have been swept away. The family is now all there is that stands between oneself and disaster, and it is as emphatically patrilineal as ever.

Although a wife now has a legal right to a divorce if she wants one, that right is hard to enforce, especially in the countryside. Even if she does succeed in getting her divorce, she will, like a widow who defies convention by remarrying, have very great difficulty in asserting her claim to her share of the family's property. Hardest of all for the widow or divorced woman in the villages is to take her own son, especially if he is an only one, into another family. As far as Chinese rural societies are concerned, a son is the property of the father and the father's family, and the feelings or the interests of the child or the mother are irrelevant. A daughter is much less likely to be fought for by the father's family. Today's population policies, which make second and further births much more expensive and difficult because of all the fines and bribes that have to be paid, only strengthen the patrilineal family's iron grip on a son. Patriarchy is alive and well in China's hundreds of thousands of villages.

Traditional family values and institutions do not fit very well with contemporary city life. Both parents normally work; they find it harder than country people do to get round the one-child-family regulations; and if they are employed by the state, they can look forward to pensions and other welfare benefits in their old age. A nuclear family may not have relatives within accessible distance. Adult children are as likely to be a burden as a support for their parents. All this means that the discipline of the older arrangements has been much weakened and that the socialization of being part of an extended family in a village does not usually happen.

A child without brothers and sisters, and probably without cousins living near by, discouraged from forming close friendships with contemporaries (because friendships could implicate him or her in problems beyond the family's control), is likely to become isolated and self-centred, and this is only exacerbated by the undivided attention of too many adults, all too eager to buy the little darling's good will and push him or her ahead. For girls there may be some advantages in not being sacrificed for a brother's sake and in being valued as their parents' only hope.

Will the generation of urban onlies who come into their teens towards the end of the 1990s be able to wean their parents from emotional dependence on them? Will they be able to withstand the pressure of parental blackmail and get on with their own lives? It could be that the experience of growing up alone will nurture an independence of thought that the older sort of family never did and that some good will come of it all for the privileged urban minority. For good or ill, the result will end the family system, with its traditional Chinese characteristics, for the urban salaried class, and will open an even wider gap between it and the teeming peasantry. We can only speculate about the sort of value system that will take its place and wonder how today's onlies will raise their children in the twenty-first century.

If the state controls on population growth that are now only partly effective crumble even further, the consequences of the ever-greater pressure of people on land will be terrible. As long as sons are the only reliable support for each peasant couple in their old age, they will continue to try to raise them, and as conditions in the poorer parts of China become worse, the family will be the only institution to which people can turn for survival. In other words, the more essential the family becomes for each, the greater the harm it will do to all. Family values of a characteristically Chinese kind have done much to bring about the crisis in which the Chinese now find themselves, and it will be to the family in its various forms that people will have to turn as other institutions prove unable to bear the strains that the next few decades will place on them. Meanwhile the family's suppression of individual initiative and sense of personal responsibility for one's own life, like its discouragement of involvement in public affairs as a good citizen, will continue to inhibit the development of other value systems.

It may be that China will have to wait for the spoilt urban brats of the 1980s to move up through the education system (which, at its higher levels, will remain closed to all but exceptionally lucky sons and daughters of the peasantry) and into positions of power in the twenty-first century before other concepts of being human will become influential. And even then the great majority of the population will still belong to the world of familism.

Meanwhile the village family is one of the few institutions that look set to survive the breakdown of the present order. The family smallholding is once more the basic unit that feeds the nation; and as much of state-owned industry staggers from crisis to crisis, the small or extended family firm is the most dynamic part of the manufacturing and trading economy. It is able to adapt quickly and flexibly to market opportunities and, where the family has connections overseas, to use them to join the world economy. Given the right conditions, the family business could be the saving of coastal China; and for parts of inland China family networks may be all that can avert or mitigate hardship as the state becomes less able to cope with catastrophe.

7. LAW

===

Law is an area in which China has inherited the worst of the past. From a formidable legal tradition that developed unbroken for some 2,300 years until the early twentieth century, and had a long prehistory before that, contemporary mainland China has retained a harshly punitive approach to serious crime, a scarcely developed system of civil law and minimal protection for the subject against the absolutist state. What has been lost includes the main defences against the abuse of judicial powers under successive dynasties: a judge's ability to be seriously punished if he fails to ascertain all the relevant facts in a case and the review of all sentences by higher judicial authorities.

One of the ways in which the force of tradition expresses itself most strongly is the grisly process of 'severe punishment in accordance with the law'. While most legal processes in China are hidden from public view, capital punishment is played as theatre in a near-traditional way, with as much publicity as possible for everything except the actual killing.

Several times a year rashes of a special kind of poster appear in China's cities, on walls carefully chosen so that they will be seen by all local inhabitants but will not attract too much attention from foreign visitors. They are notices of execution setting out, in thick, black type on white paper, the names of the dead and their alleged crimes – murder, robbery, rape, corruption, habitual housebreaking and many other offences that can qualify for the bullet in the back of the head. Each notice is marked by the immemorial sign of a death sentence carried out, a big, red tick through or beside the victim's name, a bloody gash across the cool white space and the stern regularity of the blocks of print.

All societies that indulge, or have indulged, in judicial killing love and cherish their rituals of death and are very conservative about them. China is no different. Even the position of the victim at the final moment is what everyone has learned to imagine: kneeling, with the executioner standing behind him or her, just as one knelt to be beheaded. Much of the hallowed tradition is preserved, though progress has made the actual instant of killing less public – no longer are the condemned lined up on their knees at Peking's Vegetable Market after the autumn assizes, ready for the executioner. The gun fired into the back of the head has replaced the long-handled sword with which a good killer could remove a head with a single swing while an assistant pulled the victim's plait out of the sword's way. Not for China the wasteful firing squad when one bullet is enough to blow the brains out of the top of the skull, though there are stories about messier shootings during the Cultural Revolution. Folklore insists that the victim's family is billed for the cost of the bullet, bringing the cost to the state down to nothing. An aspect of today's executions that carries tradition further is the use of the regular and predictable supply of healthy young bodies to meet the demands of senior officials and the international market for fresh kidneys and other human organs. Once executioners sold their victims' blood for its imagined medicinal value, earning a handful of silver. Now a body can be turned into tens of thousands of dollars.

The journey to the killing ground is a public performance. Once it was done in a cart, and the condemned criminals were allowed their minutes of glory, shouting to the crowd, even joking and singing snatches of opera if their nerves and voices held out. Everyone knew what to expect, and though most victims were probably in no state to put on a good display of bravado, it did at least give them a chance to go out in style. Now the vehicle is usually an open truck. The victims are made to stand with their hands fastened behind their backs. Rising above their heads are tall placards in the shape of a sword blade giving their names and offences. These days the guards will not let them shout. Sometimes their throats are slit before the final journey, or a wire noose is put around their necks. All that is left is their humiliation and the shock to all who see them as they are driven around the streets.

The sight is not one to forget. After many years of imagining it from written descriptions I saw a convoy of vehicles coming towards me while I was being driven through a rural district south of Peking one afternoon late in September 1985. Everyone in the car stopped talking as we realized that the people standing on the back of a lorry in the approaching convoy had the fatal placards above them. I cannot remember their faces, only their expressions and the horror and anger that the bowed, cropped heads and the apparent insouciance of the guards evoked. The first lorry passed by, followed by another with a second load of victims and smaller vehicles carrying the other actors in the ritual. In seconds the convoy was behind us, on its way to the small city of Zhuozhou to display its doomed passengers before taking them to the local killing ground. Conversation in our car was subdued and soon turned to someone in my companion's unit who had been executed not long earlier for sexual promiscuity with willing partners. Nobody expressed the view that the victims were getting what they deserved.

If one county could produce a dozen or so victims at once, one wonders how many were executed across China that month. The timing was significant. The traditional seasons for executions were autumn and winter, times of death in the natural world. This has turned into a modern custom of having a blood-letting before major festivals, a symbolic purging so that the country's ancient rulers can enjoy National Day on 1 October, Chinese New Year or May Day with the satisfaction of knowing that some of the dangerous young have been destroyed. Today's rulers kill many more than did their dynastic predecessors, who except in times of war or rebellion kept the number of executions to a minimum.

Executions have been a particularly strong feature of the Deng Xiaoping era, especially since 1983, when collective panic among the ruling group prompted a huge campaign against the growing crime that was one of the symptoms of the collapse of revolutionary morality since the Cultural Revolution. In the name of law and order the number of capital offences was sharply increased, and the legal process speeded up and simplified, so that most death sentences no longer had to be confirmed by Peking, appeals could be dealt with in a few days and at a lower level and victims were executed quickly. There were thousands of executions that year. Unknown numbers of the urban young were rounded up and sent to labour camps or to exile in the far west.

It was strangely reminiscent of the panic about crime in eighteenth-century England, which also saw a rapid increase in the number of hanging offences and sent tens of thousands of convicted felons to penal colonies in remote continents. Fear of social change and of hitherto subservient groups becoming too assertive as new economic opportunities enabled them to escape traditional controls, was common to the rulers of eighteenth-century London and late-twentieth-century Peking. In neither case could the repressions succeed in turning the clock back or deal with the causes of instability.

Jails have a long history in China. Their traditional function was not to be the punishment but to hold the presumed criminal until his or her case was finally decided, which could take years. When a final judgment had been made the punishment ranged from a number of forms of execution through – in later imperial times – beatings of various degrees of severity, penal exile and fines. Earlier dynasties indulged in physical mutilations. It took Western civilization to show China how to build and run a proper nineteenth-century prison, such as the one so well constructed by the British in Shanghai that it is still in use, like its counterparts around the world, those massively built and enduring embodiments of Victorian values that will probably go on creating and containing pain for centuries.

The old-fashioned Chinese prison was evidently a terrifying place even to think about. Accounts of jail conditions in literature speak of disease, hunger, cruelty and corruption. Jailers had to be bribed if a prisoner was to have any hope of tolerable conditions; and they could also be paid by a prisoner's enemies to ensure his or her death.

If the sentence was a beating and exile, bribery could lighten the blows and make the journey under escort to another part of one's own province or to a remote and unpleasant corner of the empire more bearable. Exiles were put to forced labour in the service of the state and, in the worst category, were enslaved to soldiers on the far and inhospitable frontier.

This looks like a prescription for the sort of penal slave labour economy that flourished under the Qin and has since been known elsewhere in the world. But by the time of the Qing, some two thousand years later, most beatings and sentences of exile could be commuted into a payment of silver on a scale set down in the criminal code. It seems unlikely that late dynastic China was getting any significant economic benefits from its penal exiles or that the prison population was normally very large.

As in other areas, the Republican interlude saw some limited Westernization – a few foreign-style prisons, as the treaty-port model was copied – but not enough effective state power to extend the delights of new-style prisons far beyond the big cities. Prisons were useful for holding those political opponents who could not be conveniently killed. One or two prisons in the 1930s were particularly notorious for being modern in their techniques of interrogation and brainwashing. Survivors' accounts tell of the chillingly familiar methods by which so many Third World military dictatorships deal with political prisoners. Wang Ruowang, a communist (until his expulsion in 1987) who had spent years in both Nationalist and his own Party's prisons, found the former bad and the latter worse: the People's prisons were much more systematic and unprincipled in their cruelties than their occasionally humane predecessors had been.

The People's Republic has been developing its prison and camp system since its first years. Prisons, like society outside, are divided into classes. There are the VIP establishments that were used for former generals and emperors from earlier regimes and in the last quarter of a century have accommodated senior officials out of favour for a time. Good examples of special prison treatment are that given to the former emperor Pu Yi, who was much too useful to get the harsh justice that was inflicted on lesser collaborators with the Japanese, and more recently to the well-connected journalist Dai Qing, who was dealt with correctly and given a cell to herself while being interrogated for many months in 1989. Most of the system's victims get much rougher treatment, whether they are being held in urban jails while they are questioned and their cases are decided or in the many labour camps to which nearly all prisoners are sent. Some camps are fairly close to the cities and are part of the 'labour education' system to which people are consigned without any court formalities at all. Others, which are usually worse, are in remote places in the empire's vast frontier areas where the state wants labour but would not be able to get it except through the penal system. Wherever you see a big construction project in China outside the big cities there is a good chance that it was built, in part at least, by prisoners.

Mines, heavy construction including railway and road building, farms, plantations, factories – the forced labour institutions add up to a considerable vested interest that the state has in maintaining repressive penal policies. They are also obstacles to economic progress: when the most unpleasant jobs can be done for next to nothing by prisoners, there is not much incentive for expensive investment. The slave sector of the Chinese economy thus perpetuates backwardness and encourages repression. Limited though the freedoms of the rest of the population may be, the shadow of the forced-labour institutions to which anyone can be sent merely by an administrative order is an effective reminder of the dangers of challenging the system. The serf who misbehaves can be turned into a slave. The high walls of the detention centres and jails in the cities are, as everyone knows, the gateway to the world of the camps.

Once upon a time there was a lot of propaganda about how the Chinese penal system remade its prisoners into new people, combined harshness with 'proletarian humanitarianism' and reintegrated ex-prisoners back into society as workers full of socialist consciousness. At first it was not all pure invention, as even embittered ex-convicts have written. In recent years the bottom has dropped out of that line of propaganda. As state-owned enterprises have been under pressure to cut their staffing, ex-convicts have become more or less unemployable and have been forced to make their own living, often as small-time private traders. Those who succeed in making a little money seem to be regarded with deep hostility by officialdom. Former convicts were identified by the regime as being some of the most dangerous of its enemies in 1989, and the Flying Tigers bikies – whose motorbikes were evidence that they had done well for themselves, although many of them were ex-convicts, and who had been very useful in the peaceful resistance to the army's siege of Peking – were the first group among the protesters to be singled out for arrests. Ex-convicts are also strongly represented among execution victims. By now the message to the general public is that the penal system does not save but destroys you. Another sign of a new era in penal policy is the willingness to rent convicts to foreign investors, lured by labour costs that are low even by Chinese standards and reassured to know that the workforce can be shot if it tries to leave.

The People's Republic got along without a criminal code for the first thirty years. All the legislation of the Guomindang government was cancelled, and not much was put in its place. There were some laws and other decrees covering certain offences, but others were dealt with in the absence of either published laws or openly acknowledged customary or common law. In the heady days during which the Communist Party first established state power, then socialized virtually all productive capacity while organizing uninterrupted 'class' war against its chosen victims, it did not want to be inhibited by such tiresome legalisms as a published criminal code and a law on criminal procedure. When the Party determined everything, any institution that restricted the Party was counter-revolutionary and hence a target for attack.

The small legal profession inherited from the Republic and allowed to practise for a few years virtually disappeared from the late 1950s onwards. Though a number of judges and other legal officials were retained, they were not encouraged to think or act as independent professionals upholding principles of law. Nor were they provided with legal codes and detailed instructions on their implementation, as legal officials of dynastic regimes had been. Rather they were expected to be revolutionary cadres implementing the Party's will and determining cases in accordance with general and specific instructions from the Party. The county or municipal Party secretary would provide the verdict and the sentence in any difficult case.

It has not been necessary to go through even the form of a court trial for many offenders to be punished. The struggle meeting and other forms of public humiliation could turn a respected member of the community into a pariah overnight, and anyone who objected to how victims were treated could expect to join them. During the more exciting phases of the revolution, such as the early 1950s or the late 1960s, the 'revolutionary masses' were allowed to imprison, maim and kill the targets of their proletarian wrath. Sometimes the police even helped, as in Daxing county on the outskirts of Peking in August 1966, where – according to Yan Jiaqi and Gao Gao's history of the Cultural Revolution – the local public security told Red Guards about 'class enemies' and did nothing to prevent Chairman Mao's storm troopers from killing 325 of them.

In calmer periods administrative decisions have been, and are still, enough to get people sent off for up to four years of penal labour for such offences as being fired by one's employer and having no other source of livelihood, refusing to accept job allocations or transfers, or constantly 'making trouble'. According to the 1957 'Decision of the State Council on the Question of Education Through Labour' that was republished in 1980, it needs only an application from civil affairs departments of local governments, public security departments, a work unit (a government office, public body, enterprise or school) or a parent or guardian to the relevant provincial government office for one to be sent off for forced labour. This is an administrative procedure that requires no judicial process whatsoever and against which there is no appeal to the courts provided correct procedures have been followed. It is also a form of tyranny that is hard to parallel in dynastic law.

Other current non-judicial sanctions that were not available to Qing officials and are intended to keep the citizen under control include short periods of detention by the police at their own discretion. A much more serious sanction is the cancellation of someone's urban residence licence. This enables the local authorities to expel anyone they dislike from the cities, and though reliable overall figures are not published, it seems likely that large numbers of urban dwellers have been sent into exile or returned to the villages from which they came in this way.

If all this can be done without reference to the courts, and if the courts are as powerless to intervene in these extra-judicial processes as they appear to be, it will be evident that China's courts and judiciary are weaker institutions than their counterparts in Western countries. Indeed, after over a decade of reforms that have given law a much bigger role than it had in the first thirty years of the People's Republic the most one can say is that law has been raised from an almost superfluous to a minor component in the political order.

Yet China created one of the world's great legal cultures and has one of the world's longest uninterrupted traditions of recorded law. The legal code of the Qing dynasty that was still being applied at the beginning of the twentieth century was directly descended from the codes of the states of Wei and Qin in the fourth century BC and indirectly from codes going back a thousand years before then. When Qin conquered the Chinese world its laws became the first of the imperial codes and were imposed on all Qin domains. The Qin code was adapted by the successor Han dynasty, and for the next two thousand years and more there was a remarkable continuity in legal codes and the thinking behind them as each regime inherited and modified the laws of its predecessors. Continuity did not exclude change. Qin laws were intended to bring about fundamental transformations in society and to give the state an unprecedented degree of direct control over the lives of its subjects. Two thousand years later Qing laws were more modest in their aim: defending the existing political and social order.

While some Qin laws were consciously intended to challenge earlier values that conflicted with the state's absolute power, they also enforced the traditional subjection of a son to his father's authority, even providing for the execution of an unfilial son on his father's request. And the Qing code, for all its apparent conservatism, helped to reduce social inequality by removing some of the legal privileges of the gentry.

Dynastic codes were not static, and over that long period they reflected changing relationships between and within state and society. They tended to become slightly less harsh as the large number of capital offences was slowly reduced and more of them could be commuted, penal mutilation almost disappeared (unlike torture and flogging) and, except in times of civil disorder, the death penalty was inflicted only after cases were repeatedly scrutinized until a sentence was confirmed in the capital. Once the extreme interventionism of the Qin code had been softened by the succeeding Han code, legal draughtsmen tried to reconcile the goals of protecting the absolute power of the monarcho-bureaucratic state and defending the authoritarian family relationships that embodied key 'Confucian' values.

All the major codes had much in common. They all made the administration of formal justice a monopoly of the state and its appointed officials, while leaving informal justice to families and local society. They all treated criminal-law procedures not as ordeals or contests but as processes in which the official handling the case in the first instance was acting not so much as a judge or jury but as an examining magistrate whose responsibility was to establish accurately all the relevant facts. Once that was done, it was normally fairly straightforward to determine the category in the criminal code that an offence best fitted. The code specified the penalty for each type of crime and left very little discretion to the official involved. All codes held the official handling the case personally responsible for getting it right, from ascertaining the facts to applying the correct punishment. All cases except minor ones would be reviewed by legal specialists at a higher level, and convicted criminals or their families could, if they dared, lodge appeals themselves with the higher courts. Officials who made mistakes in handling cases, including failure to establish the relevant facts, were liable to be punished themselves, even when they erred in good faith. This important safeguard in dynastic legal systems has disappeared during the twentieth century. China is now left without the defences for the accused either of an adversarial system or of one in which the judges have to fear for their own future if they have failed to get at the truth. Under the People's Republic judges have to worry more about making political mistakes than doing injustice.

Under dynastic law local communities could be left to settle many matters for themselves. The state allowed and even encouraged families, villages, merchant guilds and other groups to sort out disputes and bring wrongdoers under control. In the past, as now, informal mediation was preferred to court proceedings. The dynastic state permitted the imposition of legitimate authority by the family or the community through violence and other forms of coercion. The empire and its officials generally let patriarchs bully their families into submission. As long as a son was not killed, his father could beat him with virtual impunity for disobedience, whereas a son who merely struck his father could face immediate execution once convicted.

In criminal law, as in many other areas, the imperial state tended over many centuries to intervene less in village life and to be more willing to let families and local communities regulate their own affairs provided that the supremacy of the state's code was not challenged. But while non-state institutions were allowed to apply their own forms of discipline, these had to be consistent with the legal and moral principles of the emperor's laws on pain of severe penalties imposed by the courts. A strict code that had to be applied rigidly when it was invoked could thus have a certain looseness at the edges and could coexist with customary systems dealing with matters that the code left alone. The imperial law could ignore large areas while still keeping its option of getting involved if necessary.

A huge area of legal activity in Western cultures from the age of the Greek city states to our own time was very little dealt with by dynastic Chinese law: commerce. It was not that commerce was unregulated. The earlier imperial dynasties had tried to control it closely, even setting prices and confining trade to designated markets in cities. Later dynasties, more inclined to *laissez-faire*, let merchants and entrepreneurs get on with it, allowing guilds and other non-official bodies to resolve disputes over tort and contract for themselves. The state's courts became involved only as a last resort, and that generally when one party objected to the seizure of property or when disorder broke out.

Contracts were written so as to be self-enforcing as far as possible, often through a guarantor who undertook to make recompense if one party failed to deliver or perform. Guilds, associations of people from the same native place in another city and public opinion generally were very effective in enforcing commercial morality and upholding contracts. If you wanted to stay in business, you had to honour your deals. Commerce ran on belief in the word of known and trusted trading partners or on written contracts endorsed by reliable guarantors, who were the essential intermediaries in a commercial world characterized by a virtually infinite number of small operators. Deals were held together by complex and self-regulating patterns of interlocking obligations that could span great distances. The remarkable effectiveness of small and medium-sized non-mainland Chinese businesses in operating internationally, and especially in South-East Asia, owes much to the normative role of the common business and familistic cultures of the Chinese diaspora. These have to function in circumstances that have made it impractical to resort to the courts of many different jurisdictions, including ones in which no Chinese could reasonably expect to be fairly treated. Because the commercial economy depended so much on the reliability and trustworthiness of one's trading partners, contracts tended to be fairly simple and to avoid detail, assuming that the parties would act in good faith. There was no point in trying to achieve very detailed, legally watertight contracts if they were not going to be tested in the courts by professional advocates.

While the later dynasties kept out of commercial law as far as they could, their laws did defend property. Theft was always liable to punishment if brought before the courts. The tariff of penalties took into account the value of what was stolen, the intention of the stealer, the means used, the number of people involved and the relationship between thief and victim. Minor theft was felt both by officialdom and society to be best dealt with informally, not through the state's criminal process. The contemporary Chinese state continues to use social and administrative sanctions to deal with minor criminal matters that in Western countries would go before the courts.

Landed property was a special concern of the state, given the general principle that all land ultimately belonged to the emperor. Even when the later imperial state abandoned the struggle to allocate land and virtually recognized private ownership, it still needed to know who owned what land so as to tax it. This meant that the courts sometimes became involved in land disputes. Generally speaking, however, civil property questions were not central concerns of the judiciary, which much preferred disputes to be settled out of court. The present Chinese legal system is still at an early stage of developing the capacity to handle such property disputes. Before the 1980s it dealt with them scarcely at all.

The preference for avoiding court proceedings – one that was strengthened by the absence of private lawyers who would have profited from them – probably did more good than harm, especially considering the severity of the legal process and the opportunities for extortion that trials offered clerks, constables and other petty officials. It is a preference that is still very strong: China remains a country with fully trained lawyers by the thousand and mediators by the million.

Laws were made and interpreted by the state's legal specialists. Generalist officials at lower levels of government, whose duties included acting as magistrates, had to handle cases in accordance with the statutes, the official commentaries on them and cases selected by the Board of Punishments as offering useful guidance on how statutes were to be interpreted. Magistrates' judgments would be reviewed at higher levels of the bureaucracy, up to the Board of Punishments and, when the death penalty was involved, the emperor himself. The central bureaucracies made and interpreted laws in the name of maintaining the social, political and cosmic order. This left no room for outsiders, such as priests, to challenge the emperor's law by reference to a higher, divine law – the emperor's law

embodied the highest principles. Nor did it allow interest groups
and other representatives of the subject to agitate for changes in
legislation, or to demand the right to vote on new or existing laws,
or to argue that laws made by the emperor without their consent
had no moral validity. There was no assembly, no senate, no Magna
Carta, no social contract, no immemorial rights of the freeborn
subject, no constitution, nothing requiring any of the people to take
part in the legislative process.

The only permitted lawyers in imperial China were the state's
own legal specialists. Right into the late nineteenth century the
imperial bureaucracy was trying to stamp out the private legal
profession. It was a criminal offence to become involved in preparing
pleadings for anyone but a close relation; and even when the litigation specialist was innocent of such other offences as bribery,
intimidation of witnesses or misrepresentation of the facts in a case
he was still liable to flogging (possibly redeemable through a fine)
and exile simply for practising his profession. The assumption of
Chinese legal thinkers was that cases were hard enough to settle
correctly without letting word-twisters disguise or distort the facts
of them. The only legitimate career in the law for a private citizen
who had not won or bought his way into the regular bureaucracy
was as a legal assistant to a local official, guiding him through the
minefields of the state's legal literature and helping him to handle
cases without making mistakes. This was not a career that brought
much respect or status, though it was a living for some of those
educated for the bureaucracy who could not join the lucky few able
to succeed at exams. For all the expertise in the letter and the practice
of the law that these men could acquire, they had nothing of the
professional status of advocates in ancient Mediterranean and later
European cultures. At best they made a living and escaped the perils
of facing prosecution as 'litigation hoodlums', as lawyers in illegal
private practice were called. Officials' legal assistants had the quasi-
respectability of the permanently kept mistress instead of the oppro-
brium of the streetwalker.

Traditional Chinese law thus managed without private lawyers.
It also virtually excluded judges from making law when deciding

cases. The only legal precedents that a court could take into account when dealing with a case were those that the state's own senior legal officials selected and issued as appropriate. Trial by jury would have been abhorrent to the official legal mind. To let verdicts be made by a randomly chosen set of untrained commoners who could not be held personally responsible if later evidence indicated they had got them wrong would have been bad enough. To allow those decisions to be influenced by the relative histrionic strengths of two or more paid performers in front of a panel of ignorant jurors would have been even more atrocious.

Although the legal profession began to acquire foreign coloration under the Republic, especially in the big coastal cities, older attitudes to lawyers as selfish, antisocial troublemakers came back on top after the Communist Party won power. Given lawyers' lack of support from society and the absence of a strong tradition of an independent legal profession, they were not in much of a position to resist their virtual abolition after the socialist transformation of the late 1950s. Nor was there much of a tradition of independence to enable judges to defy the instructions of Party officials on how to handle cases. The Communists inherited the old attitude that judges were officials of the state and obliged to obey political instructions. In European countries under Communist rule much more effort was made to observe the forms of legal institutions. Even if the judges had no discretion in the handling of serious political offences, it was important to their governments that everything should appear to be correct in court proceedings. Only since the 1980s have China's courts begun to be a little less under the thumb of the local Party boss – and that has only been because the highest Party bosses have encouraged the rebuilding of legal institutions and have lifted political control to a higher level.

There has been since the 1980s something of a recovery for courts and lawyers as the authorities have tried to use law to reduce the scope of arbitrary rule by subordinate Party officials, building up a set of rules and procedures to regulate the state and society. China is still a long way from seeing an independent legal profession or a judiciary that is ready to stand up to the party state. But courts are no longer entirely in the pocket of the local Party secretary, and at least they can now require the dictatorship to make more of an effort to obey its own rules. They and the procuratorate (a formally independent supervisory and prosecution service) seem to be more assertive than they were about sorting out the facts in a case before reaching the almost inevitable guilty verdict in any case that goes to trial. (Acquittal rates are well below 1 per cent.) It is not inconceivable that the legal system may reach the standards of the Qing dynasty within a decade or so.

In China before the twentieth century the legal officials' duty to get cases right meant that a guilty verdict had to be confirmed by a confession, without which the judgment was unsafe. To avoid injustice the criminal might have to be encouraged to confess through legally sanctioned forms of torture. The intention of judicial officials who ordered torture was to prevent injustice. The result was sometimes the opposite when an innocent person made a false confession under duress. Pressure on suspects to confess remains very heavy to this day and can include the use of fetters, handcuffs and beatings.

Getting it right was also a very serious concern of the legal specialists who drafted and revised the criminal codes of successive dynasties. While codes could be adapted to changing circumstances as centuries rolled by, they were also generally very conservative. This was not only because each dynasty tended to base its code on its predecessor's but also because each code wanted to go back to the fundamentals of social morality and conduct, as laid down in the classical texts accepted by the Confucian tradition.

In the so-called Confucian classics great attention is given to gradations of authority, respect, duty and obligation within extended kinship structures and, outside those structures, in a wider society. The precise forms of action that expressed these gradations were set out in the texts on *li*, correct behaviour, which were thus quasi-legal in their effect. *Xing*, punishments, and *fa*, law, were only for a short period and in some places used as weapons to attack traditional *li* behaviour codes. For nearly all the history of dynastic regimes the law was an expression and defence of *li*.

Those who revised inherited law codes tended to be traditionalists, and even those who were not so conservative often chose to hide innovation behind familiar elements. Thus it was that for Qing legislators, as for their Tang predecessors a thousand years before them, the law code had to begin by stipulating very severe penalties for the same Ten Abominations – rebellion, lese-majesty (damaging imperial temples, tombs or palaces), treason, vicious contumacy (killing or striking a parent or other senior close relative) and so on – in a language so similar that one has to look very carefully to see if the code one is reading is from the eighth or the eighteenth century. The successive codes all recognized and defended the inequality in society and in the family that was essential to the moral and the imperial order.

The solemnity of dynastic law in action is something of which all Chinese are still much aware. In books and stories, on the stage and on the screen, the terrifying rituals of past court hearings are constantly re-enacted or reinvented, with defendants and witnesses on their knees before magistrate or judge and liable at any moment to be flogged or tortured by the guards lining the courtroom. By comparison the intimidating effect of the wigs and gowns in courts of the English type is rather mild. As a seventeenth-century manual for magistrates observed, even the humble county magistrate, who could sentence a prisoner to nothing more severe than a flogging, had it in his power to have a recalcitrant prisoner or a witness suspected of lying flogged to death. Those who appeared before the magistrate in his courtroom had every reason to tremble.

There was no room for presumption of innocence before conviction when the magistrate trying a case had also been responsible for investigating it and deciding who was probably guilty and should be put on trial. The first point at which a neutral observer would look at the papers in a case would be when a higher official reviewed a conviction. Although one finds the occasional Western-influenced jurist in modern times writing about the desirability of presuming innocence, this carries very little weight against such massively present tradition. Everyday language speaks not of suspect or defendant but of criminal. Trial – in those cases that come to court – is normally only a ceremony to confirm what has already been decided. The way prisoners are treated in show trials or sentencing rallies today, forced by guards to keep their heads bowed, allowed little personal dignity and denied the right to an effective defence, echoes the humiliation of prisoners on their knees before the magistrate in past centuries.

The attitudes to punishment that still prevail today are also deeply traditional. Whereas most offences were dealt with in the past by the family and other local social organizations, many minor offences are still dealt with by the work unit, street committee or village government. The state also uses such extra-judicial sanctions as exile, a feature of contemporary Chinese penal practice too little discussed by outside observers that is a direct reversion to Qing and earlier times, except that it is now done on a much larger scale and on the basis of purely administrative decisions. Even some of the places exiles are sent to are the same, such as the remote and inhospitable north-west. Just as in Russia, the exile policy of the last dynasty seems mild and moderate by comparison with what followed. A Qing subject could not be exiled without a court decision that had to be reviewed by higher judicial authority.

The creation of an army of forced labour in penal settlements is a return to practices much earlier than those of the Qing, going right back to the extensive use of convicts and state bondservants by the Qin regime 2,200 years ago. Then, as now, the state had a vested interest in keeping large numbers of prisoners working for it in exchange for little more than their food and clothing. Then, as now, the state used its power to benefit itself at the expense of its subjects. It is depressing to see another example of today's regime failing to meet even the standards of the Ming and Qing dynasties. Accounts of life in today's camps carry one back to the penal world evoked by the surviving regulations on the treatment of prisoners in the Qin Gulag 2,200 years ago.

If China's present criminal law is open to question as a system of justice, it could be argued that it works as a mechanism of repression – the role that Mao gave the courts and the public security in his 1949 article 'On the People's Democratic Dictatorship', which set out the main policies of his new regime. But it is fragile machinery, easily swept aside by events such as those of the late 1960s, when mob rule and local military dictatorships replaced it. It is also a system that risks destroying itself through its own harshness if it creates too many victims with too little to lose in taking it on. That was what brought down the Qin regime; and official propaganda in 1989 about ex-prisoners as one of the most dangerous groups among those who challenged the dictatorship from April to June confirmed that the state regards them as its enemies.

It is also possible that only a thoroughly repressive criminal code backed by draconian administrative sanctions will be able to cope with the troubles that the regime openly predicts for the nineties. Perhaps only a government willing to shoot a lot of its subjects has a chance of surviving and holding the state together.

To meet the standards of any kind of justice the criminal legal system needs to be either more traditional, with the checks that were applied before sentences were confirmed in Qing times, or more modern, ditching old-fashioned and authentically Chinese concepts and methods. Whether the Chinese state really feels it needs a better criminal justice system is much more doubtful: it created the present arrangements, after all, and in recent years has made them more repressive.

China remains a country in which the subject has very few rights that can be asserted against the state and its officials. Civil rights and human rights remain alien concepts with very little meaning, which the state addresses only under pressure from meddling foreigners. As under dynastic rule, subjects have a recognized right to eat, and famine is seen as a failure of government, but the right to eat does not in law override the principle of private property. To be fed, clothed and housed, and to be allowed by the government to live a normal family life, is not so much the basic minimum as the most any subject can decently demand. The time when a Chinese subject will be able to choose where to live still seems remote. So far from protecting freedom of political belief and action, the constitution still forbids it by requiring subjects to uphold Marxism–Leninism and Mao-think, and to support the Communist Party dictatorship.

Although legislation now expects the authorities to go through correct procedures when infringing the subject's freedoms (to use a profoundly un-Chinese concept), this only makes repression more regular, and defines more clearly which officials have to be involved in taking the subject's limited freedoms away.

The disappearance of community law and custom that had regulated commerce before the twentieth century, and continued to serve the more traditional parts of the economy into the 1950s, made some kind of commercial law, formal or informal, immediately necessary in the 1980s as collectively and privately owned enterprises began operating outside the command economy. A market economy, however limited, requires much more precise definitions of who owns what – or at any rate is entitled to use or dispose of it – than does a command one. A rapidly growing number of commercial disputes also have to be resolved.

These needs have created enormous problems. As the 1980s began there were very few commercial lawyers – and even they had for the most part not practised for decades – and there was hardly any existing legislation to govern the private economy that socialism had abolished in the 1950s and was now coming back to life. Under the command economy economic disputes had been dealt with administratively or through mediation and negotiation. Lawyers and the courts had rarely been involved in disputes between enterprises, units, systems and localities. Party directives and government orders had not been open to challenge in the courts. Nor had there been much incentive to be heavily involved in commercial disputes when enterprises stood to gain or lose very little from how profitable or unprofitable they were. And disputes were settled not through the courts or through negotiations backed by the possibility of resort to the courts but by the relative strength of the political backing the disputants could rely on.

The control mechanisms that kept the command economy functioning cannot be used to regulate a free market. A market must be controlled through known and impersonal rules that can be enforced. There have to be ways of resolving disputes that are sufficiently fair and accepted to give traders the confidence to operate in the market. Contracts have to be enforceable if they are to be reliable. Long-term investment requires confidence that property rights will not be arbitrarily removed.

Reviving traditional non-state institutions for regulating commerce in the 1980s was not easy. For a generation they had ceased to exist. No longer were there the interlocking networks of countless brokers and guarantors, local chambers of commerce, merchants' associations of many kinds and other social structures linking producers, dealers and customers. What is striking in the most commercialized parts of China is the success with which local institutions have managed to regulate trade outside the state's command economy. While the improvisations of the 1980s fell far short of the sorts of legal institution that enable a modern economy to emerge, they have some other implications that threaten the ability of centralized state power to reimpose its control of the vigorous non-state economy. If traders can sort things out among themselves with minimal resort to the state's laws and courts, and outside the dictates of the command economy, institutions must be developing that will favour more local economic autonomy, which in turn will undermine the centralized dictatorship.

Where did these new commercial, quasi-legal arrangements come from? There were, no doubt, memories of earlier ways of regulating commerce. Existing contacts from the days of collective agriculture and the all-powerful command economy could be used. Even before the 1980s state enterprises had needed fixers to solve problems that could not be dealt with through regular procedures. But they provided little legal or quasi-legal basis for resolving disputes, invaluable though they were in making deals.

An urgent need in the 1980s was to create a legal framework for economic activity in China that would convince foreign investors that they could bring their money, their people and their technology to China in reasonable safety. Investment called for far more legal safeguards than had buying and selling. Whereas the typical Chinese contract is brief, setting out only the main points of an agreement and leaving the details to be sorted out later, foreign investors took an un-Chinese attitude, expecting everything to be spelled out.

They wanted protection for their trademarks, software, patents and designs. They needed to know what was going to be done with the equipment and the know-how they brought in. They had to have enough control to maintain the quality of products sold under their name, to prevent their technology from being used against them in other markets and to restrict know-how to those they licensed to have access to it. Provisions for taxation and for remitting profits in foreign exchange had to be put into black and white and adhered to. There had to be protection against expropriation and the sorts of measure that had closed down all foreign businesses in the 1950s. As the Deng reforms were heavily dependent on imported technology and investment, it was no longer possible to tell the foreigner to trade on Chinese terms or not at all. This meant that China would have to accept alien approaches to commercial law.

Domestic and overseas pressures have combined to hasten the invention of commercial and property law since 1979. Lawyers too have had to be invented, often through crash courses. The courts will have to be given the power to take on commercial cases without fear of powerful bureaucracies, and society has to be made to believe that the law actually works.

This will all take time. Even in official papers and journals there are reports of do-it-yourself approaches to solving commercial problems by using force to seize an opponent's assets or take over land. The Cultural Revolution decade made life rougher and more violent throughout China, and this applies to the economy too. Ignorance of even the most basic principles of China's new commercial and property laws is widespread. Much remains uncertain and vague, such as the right of state-owned enterprises to dispose of land and other assets.

At the same time the propaganda about law has begun to unleash a potential for litigiousness that had previously been diverted into appeals to Party officials. In the world of publishing, for example, fights over royalties, once unknown, are starting to keep lawyers busy. Thus the last widow of Pu Yi had a long battle with the Ministry of Public Security's publishing house over who owned the rights to his supposed autobiography and stood to get money from the film *The Last Emperor*; and the great writer Lu Xun's family sued his publishers for some of the money owed to his estate.

Although the events of 1989 did nothing for human rights in China, they could not curb the growth of the non-state sectors of the economy and, with it, the need for reliable and effective commercial law. Even though the overwhelming majority of commercial disputes will presumably continue to be resolved by mediation and compromises reached out of court, there has to be a framework of commercial law for the informal processes to work effectively. Much has been done in recent years, but much is still unresolved, and it needs a strong faith to have confidence in the long-term stability of central legal institutions.

Yet if China is to have a fully developed market economy, and if public, collective and private enterprises are to go further with the process of change, more and more commercial and property law will have to be made and published. For private and collective enterprises to make the transition to high technology and high investment they will need a level of legal security that does not now exist and will not exist until the courts and the law are the ultimate arbiters of all economic disputes and Party officials lose the power to intervene. This ought to mean the command economy itself having to operate under rules of law, much as publicly owned enterprises do in capitalist democracies.

One would have to be an extreme optimist to see any prospect of China's legal institutions presiding over a transition from autocratic tyranny to a politics of limited conflict between interest groups, in which no clique holds power as if of right, and governments can be changed without general chaos. That would need constitutional arrangements so far removed from the present or any past ones as to be almost unimaginable. It would also require the authorities to accept the possibility of the end of the unitary state and present Chinese empire.

To bring our fantasy back to less impossible futures, property rights of individuals and collectives will have to be further defined and protected, especially against the state and its agents. Even most state-owned enterprises will need to become more like autonomous corporations. Unless things move this way, economic chaos will prevail. Though it strains credulity, we cannot exclude the possibility of the state becoming the defender of private property rights and giving the courts the laws and the authority to resist a collectivist restoration.

This hypothetical tendency would only make sharper than ever the dilemma of a regime trying to combine political autocracy and conservatism with economic innovation and liberalism. If the legal framework for a capitalist economy is weak, the price in lost development could be very high, and all kinds of political instability would follow. But the more areas of economic autonomy that law defends, the harder it will be to maintain a Party dictatorship that has less and less to do. That too will lead to instability.

When speculation is brought back down to earth, the prospects for strong legal institutions and a powerful, independent legal profession seem remote. Japan has made the long journey to being an economic superpower without becoming a lawyer's culture, and it resists very effectively attempts to impose the rule of law on the nation's rulers. Given the deep-rooted expectation in China's dominant political culture that laws are rules made by the emperor and administered by officials acting in the government's interests, it would be unrealistic to expect law to limit the powers of the state and defend the citizen against the state's considered wishes. Where it may become fairly effective is in stopping officials acting beyond their powers (as more narrowly defined than in the Mao era) and in regulating the areas from which the party state has been retreating. China's courts will continue to be organs of government, and law will at most enable the rulers to regulate the machinery of government in more predictable ways and to reduce the element of arbitrariness in how officials treat the people. Whoever wants precedents for law as a guardian of the freedoms of the subject had better look elsewhere than to China's past or present.

The colonial and ex-colonial territories on the fringes of the Chinese world have managed to combine interventionist government with more security for private enterprise than any mainland regime has ever been able to offer. Given China's size, and the absence of economic factors making the political unity of the Chinese empire desirable from the point of view of its richer areas, the central government is unlikely to encourage the economic autonomy of coastal regions by providing laws that will protect the interests of their get-rich-quick entrepreneurs against the centre's wish to milk them. Yet if the centre fails to provide adequate legal institutions to regulate commercial life, this will in turn strengthen the secular tendency of the richer and poorer parts of the empire to drift apart as different localities develop their own informal legal arrangements behind the façade of unified central legislation. This could also happen in relation to foreign companies as different parts of China become bolder in making their own rules to suit their own interests.

In legal matters the past exercises a tyranny strong enough to hinder radical change, while being too weak to control a Chinese world that has outgrown the old constraints. But despite all the difficulties better and more effective legal institutions will have to develop if potentially disastrous conflicts of interest are to be regulated without dragging China into civil war. The harsh penal approach that finds its expression in the regular replay of the hideous theatre of the sentencing rally and the long ride to the execution ground will solve none of the underlying problems of Chinese societies, and the courts will need to be a lot stronger than they are now in handling commercial and administrative matters. If this strengthening of the courts happens, it will in the long term be at the expense of the autocratic state.

8. The Party's Over

===

History's tyranny, like the history of tyranny, applies to the decades of Communist Party rule just as it does to the millennia of dynastic autocracy. The Communist Party has always been particularly conscious of itself as having a mission defined by history — history as a supra-human force. Illusions about future history and commitment to past history has been central to the failure of what was once a spectacular triumph.

Thirty years ago the propaganda machine could make a popular hit out of a song that began:

> Socialism's good,
> Socialism's good,
> The people's place is high in the socialist state ...

The song had a cheerful, catchy and singable tune; and for a year or two the lyrics did not sound too bad provided one forgot about the tens of millions who died because of socialism. But the love of conflict that was so central to Maoism led to the song's being denounced during the Cultural Revolution for not being a call to arms against the mythical bourgeois enemy. After Mao's death and the discrediting of obsessive class struggle it ought to have been easy to revive the song. It had a good tune and was free from associations with the horrors of the immediate past. But by the 1980s the song was beyond revival. It was too obvious that socialism was no good and that the common people were far from riding high. In addition, official attempts to promote the song now doomed it to failure, in contrast to the regime's ability to get the people to do almost anything it wanted in its first years.

Evidence of the failure of what the authorities call characteristically Chinese socialism as a value system to rally support in the 1990s is everywhere. Among the most telling signs are the attempts by the official propaganda machine to persuade people that socialism under the Party dictatorship is China's only salvation. There is something both desperate and pathetic about the false optimism and the assumed confidence in the inevitable victory of socialism of such ham-fisted efforts as the television series about the triumphant advance of Marxism–Leninism, *March of the Centuries* (*Shiji xing*) or books like *Theoretical Reflections after the Turmoil* (*Fengbo hou de lilun fansi*) and *Perspectives on the Turmoil of 89* (*89 fengbo toushi*). These and countless other broadcasts, books and articles hammer away with arguments that all appear to assume what would have been unthinkable thirty or even twenty-five years ago: that the audience and readers they are aimed at have little faith in socialism under the Party dictatorship. Even among many officials little secret is made of the end of the belief, apart from the formalistic declaration of faith on public occasions or for an official visitor.

Some of the most self-damning output from the Party centre's propaganda department falls back on intimidating people with the prospect that the mess would be much worse without a strong dictatorship: chaos, civil war, famine and the end of China. Similar arguments are quietly put to foreign politicians when they have been mellowed by the sort of VIP treatment few of them would get at home and are backed by a real frightener: effective Communist rule is all that stands between the rest of the world and the sort of breakdown that would have millions or even tens of millions of Chinese taking to the sea in boats and turning up on many other countries' beaches.

It was not so in the Peking I knew in the early 1960s. Despite the catastrophe that had followed the Great Leap Forward, many officials – and in those days one called them not officials but cadres (*ganbu*) – would show even in private how closely they identified with the cause. There was widespread pride in what the Chinese revolution had achieved and a satisfaction in throwing out, and keeping out, the United States that had been renewed and confirmed by China's success in getting rid of Soviet domination.

In the 1990s there is not enough confidence left in the Communist Party to have a crisis about. The ferocious satirist Wang Shuo, a Peking-based writer whose devastating and ruthless depictions of the society he lives in are only a little exaggerated – in this as in much else he is curiously reminiscent of the Evelyn Waugh of *Decline and Fall* and *Vile Bodies* – catches the end of Communist values even within the Party itself in an episode in his absurd and thoroughly convincing short novel *Don't Treat Me as Human, Whatever You Do!* (*Qianwan bie ba wo dang ren*, published in three issues of the Nanjing literary bimonthly *Zhongshan* in the second half of 1989). In this wickedly accurate fantasy the central character, a naïve young practitioner of the martial arts who is being used by a group of crooks and bureaucrats and turned into a national hero for their own devious purposes, is taken by his keepers for some indoctrination in Marxism. The only true believers they can find in Peking belong to a small group of underworld Communists who meet in secret. They are all patients in a mental hospital.

Yet once there was a Communist-run, non-socialist revolution that, for all its brutality, intolerance and violence, had a moral power to it and appeared to have the values needed to create a new and better China. It even seemed to be making a new national character by drawing on positive elements in the existing cultures.

It would be easy but wrong to dismiss the Chinese and foreign observers who saw something remarkable developing in the Communist-controlled parts of China in the 1940s. Against overwhelming odds, and through their ability to mobilize support in villages from Fujian to Ningxia, the Communists built a political, military and moral culture that enabled them to conquer the whole of the mainland Chinese empire. Only the most dedicated and tough revolutionaries survived such ordeals as the long marches of 1934–6. Only extraordinary self-discipline and acceptance of the Party's goals made it possible for the isolated Eighth Route Army and guerrilla commanders to subordinate their own interests to those of the cause during the Japanese war, even at times when the centre was in no position to enforce obedience. During the civil war of 1946–9 one of the biggest advantages the Communist command enjoyed over its Nationalist enemies was that it could use its initially much smaller forces in ways that made the best political and military sense without having to worry about the loyalty of generals whose units had to be sacrificed to the greater good of the Communist cause. Anecdotal but plausible accounts of the rival command systems in action contrast the intense mutual distrust on the Nationalist side, as senior commanders had to be on guard against political rivals, with the relative ease and success with which Communist units could be ordered to do things that were not in their own interests, such as abandoning territory they had long held and where many of the officers and other ranks might have to leave their families behind to face the reprisals of returning Nationalists.

Although the Red Army and its successors were also sharply factionalized and held together not only by shared dedication to the cause but also by draconian discipline and structures of personal loyalty, commitment to the Communist cause was stronger than these ties. Defections and surrenders were less frequent than in the Nationalist forces. The Communists were on the whole coherent, vigorous, dedicated, uncorrupt and competent. Despite the ruthless purges and ideological campaigns that were carried out in the rustic Communist capital, Yan'an became synonymous with a way of life that was frugal, disciplined and dedicated to the revival of China. Chiang Kaishek's Chongqing, by contrast, was characterized by rampant corruption, incompetence, conspiracy and the ruthless exploitation of soldiers and peasants.

When the civil war was being won in 1949 the units of the People's Liberation Army that entered the cities seemed very different from the Nationalist forces they had just driven out. They behaved properly and did not loot or rape. The officials who came with them in shabby, cotton uniforms evidently believed in what they were doing, and did not seem to be trying to enrich themselves. Though Communists, they said little about socialism but talked a lot about their kind of democracy. It was soon made clear that the 'people's democratic dictatorship' was firmly under Communist Party control. Yet it was hard to oppose a party doing such things as rapidly restoring an economy ravaged by over a decade of war, protecting the property of nearly everybody, including most business people, and addressing problems that were in obvious need of solutions. Even the widespread killings during land reform in the villages were mainly of the more privileged and did not challenge the principle of private ownership of land. Raging inflation was brought down to imperceptibly low rates. Corruption, whether by officials or business, was harshly punished. And China's part in the Korean war showed that the Communists were capable of standing up to the world's greatest military power. All these achievements were fired by a nationalism whose values were collective and very earthily Chinese.

By the beginning of 1954 the Communist Party could claim to have started building a new China and to be the first government since the irruption of the West in the middle of the nineteenth century to have made a start towards achieving the dream of making China a country that was rich and powerful. After Korea China enjoyed the welcome relief of being treated with respect, based on fear, by the powers that had for a hundred years been able to send troops and warships into China at will. Few Han Chinese were anything but delighted that Tibet, eastern Turkestan and other former Manchu colonial territories were back under Chinese control. The empire had a strong and effective central government after forty years of fragmentation under warlords. Peking had been able to dissolve the regional military governments that ran the newly conquered territories between 1949 and 1953 and to establish the rule of the Party, backed by its mass organizations in virtually every village and every city street. By 1954 almost everyone had felt the power of a Party-run political movement and had learned to be afraid of the struggle meeting, show trial and exemplary execution. In the cities the relentless and unending process of indoctrination through political study meetings had taught the people the language of the new order. The Party had replaced chaos with order, war with peace, weakness with strength, impoverishment with a modest turn towards prosperity, confusion with certainty, aimlessness with purpose. In almost all respects the Communists were performing far better than any predecessor. A national identity and value system was being remade.

The nature of that identity and those values resists brief characterization. To start with the values, though there was no sudden transformation of all that people lived by, the political situation by 1954 was one that combined a most effective and ruthless dictatorship with a lot of participation by the common people in carrying out its decisions. The culture of the political meeting was well established, and people were learning how to say what the authorities expected. Communist officials were at that time still quite approachable and uncorrupt, and nearly all except the most senior lived fairly simply. There was a sense of everyone (except those designated as enemies at the time) working together to bring about visible improvements in the lives of most people. The educated minority who had been exposed to American, Japanese and other overseas influences were only too eager to win acceptance as authentically Chinese by rejecting foreign ways, and for a time they seemed to have found themselves places in the new order. While some aspects of Chinese traditions were under attack, many others – especially a politically correct and invented (or reinvented) all-purpose Han Chinese popular culture – were being revived and used to strengthen the sense of national pride that had always been central to Chinese Communism. Although China remained extremely poor, that could still at this stage be blamed on history.

The new regime was also creating, or recreating, a sense of community in which almost everyone who did not belong to the 5 per cent of non-people was assigned a place and had something to contribute. The government and Party gave everyone a new style of language in which to talk. The struggles that the Party organized and that claimed lives by the hundred thousand in the early 1950s were against social groups that in some way actually existed – rural landlords, officials of the Nationalist government, pro-Nationalist big business, foreign powers and their Chinese associates. The party's ideology was not complete nonsense. It offered a view of China's traumatic modern history that, while open to some criticism, made a lot more sense than the incoherent nationalism of the Guomindang.

The Party that had come to power in 1949 and performed so successfully over the next three or four years was not in its actions a socialist one, even though it was committed to bringing about a socialist future that was to be followed ultimately by the extremely remote utopia of Communism. The overwhelming majority of its members had joined during the Japanese war and the civil war that followed, when the Party controlled their home villages, and membership was essential to getting ahead. If a broader political issue came into the decision to join, it was probably the Party's ability to resist foreign enemies, overthrow oppressors at home and revive China. In other words, the Communists were better nationalists than the Nationalists and ran a more powerful, effective and honest dictatorship. Had they been satisfied with continuing the policies of the early 1950s for another twenty years, they might have achieved the sorts of success we associate with the mixed state and private capitalist economies under strong government direction of Taiwan or Singapore, and the power of the Communist Party in the 1990s might have been much greater than it is; there would also have been a set of national and nationalist values that might still command respect.

While the Party's senior leaders may in 1953 and 1954 have been committed to socialism (in its Soviet authoritarian version, not in one of the humane, enlightened interpretations), there is little reason to believe that the overwhelming majority of Party members felt any pressing need to push for it. A high degree of public ownership was not the issue – the People's Republic had inherited a large public sector from the previous regime – but up to 1954 the property rights of capitalists had generally been defended, as had the rights of peasants by the hundred million over the tiny plots they held after the reallocations of land reform. Until 1954 the indications had been that all-out socialism was not on the current agenda and was still many years away. The transition was going to be long and gradual.

One of the great mysteries of twentieth-century history is why the rulers of China decided to plunge into an entirely socialist economy when they were doing so well with a mixed one. The three surges of rapid socialist transformation between 1955 and 1960 were Pyrrhic triumphs for the Communist Party and disastrous for the people. The first surge in late 1955 and early 1956 ended the private ownership of land and businesses in a few frenzied months, collectivizing agriculture and nationalizing the industry and commerce still outside state control. This rush was not forced by economic necessity or by any reasonable fear that the Party's power wasunder threat. The state-owned and collective sectors of the economy had been growing for years, and it only needed patience for anyone who believed in the inevitability of the triumph of socialism to see it happen within ten or twenty years. Nor was the Party machine demanding very quick results: Mao and his followers had to apply a lot of pressure to it before the headlong rush began. The result was an unplanned set of new problems that exacerbated the atmosphere of conflict throughout society and led to the second surge of extreme socialism, the launching of the Great Leap Forward in 1958.

If the 'socialist high tide' of 1955 and 1956 had been an attempt to catch up with the Soviet Union, the Great Leap was, among other things, a bid to assert China's superiority in revolutionary commitment and to reach the utopia of ultimate communism, with all the goods and freedoms anyone could want, through a few years of heroic efforts. Farming co-ops were swept into unmanageably large people's communes; economic rationality was cast aside as, in a spirit of storming heaven, the mobilized masses tried to achieve miraculous increases in agricultural and industrial output with enthusiasm and their bare hands. As a widely used slogan of 1958 put it,

> Communism is paradise;
> People's communes are the bridge.

Even before 1958 was out the signs of trouble were there for those who would read them, and some measures were taken to curb the wildest excesses. But when there was a chance to start recovery in the summer of 1959, by backing away from implementing the more wild-eyed policies that were already creating all sorts of difficulties, Mao turned on his cautious critics. At the meetings on the heights of Lushan, culminating in a Central Committee plenum, he started the third drive by relaunching the Great Leap, thereby condemning tens of millions of his subjects to death from hunger as wilfully unrealistic policies were continued for another year and more, plunging much of rural China into famine and inflicting on industry a depression that no mere capitalist crisis could possibly have matched.

The three-phase rush into absolute socialism did, for a while, recreate a national identity and a sense of Chineseness – not without opposition, as was shown most conspicuously by the uprising of Tibetans in Lhasa and elsewhere, who refused to be part of this. But within China proper there was not much reported open resistance. Even the revival of banditry in such famine areas as western Henan was more a struggle for survival than a challenge to the regime. There was a conspiracy of silence about the real cost of the Great Leap in which many people joined, and not only out of fear. The victims starved out of the world's sight, and the survivors were sometimes sustained by a stubborn pride in what they and their compatriots could endure.

The problems and tensions created by the triple jump into a socialist economy, and the attempts by some top Communists to limit the damage, led to the crisis of ultra-socialism during the Cultural Revolution and another decade of self-inflicted back-wardness as Mao and those who thought like him responded to the setbacks to their utopian dreams not by backing off but pressing on. It was the success of the Party's values in the pre-socialist decades that enabled it to lead the country into disaster; and it was the extremism of late Maoism that destroyed the earlier values.

Being Chinese in the twenty years from 1956 involved making conscious choices to do things the hard way, like the city kids sent to remote parts of the countryside at the end of the 1960s who deliberately did farm work with their bare hands instead of using tools, who did not rest from the midday sun in summer and who gloried in making the most meaningless of sacrifices. Few can have been more pointless than the self-destruction of Jin Xunhua, a former Red Guard who drowned in August 1969 in a vain attempt to recover from a swollen river a floating telegraph pole that was no longer part of a communication network but was simply a length of driftwood. The incident was given the full treatment by the propaganda authorities, who made no attempt to hide what by any standards but Maoist ones would have been a waste of a young life. They turned it into an act of martyrdom. It was almost as if the very disproportion between the possible gain and the actual loss was something admirable in itself and another sign of a national moral superiority: nowhere else in the world could match the pure revolutionary dedication of China's proletarian youth armed with the invincible thoughts of Mao Zedong.

Such deaths did not seem unusual or shocking in the late 1960s after years of purposeless killings in the persecutions and local wars of the Cultural Revolution. Indeed, willingness to make and exact sacrifices that benefited nobody was an outstanding feature of late Maoist culture. The converse of this was that rational cost–benefit analysis of anything was made very difficult for over twenty years from the middle 1950s.

Why had China's rulers chosen to try to remake their country this way? They had not been forced to take the course they did. They had chosen the Stalinist world-view, translated it into Chinese idiom and stayed with it despite their intense suspicion of Soviet intentions, which went back to the 1930s. Unlike the satellite states of Eastern Europe, their lands were not occupied by the armies of the Russian empire, and they dealt ruthlessly with their own potential pro-Russian quislings. For all the public propaganda about learning from the Soviet elder brothers (sisterhood had little place in 1950s rhetoric), there was at the top only limited respect and affection for neighbours regarded as the heirs of the Tsars and often despised for only half belonging to the civilized world. It may be that the wish to be redder than the Russians, which became perfectly clear by the beginning of the 1960s, was already a factor in decision-making in the mid-1950s.

Was there a cultural explanation? No Chinese government anywhere has ever believed in untrammelled freedom for private enterprise, but there have been wide differences in how far regimes have gone to control it. Few have tried to suppress it or nationalize it altogether: the nineteenth-century Taipings made the attempt in their early years, when the lunatic fire burned brightest, but they soon gave up; and one would have to go back two thousand years and more to find earlier efforts to eliminate the private economy. While it would be easy enough to show snobbery and prejudice about merchants among officials from antiquity to our own times, private manufacturing, trade and land ownership had been accepted, and even defended, by the state for a millennium. No adequate answer can be found in the dominant culture.

Were the Communists then caught up in a massive resurgence of the chiliastic urge that has long been latent in many Chinese popular cultures, the longing to change the world suddenly, violently and totally, destroying anyone who stands in the way of the dream? This is one of the elements in China's cultural mix that is in direct contrast to the conservatism and the rational calculation of interest that are much more conspicuous features most of the time. It is as if the success of the reforming approach in the early 1950s was becoming increasingly unacceptable to Mao and those who felt like him. They needed action, movement, change. Mao was not the sort of emperor who could hold himself in check for very long or could feel comfortable with steady plodding. Until his final decline he needed to make things happen. State-building and gradual progress was too boring; and peace in Korea deprived him of the adrenalin rushes of warfare to which he had become addicted in the twenty-six years up till 1953.

Another factor that must have contributed to the decision to act was the extraordinary power that the Communist regime had given itself through its success in building up its own enormous apparatus and all the other structural systems that made up the new order. The Party machine could give orders that would actually be obeyed right across China. It could mobilize the labour and change the lives of hundreds of millions of people. To expect Mao to have this power and not to use it would have been as unrealistic as to give a pyromaniac a box of matches and a can of petrol and hope for no fires. Mao loved and needed upheaval, movement, chaos; and he had enough support in the Party and the population to be able to undermine the rather stable dictatorship of the 1950s.

Whatever the causes of the historic change, the headlong rush towards the elimination of private property transformed the meaning of being Chinese between the middle of 1955 and the middle of 1956. This newly created version of Chineseness was reinforced in the anti-rightist campaign of the next year and in the Great Leap Forward of 1958 and was put to the test in the famine and general economic catastrophe that followed it. The split with Moscow gave the new identity a more sharply defined nationalist character. China, no longer content with plodding along behind Russia on its road to the Communist utopia, had to be the most socialist, the most revolutionary, the most advanced. In the 1960s the Chinese claim to be showing the way forward at the very time when the Soviet Union was losing much of its appeal was a claim taken very seriously by many on the left in Western countries. There was in the early 1960s a widespread perception – more in western Europe than in the United States – of China as a country where communist rule was somehow more acceptable than in the Soviet Union and eastern Europe. I remember believing then that with all its faults – some of which were a lot clearer to me after living in Peking for a couple of years – Chinese socialism worked and was decidedly better than what China's past and other Communist states had to offer.

A socialist national identity did appear to be widely accepted in China. Not, I think, the wilder extremes of Maoist fanaticism, which only ever really appealed to minorities, but a shared vision of China as different from, and morally superior to, richer and militarily more powerful countries. The hostility of the United States was not entirely unwelcome, even to the American-educated élite, especially as it showed that foreigners were afraid of China.

When China became a nuclear-armed state and the great powers could no longer do a Hiroshima on it, that was more gratifying still. This national assertion went with a deep-rooted suspicion of Western individualistic values and an attachment to the collectivist, or at any rate familist, traditions of the past. Had the Communist Party stayed with the pre-1955 policies of a gradual transition to socialism and the steady development of a cohesive and stable bureaucratic state, there is every possibility that China would now be a richer and duller country than it is. But the founding emperor of the new dynasty willed otherwise and ruled out that sort of national identity.

Mao's doctrine of an unending struggle between a 'proletariat' and a 'bourgeoisie' as the fundamental issue in Chinese life since the socialist transformation made no sense at all socially, economically or politically in a country that had never had many proletarians or bourgeois. It gave an extra zest to the self-definition of some Chinese, who saw themselves as belonging to a class that was entrusted with destroying a bad world order and also assured by history that it was scientifically bound to win. This simple red-and-white view of the world was clearer than the complexities of the Party's previous doctrine of a people's democratic dictatorship that was an alliance of several classes. For the common people it had the additional appeal of locating the leadership of the imaginary bourgeoisie in the highest levels of the Communist Party itself, thus making it possible to take out one's resentments on senior officials without having to challenge the Party as such. That this notion was attractive to the Party's subjects was proved by the speed and enthusiasm with which many of them took it up and acted on it during the Cultural Revolution.

Political fervour never lasts. Mao's chiliastic urges had brought not an earthly paradise but the biggest famine in history, followed by the internecine madness of the Cultural Revolution, in which every revolutionary ideal was betrayed. The sincerest followers of Mao ended up the most bitterly disillusioned.

By the end of the 1970s socialism was a bad joke. The official cliché about the 'superiority of the socialist system' was popularly used as a tag for anything in Chinese life that did not work. To make people believe that things might well be even worse than they seemed, they only needed to be told that there was an 'excellent situation', a term used by bureaucrats since the great famine of 1960–62 to cover disaster with words. Those who had once sincerely believed that capitalist society was quintessentially evil now longed to be part of it.

There was something sad about the end of ideals. It had been nothing remarkable in the first decade of the socialist economy for people to show great altruism. The Great Leap Forward and the Cultural Revolution demanded and received countless heroic sacrifices that helped turn folly into catastrophe. It was faith as well as terror that drove people into such absurdities as trying to multiply total harvests by halving the amount of cultivated land and planting the seed many times more closely than normal, or clearing forests to fuel blast furnaces in which useful iron and steel objects were melted down into useless pig iron, or dying to save a log of wood.

The first decade after the death of Mao in 1976 was the Communist Party's last, slim chance to rebuild a working value system that could accommodate both what was needed to pull China out of backwardness and the Party's claim to maintain its dictatorship.

This has proved impossible. The dictatorship cannot tolerate fundamental political reforms that would weaken its monopoly of power but without which backwardness is ineradicable. Throughout the 1980s and into the early 1990s the balance and influence at the court of Deng Xiaoping has swung between those who would save the dictatorship at the expense of the country – or, as they would put it, preserve the leadership of the party so as to save the country from disintegration and chaos – and those who will accept the weakening of Party power so that drastic changes can be made that might deal with some of the basic problems.

The argument pushed very hard in official propaganda, especially since the 1989 Peking killings, that only the Party dictatorship can keep China from much greater horrors, is uncomfortably difficult to dismiss. To be sure, continuation of the dictatorship can only lead to one set of disasters or another, and the regime is so badly riven by divergent interests that its chances of preserving even a dead, static order for long are poor. But are there other possibilities, other value systems, other ways of organizing human life that have a chance first of establishing themselves and then of doing better for the people of China than their present rulers?

Plenty has been said and written on such matters in China and around the world in recent years. One model of salvation that has been held up is the so-called Confucian one; other values of which much has been made are those of democracy and capitalism. The 'Confucian' value system is one that the Communist Party in its decline has tried to cling to. This comes after decades of bitter attacks against the Confucius business. While this change of heart is more amusing than surprising – the Communists have always had much of the Chinese past in their views of the world – it is also an admission that their own values have failed.

9. CONFUCIAN, BOURGEOIS AND DEMOCRATIC CONFUSIONS

It is not only the veterans of the once revolutionary Communist Party who have been turning to Confucius and the values associated with him, even to the extent of staging fancy-dress ceremonies in honour of the man they used to denounce as the enemy of progress from his own times until our own. The sage has also been imposed by other authoritarian Chinese regimes, from Taiwan to Singapore, as an object of compelled veneration and seems set to resist being consigned to history for a long time yet.

Over the last decade or two Confucius has been dragged by the topknot into discussions of matters that it would have been beneath his dignity as a junior member of the Zhou aristocracy to notice or talk about: trade, economic growth and the outrageous notion that the lower orders, and even women, should play a part in the government of the country. That a man who could not accept the changes taking place in his own time, around 2,500 years ago, and who set his face resolutely towards a past that even then was 500 years distant is invoked as a guide through the present and future uncertainties of the Chinese world is a symptom of the depth of the crisis.

Confucius was no fool, and one does not have to share his despairing vision of recreating a stable and highly unequal social order based on hereditary status to find perceptiveness and common sense in his advice on how to make such a society work. But the political philosophy that can be pieced together from the brief and often cryptic remarks attributed to him in the collection of his sayings that was put together after his death as the *Lun yu* (*Analects*) is one of questionable relevance to the present needs of the Chinese world.

Yet the package of values loosely labelled Confucian (although they include many elements that antedate Confucius by centuries and others that are much more recent) has been credited by some observers with the spectacular economic growth in recent decades of Chinese societies in Hong Kong, Taiwan and Singapore — in Singapore the elected dictatorship has even adopted a plastic Confucianism as the national ideology — and also with the economic successes of Japan and South Korea, countries whose inherited high cultures are both dominated by Chinese imports. It has even been argued in Australia that countries with European and Europe-derived cultures ought to be Confucianizing themselves as fast as possible in order to survive the economic onslaught of East Asia in the next few decades.

If 'Confucian' values really were the answer, then China would need only to suppress all rival and threatening values in order to emulate its wealthy neighbours. Indeed, the whole Chinese and Chinese-influenced world would, many centuries ago, have reached such prosperity and power through industrial and military supremacy that East Asia would have dominated the globe long before Europe's modern industrialization began. Yet this did not happen. It was only in the 1970s and 1980s that Japan became an economic superpower, able to challenge the United States and Western Europe. If the man behind Japan's recent rise was Confucius, he was in no hurry: it took him around 2,500 years to prove his economic efficacy.

It would be rather easier to find factors encouraging late-twentieth-century economic growth on the edge of East Asia that have nothing to do with China's past. Only when these alien, Western factors came into play were certain elements within some inherited East Asian value systems able to bring about successful capitalist development.

One such group of factors was connected with nineteenth-century European imperialism and the success of Japan in copying and joining the imperialist club. Where European powers set up their colonies and concessions in East Asia they imposed their principles of commercial law. Even more significantly, they removed some territory from the direct control of the Chinese state, creating enclaves where Chinese entrepreneurs could set up in business fairly secure from the kind of arbitrary impositions and interference by officials that so effectively restricted development in China. Japan, whose feudal pre-modern political structures had left space for merchants to establish long-lasting and powerful business houses, moved rapidly in the second half of the nineteenth century towards encouraging both private and state-sponsored modern capitalist development. Apart from Japan all the East Asian countries that have prospered in recent decades were colonies either of Britain or of Japan for generations before the Second World War. In mainland China the principal heavy industrial base that the Communists inherited in 1949 was in the north-east, the Manchuria that had been under various forms of Japanese control for thirty years or more before the surrender of 1945. The argument that colonial rule and the adoption of some Western institutions has been an essential precondition of modern economic growth in the Chinese world is not welcome to those who, like myself, have no liking for colonialism, but it is much more plausible than attributing recent successes to the superiority of Confucianism. Self-evidently there must be elements in value systems inherited from the past that were also favourable to successful capitalism; but those elements were not strong enough to work modern economic miracles anywhere in China before the Western irruption or to create modern industry in such 'Confucian' territory as North Korea, Vietnam and most of China up to the present.

Another group of factors is more recent: the willingness of Europe and North America after the Second World War to provide Japan with its newly industrialized sidekicks with the most un-Confucian external conditions needed for rapid industrial growth: science-based technology, credit in the early stages and relatively unprotected export markets with a voracious and ever-growing appetite for unnecessary imports that they were willing to run up huge debts to pay for. Japan also had the double good fortune, in the critical quarter of a century after the Second World War, of not being permitted to waste much money and resources on arms and armies and of having safe but profitable wars near by, in Korea and Vietnam, on which to cash in. Although the relative advantage of, say, West Germany and Italy in carrying lower military burdens than their European competitors was not as great as Japan's, so that their growth was not as rapid, they too show that it was possible to out-perform the United States and Britain simply by carrying a lighter handicap of military expenditure. (Taiwan, however, has supported very expensive armed forces and prospered too.)

Despite the historically weak connection between Confucian values and rapid economic growth – it is unlikely that there were big increases in the per capita output and consumption of material goods in the Chinese world over the thousand years before the Qing dynasty fell in 1912 – a selective reinvention of Confucian tradition has been useful to post-colonial regimes in the Chinese and Chinese-influenced worlds when combined with European economics, commercial law, science and technology. This spurious Confucianism, which might be compared with the invented traditions of chivalry much used in the indoctrination of the sons of the English ruling classes in the nineteenth and early twentieth centuries, serves to counteract dangerous tendencies that are also part of the Western culture package, such as human rights that the individual can defend against the government or the encouragement of younger generations to assert themselves as their elders' equals. With its emphasis on the values of the authoritarian family and the authoritarian state, and its disapproval of social conflict and political extremism, latter-day Confucianism is clearly meant to be a stabilizing force in a rapidly changing world. But for it to work it needs dynamic, alien, Western institutions and forms of economic organization. It also needs more modern types of authoritarian rule than a party dictatorship under an emperor. A lot would have to change in contemporary Chinese political culture before a Singapore-style, efficient and effective 'Confucianism' could be any answer to mainland China's problems. As things are, talk of Confucius and Confucianism in China are signs of a wish to reject the other values that have made Taiwan, South Korea and Singapore prosperous. In the absence of the dynamic factors that have transformed those other countries the familistic values we have already examined are much more likely to impede than to support change and development. In particular, China is still under the rule of a thinly disguised, pre-modern imperial bureaucracy, unlike those former colonies.

Perhaps we should worry less about Confucianism, whatever that might be taken to be, and look at the values of merchants to see whether some indigenous capitalist or bourgeois traditions might turn out to be the possible inspiration for an escape from the clutches of bureaucratic autocracy.

The value systems of traders and manufacturers in the Chinese world are centrally important to any analysis of economic successes and failures over the long perspective of 2,500 years and the shorter one of the last half century. What makes Confucius so inapt a patron of these values is that he was an aristocrat who despised the pursuit of profit and the 'little people' who were devoted to it. His ideals of gentlemanly behaviour were adapted from those of the hereditary aristocracy of the early part of the first millennium BC and were concerned with maintaining the correct social order. This order, already dead in Confucius's time, was one in which gentlemen supposedly had things nobler than trade with which to concern themselves: duty, benevolence, traditional high culture, good government, proper family relationships, the observation of eti-quette and setting a good example to the lower orders by fulfilling the obligations of the station in life to which one was born. Neither Confucius himself, as he emerges from his recorded sayings, nor the education in texts that can be called Confucian for the sons of the gentry who wished to pass the imperial examinations for govern-ment office had much to offer peasants, artisans, manufacturers and traders. To be sure, Confucian-educated bureaucrats were not necessarily bad administrators of economic matters. To its very end the imperial state ran factories and other economic enterprises with varied success. Its officials observed some aspects of the economy closely and intervened, where they could, to regulate parts of it and make it perform correctly by their standards, as when they tried to narrow fluctuations in grain prices. They could co-operate with merchants and their guild organizations and might be involved in trade on their own account or through other members of their families. Some officials also came from trading backgrounds themselves, they or their fathers having bought their way into the bureaucracy and the much higher social status that went with it.

Though the distinction between officials and merchants was in reality a blurred one, Confucius and the classic texts of Confucian tradition offered little of specific relevance to merchants as distinct from other members of the human race. The only reason for a merchant to give his sons a full and expensive education in the Confucian classics would have been to equip them for an escape from their class into the ranks of the mandarinate.

Western academic perceptions of China have nearly all been so heavily influenced by Chinese official cultures and their proclaimed values that bureaucratic Confucianism is often, and quite wrongly, taken as the dominant value system for most Chinese before the twentieth century, just as the rhetoric of Marx and Mao, imposed by the Communist Party, has been thought by many foreigners until very recently indeed to be what most, if not all, Chinese have believed in during the last forty years. (A variant of this illusion is the old China Lobby myth that the people of Taiwan and − if only they had been allowed to express it − of the mainland were passionately devoted to the Guomindang's ideological mishmash.) Confucian and Maoist historians have downplayed the cultures of merchants. Both have been prepared to allow merchants a place in their scheme of things but not a dominant one. They have concurred in treating private profit as not quite nice.

In the 1950s some Chinese historians took their Marx, or rather Engels, a little too seriously for their own good and brought together evidence pointing to the burgeoning of China's indigenous mercantile and manufacturing capitalism in the second millennium of dynastic rule. The ascendancy of Maoist values in the 1960s meant that they had to shut up. By then there was no room for a theory that would, in the standard Engels model, have seen China's so-called feudalism well on the way to being replaced by a home-grown capitalism but for the intervention of the West in the nineteenth century. Had that view of China's natural historical development been accepted, it would have undermined arguments concerning the historical necessity for the Communists to take power and, soon afterwards, impose their socialist transformation. The more evidence that was found that did not fit in with the meaningless categorization of China on the eve of Western irruption as 'feudal', the harder it became to justify the Communists' claim to have completed successfully by 1953 an anti-feudal as well as anti-imperialist democratic revolution and therefore to be required by the implacable logic of history to go on to socialism, the next and higher stage of human society. By 1962 there was no longer a place in the Maoist vision for the bourgeoisie in the ranks of the 'people'; nor was there room for them in the redrawn picture of the past as a powerful force for progress.

Only with the change in Party strategy from the end of the 1970s could the entrepreneurs of earlier centuries be posthumously rehabilitated. As is the way of things in China, the switch in current policy required an instant readjustment in the official historical mythology. The 1950s research was reprinted, and new monographs and documentary compilations on native capitalism were published. The evidence gathered in the 1950s and the 1980s is now easy to find. Although much more reinvention needs to be done before we can form reasonably detailed pictures of the lost worlds of traders, there can be no doubt at all about the capacity of the commercially oriented to make economically rational decisions and to create and maintain the conditions for successful business within the limits of what states have permitted.

About 2,400 years ago Bai Gui, a man of the Zhou royal domain and therefore probably a descendant of the Shang people who became great traders after their dynasty fell around 1050 BC, expressed his principle of working against market trends. He enjoyed watching changes: 'What others discard I acquire, and what others want to take I let them have.'

Early in the sixth century AD Liu Bao, a leading merchant in the capital Luoyang, 'had a station in all the leading centres of the provinces and prefectures and kept ten horses [some texts read 'a horse'] in each of them. He observed the movements of the prices of salt, grain and other commodities everywhere; he traded wherever boat or cart could go or foot could tread.'

In the thirteenth century Marco Polo reported mercantile activity in China on a scale that so dwarfed Europe's that Europeans could not believe what he told them after his return from Asia. By then the most advanced regions of China – especially the Lower Yangtse valley and the south-east coast – led the world in commercialization and in the sophistication of private economic institutions, including paper money, that worked for centuries until taken over, abused and destroyed by governments. This enormous commerce was carried out by a vast number of small business concerns. If by the eighteenth century there was little investment in labour-saving machinery or in improving the quality of arable land, that too was rational. Human labour was generally cheaper than machinery, and a landowner did not need to improve land to get high rent for it. Land was, besides, a low-yielding investment made for security. Much higher returns could be had from usury or trade.

Even in the hard times of the second half of the nineteenth century, when the Chinese state was proving less and less capable of defending its sovereignty, Chinese mercantile networks were remarkably effective in preventing foreigners from extending their control of Chinese export industries upstream from the treaty ports. The West never succeeded in taking over the production of tea in China, for example. Chinese intermediaries rather than foreign companies usually brought goods to the ports for export. Chinese merchants thus kept profits that might have been given away if the state had been in charge of the economy.

During the disorder of the Republic business communities adapted quickly to the chances offered in and around the treaty ports to develop forms of manufacture and trade that were new to China. The cramped, overcrowded and dark little factories that sprang up around the foreign concessions in Shanghai during the first half of this century remain China's biggest concentration of producers of relatively high-quality light industrial goods and continue to pull far more than their weight in the national economy.

In the late nineteenth and early twentieth centuries producers and distributors far from the foreign enclaves also showed that they could change in response to new opportunities. Where railways gave them access to new markets farmers altered their crop patterns. The hand spinning of cotton was abandoned when mill-spun thread made it pointless, but some weavers away from the big cities adopted enough cheap foreign machinery – intermediate technology, to use the jargon of a later age – to keep their industry alive. When the damage and disruption of the Japanese war and the civil war that followed it were ended by the Communist reunification, private industry and commerce responded to the economic opportunities of the new order with both enthusiasm and success for as long as they were allowed to. Their reward was to be the elimination of nearly all private business by 1957 and the reclassification of the bourgeoisie and petty bourgeoisie out of the people.

A quarter of a century and a lot more destruction later, merchants and entrepreneurs were allowed to raise their heads again, but only on a provisional, probationary licence. It was like allowing trees to grow again after being cut down: instead of strong trunks, what appeared were vigorous little shoots that could, when necessary, be coppiced once more. The Communists were willing to allow a lot of small and easily controllable enterprises to grow in the 1980s, but they were nearly all tiny family businesses that filled the gaps left by the clumsy and inefficient publicly owned sector. As Wang Gungwu, the perceptive historian who is Vice-Chancellor of Hong Kong University, has pointed out, the Communists are much more comfortable with big and powerful enterprises that are wholly or mainly foreign-owned than they would be with a strong Chinese bourgeoisie that found some political muscle. Deng Xiaoping, Chen Yun and the other gerontocrats, like other officials a generation younger, can still remember how they expropriated foreign-owned enterprises in the 1950s, and they know they could kick foreigners out again in the 1990s if it suited them and if they were willing to risk the destruction of the national economy.

Powerful Chinese businesses might take a lot more shifting. It will be many years before the lesson of the Stone Company is forgotten. Stone, much publicized as a Peking success story in the 1980s, was the small private computer company that in the 1989 crisis backed the protest movement with its resources, something IBM or Sharp would never have done. Stone has since been disciplined, and its founder has gone into exile. Even the apparently tame CITIC, the China International Trust and Investment Corporation, may turn out not to be as reliable a way of using and controlling rehabilitated survivors of the 1950s capitalists and their money for the benefit of the regime as it once seemed.

There is plenty of evidence that China's business cultures have long been able to flourish if only they were allowed to, but for over two thousand years states have preferred to keep business divided, confined and controlled. The Guomindang on Taiwan has been a little different. Obliged by its dependence on the United States in the 1950s and 1960s to give private enterprise a better deal than it did when it ruled the mainland, it had to permit private firms much more freedom to develop. The Taiwan economy remains a mixed one, with substantial state-owned enterprises existing alongside a flourishing private sector. The Nationalist regime may yet come to regret allowing Taiwanese interests to develop an economic power base strong enough to enable them to mount a strong campaign for the island's self-determination, the prospect that horrifies both Nationalists and Communists: they agree that Taiwan must remain a part of China.

Despite the successes of private capital in Taiwan, Hong Kong and Singapore, and despite the triumphant revival of private farming and small private business in China over the last decade, the values of free enterprise are most unlikely to replace bureaucratic values as the dominant ones in China as a whole. Chinese entrepreneurs have known something approaching economic freedom only in circumstances such as those of colonial Hong Kong, where they were not living under Chinese bureaucratic rule. On the one hand, business people have rarely been willing to assert their own political demands against the absolutist state; on the other, the state has kept them in their place.

Today's officialdom has at least as strong an interest as any of its predecessors in preventing the development of large and well-capitalized private businesses with the resources to take on the state-owned enterprises. Inefficient and overstaffed though most state enterprises are, they are still so heavily protected against competition that some of them yield the huge profits and tax revenues on which the government depends for most of its income. Big state enterprises also provide huge numbers of secure jobs that enable officials to keep their personal structures of patronage. Even the loss-making factories have to be kept going because there is no way of coping with the disruption of closing them down and providing for their present and retired employees. The party state has shown that it can get along without collective agriculture, which was at least as much of a liability as an asset, but it has to hold on to its mines, factories and railways. The dictatorship has good reason to be hostile to any private big business that might emerge. Nor does it have any interest in allowing independent trade unions that might be able to force economic or political concessions from state employers.

Under the dynastic system the state's concern to keep merchants away from power was mainly a political one, and it did not often try very hard to compete with them economically. Trade was regulated to a greater or lesser extent but, for the most part, was left to private merchants. Yet even in those circumstances merchants and other interest groups had rarely challenged or tried to limit imperial absolutism. Today's central government in China is more hostile to private enterprise on principle than were its dynastic predecessors (soft words about entrepreneurs come from the head, not the heart). It also stands to lose far more, economically, from private competition than any earlier regime since the Qin fell over 2,200 years ago. Entrepreneurs know very well how harshly business was treated by the Communist Party in the 1950s. The chances of a capitalist solution to the woes of the Chinese empire are as a whole not bright. Whether capitalism of some sort might work in parts of coastal China is another question. For that to happen the weakening of central power will have to go further.

★

There is no need yet to take too seriously prospects of democracy
and democratic values in China, where democracy and political
freedom mean little in any of their Western senses – and as these
are European concepts, it is appropriate to apply European meaning
to the terms. From time to time Westerners like to persuade themselves that Chinese culture is essentially democratic. One of the
century's most eminent American sinologists once even recruited
Confucius, that convinced defender of an authoritarian and unequal
social order, as a democrat; and since the 1911 revolution there have
been those eager to classify one group or other of men with guns
as China's champions of democracy. Since the loss of the mainland
by the Nationalists the implausible term Free China has been used to
describe Taiwan under what is still essentially a military dictatorship.
Among the clichés about 'People's China' since 1949 have been
ones about it being democratic, or becoming more democratic, or
granting greater political freedom, despite very little evidence to
justify any such propositions.

Democracy does not have much of a past in China. As far back
as records go, states have always been absolutist, and no Chinese state
has ever been effectively challenged except by a rival absolutism. The
main variation in the twentieth century has been that the absolutisms
have been much more straightforwardly based on military power,
even when, as the Nationalist and the Communist dictatorships both
have done, adopting the form of the absolutist party in the Lenin
style.

No general election based on universal adult suffrage, a secret
vote and an unrestricted choice of candidates has ever been held in
the Chinese world. There has never even been much of a demand
for representative government outside such minorities as intellectuals
under Western influence. In the first half of the twentieth century
democracy was much talked about but only in ways that point to
a sinification of the concept: it signified things other than leaving
the choice of government to a majority vote of the whole adult
population. As Andrew Nathan has pointed out, it has nearly always
been taken to mean what some small minority or other has decided
is best for the people. Chinese democracy means the people doing

what their self-selected betters tell them to do for their own good and the good of the nation. The idea that the common people should choose their own government, and that political groups should accept the popular verdict, has seemed alien, even improper, to the various political establishments of the Chinese world. Very few educated Chinese can see the point of allowing the uneducated majority the chance to make the wrong choice.

The absence of traditions that can meaningfully be called democratic marks not only ruling-class cultures but also popular ones. Democracy requires a notion of equality, at least when citizens or members of a group are making the choices that they are permitted to make. The family and quasi-familial structures characteristic of Chinese cultures are, as we have seen, in their essential nature unequal and depend on the finest gradations of status if they are to be held together. The state itself has always been authoritarian and concerned with the ranking of its subjects. Some regimes have recognized and defended inherited social and political status, as during the thousand years and more before 400 BC or in north China during the fifth and sixth centuries AD. Other regimes have tried to distribute status for themselves, using rank as a reward for service. This was the approach of the state of Qin in the third century BC and of virtually all Chinese governments during the last thousand years. There was not even a myth of popular sovereignty before the twentieth century; and the twentieth century has seen more emphasis on popular participation than on the people's right to decide. Responsibility for ensuring that subjects are properly looked after has generally been regarded as one of the duties of a monarch and his officials. That subjects should choose for themselves what their best interests are and who should lead them has not been part of the tradition.

Other parts of the world with strong familistic values have produced or accepted participatory or representative institutions of government, and in some other countries even tyrannies have had to preserve the forms of representative or oligarchic government. In Europe and in countries whose values and institutions have been largely derived from Europe, for example, survivals of tribal assemblies continued to be part of the political structures of post-tribal states. Athens kept its direct participatory democracy for centuries; and though participation was limited to male, free Athenians (excluding females, slaves and colonials), it was no mere form. The Roman Republic was even more of an oligarchy, reserving most power to its senators but still leaving some political influence to the people. Even though the transition to the principate left the senate an empty shell, emperors still needed to preserve it for the sake of appearances. Tribal assemblies were important among the Germanic people too, surviving the rise of monarchies to develop into modern parliaments. Europe's tyrants and would-be absolute monarchs could never eliminate the concept, or at any rate the memory of the concept, that a king needed the consent and the involvement of the aristocracy or of representatives of the people.

Chinese written tradition preserves some evidence of popular consultation, if not decision-making, in remote antiquity. A number of political theorists in pre-Qin times, Mencius notable among them, argued that a true king had to have the consent of the people and that in the last resort a bad ruler could be legitimately removed by a popular uprising. But we should not make too much of these traces of what might once have been. There is no evidence to point to an ancient concept of popular sovereignty, as opposed to popular consent to government. The evidence of consent that has been cited in official history and propaganda down the centuries has been much more concerned with material prosperity and the absence of disorder than with positive statements of support for a regime. One is tempted to compare official attitudes to the common people with those of decent and compassionate stockbreeders towards their cattle: if the subjects were placid, well fed, properly clad and housed and able to go about their normal lives, they had everything they could expect from a government. Content was equated with consent. The people's right to choose was narrowly restricted to the right to reject a totally atrocious regime that made life impossible for them. It remains an assumption of Chinese governments that all of their subjects who are not in open rebellion accept and support them. There is to that way of thinking something utterly unacceptable about putting a country's political future to the hazard of an election.

Even a public opinion poll on the popularity of a regime would be a deeply offensive attack on its legitimacy if its findings were made available to all – hence the ban on Chinese researchers' making such survey data available to foreigners even when foreigners pay for their collection. Chinese governments have been collecting their own confidential intelligence on their people's views for over two thousand years, as when the Han dynasty's secret police gathered folk songs and sayings as indicators of what the people were thinking, but this is not the same thing at all as allowing open expressions of public disapproval. In a classic example of repression from the fourth century BC the notorious architect of Qin's state absolutism, Shang Yang, executed not only the critics of his policies but also those who praised them. While that was thought by the mainstream of later orthodox political thinking to be going a little far, the crowd had no place in public life. Under the later dynasties the masses were not expected or allowed to line the streets to watch when the emperor left the palace: commoners had to make themselves scarce or, if that was not possible, prostrate themselves. Nor was there much place for public oratory on the issues of the day apart from some rather dreary (or so it seems from descriptions) indoctrination in the imperial view of morality.

The communists have made much use of the crowd over their seventy-year history. There were the angry crowds of struggle meetings against landlords, rightists, counter-revolutionaries, capitalist-roaders (the code term for Party officials who modified extreme Maoism) and others cast in the role of enemy. There were in the earlier decades of the People's Republic huge, well-organized demonstrations of loyalty, as on national days and other occasions for which the wide expanses of Tiananmen Square were turned into a sea of heads. Oratory played a curiously small part on these occasions. Mao very rarely spoke to the people, and recordings of Lin Biao addressing the great Red Guard rallies of 1966 reveal a thin voice reading a script badly. Although Zhou Enlai's performances on these occasions were less feeble, it is evident that rabble-rousing spoken rhetoric was not essential even in the emotionally highly charged early months of the Cultural Revolution. The Chinese revolutions had no Robespierre, Trotsky or Hitler to set their crowds alight.

Nor has any Chinese political leader tried to use the artificial intimacy of talking to the people quietly in their homes through radio or television. Perhaps both the public harangue and the quasi-private chat lack dignity: they are not what history has taught people to expect of rulers. Emperors and mandarins communicate their wishes through the written word. They issue orders or instruct their subjects; they do not cast their dignity aside to speak in public. In China power does not speak — it writes.

Yet the Communists have used the spoken word, and at endless length, in the meetings that are central features of their political culture. The small group meeting was the most important single method of indoctrination and control they used in the decades when their revolution was still alive. Even since the death of the revolution the meeting persists as a required ritual. The Communist political meeting has little or nothing to do with democratic decision-making or with arguing issues out. Meetings are organized from above and given clear goals, such as studying a political document or dealing with an errant member of the group. If it is a study meeting, the desired outcome is that everyone present should reproduce as accurately as possible the current official line in the current official jargon. There is no room at this kind of meeting for argument or for personal opinion. It does not even pretend to be a neutral forum in which rival views are presented on the basis of equality. Nor is it an occasion for individuals to express their own views. If it is a meeting for criticism, nothing can be said in defence of the chosen target. The meeting has next to nothing to do with people reaching their own views or making their own decisions. Instead it is a medium through which higher authority maintains and strengthens its control. However, like much else about Chinese communist ways of doing things, what was once most powerful and effective is now empty. The small group meeting is no longer what holds an empire's thoughts together and keeps them at one with the centre. Although billions of hours are still wasted each year on trying to do the impossible, the principal result is probably to intensify alienation from the system.

Not enough is known by outsiders about how the meetings that have to make decisions actually function. Whether at the highest levels of power or at the grass roots, very little is published about their proceedings. If minutes are kept, they are secret. When accounts do come out, as happened during the Cultural Revolution or, more recently, in the reports of the 1959 Lushan meetings that ensured the continuation of Great Leap follies, there is usually a polemical purpose: someone's part is being discredited and someone else's defended. Fiction and film rarely portray lively debate or reasoned argument when showing high-level meetings. Authority nearly always gets its way.

A characteristic feature of virtually all Western democratic institutions, which does not fit in with either traditional or modern Chinese attitudes on how disputes should be resolved, is the practice of making decisions on a majority vote. In cultures that accept regulated conflict and disagreements as legitimate parts of both public and private life it may be intensely distressing to have one's own preferred outcome rejected by a committee's eight–seven vote, but provided the rules are followed the decision will be valid, accepted and implemented until it is reversed by a majority going the other way. This is much less likely to happen in China, where the overwhelming preference is for consensus.

Unless the issue is one on which the dictatorship is willing to compel obedience, any actor whose compliance is needed for a decision to take effect can block it. It is as if everyone has a veto. Collective decisions have to be near-unanimous to have a chance of being implemented. This applies both within and between communities, units and systems, and from the highest levels of the Party to the neighbourhood. This can be a check on power but only when people are allowed to block the decisions that higher levels want made; and it makes for inflexibility in action by allowing a conservative veto. Under the ancient and modern dictatorships and their myths of unity lies a combination of conservatism and a kind of anarchy. All this has little to do with the basic acceptance of the rules of limited social conflict that is essential if any democratic structure is ever to be effective. One thinks of autocratic regimes as imposing a harsh discipline that has everyone obeying orders, but life in China is not like that. The negative resistance to authority to which the unfree have to resort is just as far removed from the political culture of democracy as is the dictatorship that rules them.

Another characteristic of democratic politics is the acceptance of diversity, suspicion of any person or group claiming absolute wisdom and tolerance of a fairly wide range of beliefs and values. There is a sense that majorities should not try to destroy minorities because diversity of view is desirable in itself; that today's winner may be tomorrow's loser; and that all have an interest in preserving the rules of limited conflict that is more fundamental than their interest in the outcome of any particular dispute, however painful that outcome may be. It goes with thinking about politics (in the widest sense) in terms of shades of grey rather than black and white and accepting the legitimacy of various influence groups jostling for advantage, forming alliances and doing deals. Wheeling and dealing, like factional conflict, are the stuff of Chinese politics too, but it has never been thought proper to admit it. The reality of factions in the bureaucracy itself goes as far back as remote antiquity, but they have always been treated as wicked and wrong. Even today the propaganda rhetoric continues to mask conflicts within and between the power structures, systems and units that make up China's party state. A Leninist party can no more recognize formally the factions that compose it than could a Confucian bureaucracy.

Familistic values do not help democracy either. The closed circles of obligation and the relatively weak sense of being an autonomous individual that are features of those values do not encourage a sense of having a non-reciprocal obligation to be involved in the affairs of the nation or the community, irrespective of whether one stands to gain personally from the involvement. Democratic and poten- tially democratic cultures recognize open and general obligations that are not necessarily reciprocal. They depend on responsible individuals doing things for the public good that they are not compelled to do. A functioning democracy needs a lot of people who take the trouble to vote even when they know their ballot paper will decide nothing and when voting is not compulsory, who pay most at least of the taxes they could evade, who work for public causes and community groups, who hand in lost property, who do not pass by or simply stand and watch when they see a stranger in trouble, who will give their blood for strangers and who do many other things that are of no direct benefit to themselves or those close to them and are not repayments of personal debts of obligation. I know that in giving blood I am not significantly increasing my chances of receiving blood should I need it, but I also know that in giving blood I am doing a tiny bit to keep the society in which I live tolerably humane. It is not that nobody does any of these desirable things in China or that most citizens do in the West; rather, it is that all of them are more effectively encouraged by the value systems prevailing in the West and take much more effort in China.

Democracy needs many more horizontal networks of communication crossing institutional boundaries than Chinese political culture permits or encourages. The strength of mutual obligation and dependence in the work unit or system makes for very weak links across unit and system boundaries. Units, held in the vertical structures of systems, have good internal and vertical communications but bad horizontal ones with other units and systems. Vertical communications suit autocracy.

It is not only political diversity and sectional interests that do not receive recognition. The authoritarian values of China's pasts and presents cannot accommodate the coexistence of rival and fundamentally incompatible views of the world and of human life. The state is absolutist and does not recognize that groups or individuals may have rights that can be held against the state's interests and wishes – an obvious example is the refusal to allow non-Hans, such as Uighurs, to define themselves as non-Chinese and claim political independence. Similarly, the mentality that has been created over many centuries by traditional and contemporary education is one that acknowledges only one legitimate world view, only one set of criteria by which all things may be judged. Confucius was a tireless

but completely authoritarian teacher who imposed his interpretation
of tradition even while denying that he had invented it himself.
Rote learning and unquestioning acceptance of what teacher says
are not good preparations for thinking for oneself. The foreign
notion that one can and should hold all or nearly all of one's opinions
provisionally, accepting that on many issues other views and
interpretations may be just as good or better and that new evidence
may require a change of mind, is deeply disturbing. In democratic
cultures it is often thought to be a good thing to challenge com-
placency by confronting people with views they do not share,
and arguments over controversial issues can even be a form of
entertainment in home, bar or television studio; China's dominant
cultural traditions abhor anything that challenges orthodox views.
Rival views are heresies to be crushed for the general good. Confucius's influence on education remains very great.

The abhorrence of diversity is well illustrated in the book that
purportedly records the teachings of the thinker Mo Di in the late
fifth and early fourth centuries BC. Mo Di founded a totalitarian
political party to argue and fight for his views and had to contend
with rival opinions – which made his later followers develop the
skills needed to convince neutral hearers by force of argument,
without relying on the authority of tradition to batter them into
submission. But though Mo Di and his Mohist successors operated
in a temporarily pluralist world and developed a neat line in chop
logic for demolishing rival views in debate, their aim was to impose
their own rigid orthodoxy. For Mo Di diversity of opinions was
wrong because it led to division and conflict, and the world would
not be properly ordered until all people thought the same thoughts
as those of their supreme ruler, who in turn derived his thinking
from heaven.

In Mo Di's vision of the origins of human society there was a
time in remote antiquity, before authority was established, when
everyone in the world had a different set of values, so that even
within the family there was hostility between father and son and
between elder and younger brother, and society's surplus resources
were wasted instead of being used where needed. This world of

disorder and anomie could be put right only by having the best, wisest and cleverest man chosen as Son of Heaven to set up an authority structure and announce that 'All who see or hear of what is good must report it to their superiors. All who see or hear of what is bad must report it to their superiors. What the superior thinks right they must think right. What the superior thinks wrong they must think wrong ...' The Son of Heaven was to put the world in good order by reducing the world's diverse value systems to a single value system.

Other schools of thought disagreed with some of the specific teachings of Mo Di and his later followers, which disappeared as a distinct intellectual tradition in Han times, but they would have agreed with his intolerance of diversity in political and moral values. Even though in the later centuries of dynastic rule there was a tendency to combine Confucian, Daoist and Buddhist teachings, this was done by maintaining the absolute supremacy of modified Confucian values in government and social life and by avoiding as far as possible awkward questions about compatibilities. Above all, in the two thousand years of dynastic rule there was no concept that disagreement on political issues was legitimate, let alone desirable. Though the conventional historical narratives tell of fierce factional and policy struggles within the senior bureaucracy all through the dynasties, these differences were seen as pathological symptoms. Rivals tried to destroy each other, driving defeated opponents into disgrace and exile, sometimes even to death, which made an official career a dangerous one to follow. One rarely finds the view expressed that disagreement and conflict are normal, healthy and even essential to political life. Nor does one often come across stories of political opponents able to enjoy the sort of off-duty camaraderie across party lines that tempers the ferocity of partisanship in mature parliamentary democracies and makes for a certain stability based on controlled and regulated conflict.

I remember the illusions of 1966 and 1967 that were created by the extravagantly titled Great Proletarian Cultural Revolution. The impression was given that the common people were finally taking their destiny into their own hands and organizing themselves so that they would be politically free of Communist Party control. To someone who had lived and worked in the Peking of 1963–5 this was a long-overdue rebellion against a stultifying and Confucian-minded imperial bureaucracy that even then was remote from its subjects. Time soon showed even the credulous foreigner that democracy had nothing to do with the struggles that were taking uncounted lives. The Red Guards, Revolutionary Rebels and all the rest of them were being used to create a tyranny that was even worse than the one they fought against.

Although all sorts of latent conflicts in society came to the surface, no issues were settled by the local participants in the chaos. Everything was ultimately determined by the outcome of power struggles at the top. When the Party bosses were divided there was blood on the streets, and when a new deal had been stitched up the street fighters were bundled out of the cities. What should have been a chance for some kind of participatory politics turned out to lead only to new forms of old dictatorships, whether on the small scale of Red Guard and Rebel fighting gangs or the much larger scale of reimposed central autocracy.

Talk of democratic futures for China is very pleasant, as is the notion that some individuals and groups are heroic fighters for democracy and freedom. The perpetrators of the Peking massacre of 1989 are so obviously tyrants of a most repulsive kind that we tend to assume that those they crushed were not only on the side of the angels but also serious about representative government. The problem about such assumptions is that the rhetoric of democracy in protest groups within China in 1989, and outside China among political exiles since the slaughter, is rarely matched by democratic behaviour. The enemies of the Communist dictatorship seem to have an incurable tendency to set up authoritarian organizations themselves or else to give up politics.

If there were a real pressure for democracy (in the sense of freely elected representative government) within Chinese cultures, it has to be asked why the Chinese of Hong Kong, who have had a better chance than any others over the last century and a half, and especially over the last forty years, to fight for and win a measure of self-government, did not even try to get it until after their fate had been sealed. That the people of Hong Kong did not demand full independence can be explained by the general sentiment that it would not have been proper for a territory taken from China by force of arms to separate itself not only from British colonial rule but also from China. What is less immediately obvious is why the residents of Hong Kong did not insist on taking control over the internal affairs of the colony through effective representative institutions in the decades following the Second World War, when in almost every other British colony there were pressures for self-government or independence. Apart from the violence of 1967 (which China organized and stopped once it had served its purpose), and the belated campaign for democratic rights that became a force only after the territory had been sold down – or rather up – the Pearl River and a serious one after April–June 1989, Hong Kong has been the most politically docile of colonies in the last half-century. While in the last few years the professional classes have made the running in the belated and doomed democracy movement, business interests have been strongly against letting the genie of self-government out of the bottle. Hong Kong has shown once more that Chinese bourgeoisies would rather accommodate themselves to governments than get involved directly in the struggles for political power. Peking's reminders to the colonialists and to the colonized that it did not want anyone demanding or getting representative government in the territory do not quite explain why this educated, literate and well-informed populace was never really interested in running its own community affairs and did as it was told. The overwhelming vote for democracy in the limited elections of 1991 was an encouraging sign of a profound change among the great majority who cast their ballots. One hopes that it has not come too late. There are also grounds for seeing an end to popular acceptance of dictatorship in Taiwan.

It is still too early to tell whether Taiwan, which appears to be on but not yet over the brink of the nearest thing to democracy the Chinese world has yet seen, will be allowed by forces on and off the island to burst the bonds of dictatorship. Singapore has perhaps set an example to the rest of the Chinese world in how to run an elected dictatorship that prides itself on its authoritarian approach to the rights of the citizen.

While democratic rhetoric will long continue to echo around the Chinese world, just as it has throughout the twentieth century, there is no realistic prospect that democratic values will be dominant in it for a very long time to come. This is a prediction that I hope but do not expect will prove to have been unduly pessimistic. How delightful it would be if, in a few years, we could be saluting the achievement of what now appears impossible. Meanwhile we can hope that what appears to be an attractive mirage will turn out to be something more substantial than hot air.

10. GODS, GHOSTS AND GERMERON

If democracy in any European sense, like pluralism and tolerance of antagonistic views, seems to be far away from all but the fringes of the Chinese world and the prospects of capitalism or Confucian traditions offering a value system that can work appear dim, what else is there that might provide some kind of normative framework for future Chinas? Thousands of years of bureaucratic despotism, built on authoritarian family structures, permeate the minds of those who have been brought up and educated in that environment, making escape from the mental patterns of tyranny very hard. I have argued that it took alien colonial power in Singapore, Hong Kong and Taiwan to break the continuity of Chinese bureaucratic rule and to permit growth and development within structures that were strongly influenced by foreign models. Such a break in continuity is out of the question for China as a whole: the Chinese state has the military power to prevent that, though it is conceivable that coastal regions, drawn by the prospect of doing better on their own, could slip out of the centre's economic control.

There are other value systems and influences that might bring about change, and the most powerful of them are outside the dominant traditions of past and present ruling bureaucracies. None of them seems likely to have much to contribute to a revived Chinese empire that would be capable of overcoming enough of its problems to hold itself together for another century or two. Some appear to be forces for division and destruction.

In many other parts of the world religion has been a vital

component of nationalism and people's sense of national identity. Religion can give nationalism an emotional power rarely found in its absence, endow hatred of other groups with cosmic significance and provide symbols and myths to hold a nation together. Religions are most unlikely ever to hold the Chinese empire together. Their part is, and will increasingly be, divisive. Religions are central to the non-Chinese identity of Tibetans, Uighurs, Mongols and some other subject peoples in the empire, dividing them from the Han majority. As in other countries, persecution of national religions has only strengthened the hold of Tibetan Buddhism and of Islam over their believers and sharpened the edge of their nationalistic militancy. These religions will continue to resist the attempts of the imperial bureaucracy to control, tame and weaken them. Islam in particular has great potential for division. Millions of Muslim speakers of Turkic languages in what has since the nineteenth century been chauvinistically called the New Frontier (Xinjiang) by Han Chinese are bound to be stirred as the Turkic-speaking Muslims in the south-east of what is now the Soviet Union assert their own national and religious identities and move towards either relative, perhaps even absolute, political independence or else a much stronger position in a remodelled Soviet Union stripped of some of its European republics.

There is no prospect of religion uniting all the Han Chinese, let alone the whole Chinese empire. This is not because there is no religious belief among the Chinese. Although the Confucian and communist high cultures have little time for the numinous, and it is over a thousand years since Chinese Buddhism was characterized by the kind of mass devotion and large, rich Church organization that have marked Tibetan Buddhism into the twentieth century, there is plenty of religion in China.

The religions of the Han Chinese that may count politically in future are not necessarily the obvious ones, Buddhism and Daoism. These officially recognized and controlled religions that have a legal status and are allowed to maintain some temples and clergy in exchange for a recognized though subordinate place in the state's outer structures do not appear to pose much of an immediate threat to the Communist Party dictatorship. The licensed Buddhist and Daoist shrines have flourished in recent years as they never did before under Communist power, drawing worshippers and donors in great numbers and having no shortage of would-be novices wishing to prepare for a religious life. But state-licensed Buddhism and Daoism are to a greater or lesser extent compromised by the accommodations they have reached with the regime and have, besides, accepted for many centuries state control resulting in something similar to their present lack of independence. The official Chinese Buddhists in particular have allowed themselves to be used in cultural propaganda and diplomacy and perhaps have even seen in the state's recognition some compensation for the rather low esteem in which the Buddhist clergy has long generally been held (unlike the clergy in, say, Tibet or Thailand). That even the sanctioned Buddhists might play a part in future resistance to the present dictatorship is possible – some took to the Peking streets in May 1989 – but much would have to change before Buddhism recovered anything like the dominance it had 1,500 years ago.

Daoism, in its bureaucratically approved form as an organized religion with a professional clergy, is smaller in scale than Chinese Buddhism but also less conspicuously compromised. Members of the Daoist clergy tend to keep themselves to themselves more than their Buddhist counterparts and have been less involved in propaganda performances for foreign audiences. Institutional Daoism is, besides, only a small, formalized corner of a vast and chaotic sea of popular beliefs, the multifarious indigenous religious traditions of the Han Chinese peoples, many of which are still decidedly alive.

Before returning to native religions, two other official minority religions should be considered briefly: Catholicism, a seventeenth-century transplant from Latin Europe, and Anglo-American Protestantism, introduced in the nineteenth century. The two religions have always been seen as separate faiths in China. There is not a word in Chinese that unambiguously includes the two, and they do not have the same god: the Catholics worship Tianzhu (the Lord of Heaven, a word of Buddhist derivation) and the Protestants, Shangdi (the Supreme Ruler, a deity of Chinese antiquity). Each faith had acquired several million believers by 1949, and each was compromised in the eyes of non-believers by its foreign associations. In the anti-imperialist atmosphere of the Korean War and after, there was a strong element of national self-assertion in throwing out (in some cases after imprisoning) the foreigners who had run China's Churches and bringing both Catholic and Protestant Churches under the control of the first Chinese government strong enough to do what all its predecessors for the previous hundred years would have liked to do. The nationalized Catholics, who were forced to break from Rome, and the Protestants, who were driven together into a single organization, were rewarded for their obedience to the Party with new persecutions during the Cultural Revolution decade. With the end of the 1970s came some tolerance of religion, and as the restriction eased it emerged that even the officially licensed faiths had doubled their memberships during and after the years of greatest repression. The collapse of faith in Maoism benefited all other religions, varieties of Christianity among them. Catholicism and Protestantism, like Islam and Buddhism, gained enormously from having been attacked under Maoism; but these creeds remain potentially divisive. In addition, the great revival over the past decade of the underground Roman Catholic Church that has maintained its loyalty to the Vatican and the rapid spread of private Protestant sects through house churches that are outside official control mean that a multiplicity of Churches Militant will be marching as to war, not least with each other, in the years to come. Some will have support from foreign organizations whose wild-eyed doctrines make Maoism appear reasonable. China's ill-educated masses could prove receptive to any and every kind of evangelism.

The vacuum of faith among the Chinese that followed the death of Maoism was filled not only by the many brands of Christianity – which, added all together, might command the allegiance of perhaps 2 to 3 per cent of the population – by Islam and by state-sanctioned Buddhism and Daoism but also by the extraordinarily rich variety of beliefs that make up the folk religions of the Chinese. One way of defining popular religion is as the religious beliefs and practices that are not approved by officialdom. In recent decades folk religion has been dismissed by the Communist Party as superstition and suppressed. This is nothing new: dynasty after dynasty tried to suppress potentially subversive unorthodox religious organizations and practice. Under communist power there has been freedom of religious belief on paper and sometimes, within narrow limits, in practice. The current Constitution of the People's Republic does not even pretend to guarantee freedom of all religious activity, restricting the state's protection to 'normal religious activities'. As an official propagandist wrote recently, 'the state strictly distinguishes citizens' normal religious activities from the illegal activities and criminal offences perpetrated under religious disguises', which are to be 'stopped and punished' (*Beijing Review* 4, 1991, p. 15). Official religious freedom applies only to what the bureaucracy recognizes as religion and has under its control. There is no freedom for what it classifies as superstition or for unofficial religion, even on paper.

It is hard to generalize about folk beliefs throughout China. Because of very long-established official attitudes, ranging from lofty disdain through condescension and mild curiosity to active hostility, and because peasants have not left records of their beliefs, published accounts are patchy. While cultural anthropologists have good data on the peripheral territories of Hong Kong and Taiwan, for most of mainland China the recording and mapping of folk religion is still at a preliminary stage. It emerges very clearly from all sorts of Chinese and foreign accounts that folk beliefs that were supposed to have disappeared under the pressures of the secular faith of Maoism as village society was transformed have emerged from the ruins of rural socialism stronger than ever. A fairly general characteristic of popular belief is polytheism, with communities each having their own pantheon of deities, from humble ghosts and spirits of stove and place up to the senior divinities taken from Buddhism and Daoism, apotheosized figures from recorded history and the borrowed gods of non-Han aboriginal peoples. Gods, spirits, ghosts and demons all have their areas of competence, and all have to be kept happy if one is to avoid troubles. Sometimes ordinary humans can deal directly with supernatural forces; sometimes they need the mediation of a male or female shaman, who may become possessed by a god or spirit. Relations with the supernatural world are not so much a matter of devotion as of doing deals in order to win or hold on to favours or to avert disaster. They are extensions into the supernatural of the closed circles of obligation that hold the human world together, including the way officials are placated with gifts. The suspicious and even hostile attitudes of Chinese states towards folk religions down the ages have ensured that local cults have remained local. There is not much evidence that folk religions of this kind, which are essentially concerned with maintaining and regulating normal life, have ever played, or are likely to play, much of a constructive or destructive role in national affairs. Nor are they likely to be the sources of value systems that could help to rebuild the Chinese empire. It is much more probable that they will continue to be essentially conservative and to maintain traditional attitudes – in other words, they will keep villages mentally in the Middle Ages. They may also serve to strengthen local loyalties, given the strong localism of most popular cults.

Another kind of folk religion is far more dangerous. Unlike the everyday cults that are concerned mainly with keeping life going, the other tradition is something quite different. It is like an underground river of fire, coming to the surface only when social and political structures are under strain or cracking. It has borrowed the language and images of many different ideologies and religions down the centuries since it made its first big eruption in AD 184 in the form of the rising by 300,000 members of the Yellow Turbans sect that brought death and destruction to the Han empire and dealt the dynasty a shock from which it never recovered.

The essence of this tradition is a terrible vision of the present world as an evil one ruled by demonic forces that have to be destroyed through cleansing violence, so that a new age may be ushered in. In this vision the forces of justice are led by divinely inspired leaders who recruit a core of dedicated followers into a more or less secret organization. They promise great rewards when the new Son of Heaven replaces the corrupt ruler and brings about the promised golden era. Those who join the organization stake their lives on their beliefs, as death may be the penalty for belonging to a subversive sect, especially once it has been involved in rebellion.

Most of the time such sects keep very quiet, attracting as little attention as possible and indoctrinating the members of the organization's inner core. When the time comes to expand, visible activities may be apparently harmless ones, such as worshipping some local deity or training village boys and girls in the martial arts. The sect may also be masked by a legal organization, such as an officially recognized militia or religious body.

The longest-lasting sects are those that are most patient. Investigators in the 1950s were told how the White Lotus sect in the nineteenth century distinguished between those initiated into the secret, inner core — once in, they were never allowed to withdraw — and the outer, mass organizations that could be built up rapidly in times of crisis and disorder, as when village youths were recruited into fighting units in parts of the Shangdong in the 1860s. Although a sectarian rising and the inevitable harsh repression that follows will inflict terrifying losses on the visible parts of the sectarian organization, the White Lotus tradition burrows deeper underground again, only to surface again a generation or so later. Whether actual White Lotus organizations survive persecutions is not clear. It is perhaps more likely that what survive are ideas, memories, the seeds of future organizations that can germinate when the conditions are right once more, as has happened over and over again for 1,800 years and continues to do so.

The religious colouring of the millenarian risings has changed over time. The Yellow Turbans used Daoist language, as did some other rebellions during the next 250 years. Some would-be cleansers of the world with fire and the sword took on a Buddhist colouring, as when in 515 the Mahayana rebellion, led by monks, proclaimed the new age as a new Buddhist era under the slogan 'A new Buddha is born: away with all the old demons.' Others seem to have had Manichean elements. During the Middle Ages there emerged the tradition of the Birthless Ancient Mother, sometimes in association with Buddhist deities, as the patroness of rebellion. To this tradition belonged the White Lotus.

In the nineteenth century one of the most destructive of all attempts to save China through divinely inspired slaughter, the Taiping Heavenly Kingdom, took on some of the language and concepts of Protestant Christianity, though the Taipings' underlying and essential message remained the same: kill the demons and bring about a brave new world under a divinely appointed monarch. This time the demons were the Manchus, and the heavenly ruler, Hong Xiuquan, assured the world that he was the younger brother of Jesus Christ. The revised version of traditional fanaticism achieved the rise and fall of the Taiping Heavenly Kingdom at the cost of tens of millions of lives. A more old-fashioned expression of the underground religion at the turn of the nineteenth and twentieth centuries owed much to the ideological and organizational arche-types associated with the White Lotus tradition, whether or not it should be regarded as a White Lotus outbreak: the Yihequan or Boxer movement, which used the methods of the hidden faith in organizing popular resistance to Christian missionaries, armies and converts. The Boxers were defeated, but their anti-foreignism was effective enough to give the Western powers a much worse fright than the Qing state ever had: when the Boxers were not butchering unarmed Chinese Christians they fought the foreigners and died with unnerving courage.

While major eruptions of the underground chiliastic tradition affecting large regions of China for years have happened at quite long intervals, usually several decades, smaller outbreaks are much more frequent. Nearly all potential risings are crushed when a would-be messiah has only a handful of followers and tend not to find their way into the printed record. As we have seen, there are signs that as communist rule grows shakier village Sons of Heaven are appearing frequently to lead attempts to found new dynasties. So far these movements have all failed, but they are signs that the underground river is coming nearer the surface. They hint at the destruction some such movement could achieve if it were able to mobilize peasant discontents on a larger scale.

These potential forces of darkness should not be underestimated. There is a huge reservoir of frustrated energy in rural China, especially among young men, who are not immune to the appeal of violence in a wild, irrational cause. It is hard to imagine that millenarian movements could play any constructive role in re-building the shaky edifice of the imperial state, though they could do much to hasten its dissolution. Other forms in which the underground tradition might find expression could include movements related to militant, unofficial Christian and Islamic groups.

In the past sectarian violence was often closely associated with techniques of the martial arts, physical exercise and the cultivation of mind and body. The Boxer movement, for example, won its English name from the amount of time that its adherents spent on practising the martial arts. Itinerant teachers of boxing and other fighting skills, plying their trade at fairs, have often been heroes and models to village boys. Other masters can still draw in young disciples from far and wide to be trained by them.

The Communists' victory in 1949 owed more than is generally acknowledged to their ability to draw to the surface and control these underground millenarian traditions, offering cleansing viol-ence as the way to a new and better world. Mao in particular never lost his fascination with the power of a people in arms breaking out of bureaucratic control: he loved what he saw in the Hunan countryside in 1926 of a peasant movement full of spontaneous militancy. Forty years later he turned China's teenagers loose in attacks on the very bureaucratic structures he had brought into being, allowing them to help themselves to the contents of the army's weapons stores so as to make their internecine battles as deadly as possible. The enthusiasm that a significant minority in town and country then showed for fighting, which was presented as part of a cosmic and quasi-religious struggle between good (Chairman Mao's proletarian line) and evil (the bourgeois line of the small handful of people in power who were taking the capitalist road), is a reminder of the continuing destructive potential of some forms of religion and quasi-religion in China.

While a re-run of the Cultural Revolution is most unlikely — few people outside the Party and state apparatus would go to the barricades to defend socialism and not so many inside it – the potential for new and old forms of upheaval is now enormous. Maoist belief in socialism may be dead, but Mao's teachings about the inevitability as well as the desirability of conflict in society still have an influence. There are huge numbers of people experienced in handling weapons of war. Underground millenarianism is now much closer to the surface. Revived mass interest in the martial arts goes alongside the growing influence of *qi gong* masters who claim the ability to exert paranormal forces through their control of mysterious *qi* (vital energy). All sorts of traditional values are being elevated over modern scientific rationalism with the help of some of the Party elders.

It is not inconceivable that these forces for disorder could form inflammable mixtures with elements of the present Party, state and military structures. Such a coalition could be dangerously provoked by growing national tensions between ethnic groups and the increasing influence of such foreign influences as the many varieties of Christianity and Western concepts of democracy, individualism and human rights that remain appealing to urban élites and infuriate traditionalists.

Confucian notions of hierarchical order, social harmony enforced by the state and the subordination of individual to group needs will not necessarily prevail against these disruptive forces. When one adds some other factors making for chaos, the long-term prospects for a peaceful rebuilding of the Chinese empire look bleaker still. China's pasts have bequeathed terrifying and apparently inescapable legacies. Where traditions have decayed what fills the space they leave is not necessarily an improvement.

There are tales from two thousand years ago and more of knights errant who nobly and gratuitously took on powerful evildoers for the sake of righting wrongs. Such stories have been reworked by storytellers, dramatists and novelists. They continue to please audiences with their comforting fictions about a world in which bullies get their come-uppance from altruistic heroes. It is doubtful whether there is much more factual truth in the stories than in the tales prettifying the ironclad gangsters of medieval Europe as paragons of chivalry. The real or invented wandering knights of ancient China have in any case no more to do with contemporary China than the heroes of *Le Morte Darthur* have with today's England.

A later tradition brings heroic violence lower down the social scale and closer to our own times. It is a tradition that for the last four or five hundred years has been for many people far more attractive than anything that Confucian orthodoxy, Communism or any of the recognized religions have had to offer. There is no abstract noun by which to label this tradition, which has rarely been thought worth the serious attention of Chinese or foreign scholars, but there is a word for the heroic figure it celebrates.

Hao han literally means 'good man', but it does not carry any suggestions of moral goodness. 'Tough guy' implies some of the meaning, as does 'hero' or 'good bloke', though no English term expresses all the reverberations of the Chinese words. A *hao han* can handle himself in a fight or battle. He has the weapons skills of the soldier or the bandit, not the general's mastery of strategy. He likes the challenge of single combat with a worthy adversary and will respect him if he has what it takes to be a *hao han* too. He fights for honour, *yiqi*, which requires him to stand by his mates even if that means forgetting all his other obligations to family, community and monarch. A true *hao han* is ready to throw everything away – life, family, property, position – for the sake of *yiqi*. A friend on the run asks for shelter, and the *hao han* has to give it without a moment's hesitation, though by conventional standards he has no obligation to the fugitive and is also leaving the people to whom he does have duties open to frightful reprisals from the authorities.

Yiqi does not count the cost. That is the source of its appeal in a country where everyone is brought up to have a carefully graded sense of duty, and the family normally locks one into closed circles of obligation. The image of the *hao han* who can forget about all that for the sake of a splendid gesture makes sense as an imaginary rejection of the bonds of social and family obligations restricting people in the real world. So too does the violence, often gratuitous, with which the *hao han* of stories and novels chop up their enemies

and innocent onlookers alike and pound people's heads to ham-
burger meat. In real life one has to put up with people who make
one's life a misery.

A *hao han* has no time for sex: he would much rather be drinking
or fighting with his mates and does not want family responsibilities.
Money has no interest for him either: he 'takes honour very seriously
and does not care about money'. Men in real life are not usually
free from either of these concerns. A *hao han* has very little time for
books and for scholars, who are pasty-faced, weedy, sly and probably deserve to be killed. Instead of observing the rules of the social
order the *hao han* lives for honour and gratuitous violence, eating
huge dishes of meat and downing prodigious quantities of liquor
(unlike the ordinary family, which has to calculate its consumption
and limit it to as little as possible, enjoying meat and alcohol only
in small quantities on special occasions).

While women as sexual beings are dangerous to a *hao han* – they
weaken and entangle him – the *hao han* ethic is not entirely hostile
to women. A woman who does not trade on her sexuality and who
fights like a man can be accepted as a quasi-*hao han*. An aged mother
can be rescued from hardship by a *hao han* son as long as this does
not interfere with his relationships with his mates.

A *hao han* does not have to be fighting for anything in particular.
He needs no cause. His sense of discipline is strictly limited: he will
obey those to whom he owes personal loyalty, such as the leader of
his band, as long as the leader keeps his confidence, but even this
loyalty is conditional on the chief's living up to the demands of the
unwritten *hao han* code. A chief who is too interested in money or
sex or who does not treat his top *hao han* with enough respect can
be killed without a moment's hesitation.

Such a set of values as the one outlined here obviously belongs
to the world of fantasy, especially the fantasy of adolescent boys of
all ages. The *hao han* always has been a figment of the imagination,
something many young men have wanted to become or to be
thought to be, and it is a safe guess that few people have ever lived
out the dream in real life. It is much easier to put together a picture
of *hao han* values from such fictional sources as the late medieval

story cycle *Shui hu* than from accounts of real life. And yet these values have been very influential for centuries.

They offer models of action that put much more emphasis on individual heroism and the big, bloody gesture than on discipline, restraint and acceptance of one's place in the social order. When the Communists were struggling for power they both feared indiscipline from their people trying to act out *hao han* fantasies and tried to counter the appeal of *hao han* values. Usually they were against the *hao han* style and deliberately avoided the swagger, boasting and flamboyance that were essential to it. Instead they promoted the image of modest, disciplined, quietly-spoken heroes who put the cause of the Party and the people first. For the communists the *hao han* style was associated with bandits, soldiers on the other side and other undesirables.

Ultimately *hao han* values have always been destructive. They glorify gangsterdom. Although they have given emotional power to great rebellions, especially in north China, they have also prevented them from going beyond destruction to building something new. While they have had a strong appeal as a fantasy escape from the trammels of society, as a guide to action they have always led to trouble. *Yiqi* as celebrated in *hao han* stories may have helped to bond criminal or rebel gangs together, but that is about all that can be said for it as a force for social solidarity.

Yet even the *hao han* tradition, antisocial as it was, looks good by comparison with what has replaced it in the last quarter of a century. Ever since Mao demanded an assault on certain traditional values and the Communist Party's new order during the Cultural Revolution, there has been a resurgence of a related value system that probably has its roots in the urban criminal underworld of late dynastic times. The term used for it by criminologists in China is *germen* (or the even slangier *germeron*) *yiqi*. *Yiqi* is the same word as the *yiqi* honour of the *hao han* tradition and *germen/germeron* means something like 'mate' in England and Australia.★

Germeron yiqi could be regarded as *hao han* values without their

★ *Germen* and *germeron* are both pronounced with a hard 'g'.

few redeeming features. It belongs not to imaginary heroes but to real criminal gangs, and it is far cruder than its predecessor. *Germeron* values are even more elusive on paper than *hao han* ones, as there is no equivalent to the *Shui hu* stories to serve as a canonical source. Reading in recent Chinese fiction about urban youth sent to the countryside in the late 1960s, and about the same generation and its successor in the cities of the 1980s, does, however, point clearly to the spread of the language, and perhaps, the attitudes, of criminal gangs among the social groups that once were most taken with Maoist values.

Lao Gui's purportedly autobiographical novel, *Dusk, the Colour of Blood* (*Xuese huanghun*), about former Red Guards in Inner Mongolia in the late 1960s and early 1970s, is one of the more sensational and depressing accounts of life on the frontier as the Cultural Revolution devoured its own children. In the alienated world of the army-run camps the hero tries to use *yiqi* and appeals to mateship as a way of forming bonds with one or two individuals who will stand together. Honour turns out to be weak. The increasingly disillusioned young people include some who, like the hero, work out their frustrations through savage fighting. It is a world in which almost nobody can be trusted and respect can be won only by being a harder and more ruthless fighter than the others. If you do find someone who does not let you down, and you are bound to him by a debt of *yiqi*.

The values of mateship and *germeron yiqi* cut right across those of the official culture promoted by the Communist Party and were also alien to the Confucian-influenced values of the educated. When the writer Cong Weixi was thrown into prison during the great persecution of the regime's critics in 1957–8 he was horrified at being brought face to face with the professional criminals who, when talking, revealed that among themselves the demands of mateship and 'honour' counted for much more than the regime's values. To Cong Weixi in 1958 underworld values and language were strange and shocking. Educated people in the cities twenty-five years and thirty years later were themselves using that same criminal slang in preference to the approved language and appealing to the same values. Mao's Cultural Revolution turns out to have destroyed its own most effective weapon – its militant quasi-Marxist language – and to have left a gap to be filled by the language of the underworld and the prison camp.

Thus it is that the contemporary street-sharp young men and women who in various ways hustle for a living in the pages of Wang Shuo's fiction talk like criminals, frequently use *germen*, *germeron*, or its female equivalent *jiemer*, as forms of address and resort to official language only when they are trying to con someone. Indeed, in one of Wang's wildest and truest inventions even old-fashioned *hao han* language is invoked as part of an attempt to revive a lost world for nefarious purposes. But the comfortable, everyday language that distinguishes the Red Guard and later generations from their elders remains the language of the prison cell and labour camp.

By addressing someone as *germeron* you claim a kind of solidarity as a fellow outsider, a quasi-relationship that has more human warmth than does officially approved comradeship. It is a slightly subversive gesture, even when it goes with nothing more than a request for a cigarette, because it is language that the regime dislikes. The word can also be used with a heavier meaning, signifying a claim or demand to form a bond that you cannot honourably break. If you let a mate down, you have no honour, and he can get his own back on you. As with the *hao han* values, swagger and gratuitous violence win respect under this set of rules. But they do not include the *hao han* taboos on sex and interest in money or the pretence in *hao han* fiction that all heroes are ultimately on the side of justice. *Germeron yiqi* has no time for sentimental notions about robbing the rich to help the poor or putting the world to rights. It is what holds two or three prisoners or ex-cons together against the world. Although strong but narrow loyalty to one's mates and the wish to put on a good show can have a greater significance, as when the Flying Tigers bikies provided communications in the resistance to the siege of Peking in 1989, *germeron yiqi* is normally an influence for destruction only. Perhaps for that reason it is an attractive model for a generation without any ideals or illusions: it offers a way of being meaningless with style. Although you have nothing else, at least you have freed yourself from the mental grip of authority, even if only by trading one ancient tyranny – the bureaucratic monarchy and its ethic – for a modern version of another old tradition that has no solutions, only a certain panache. It is, in its way, another and more flamboyant expression of the nihilism that is the shared position of many Chinese young and perceptive enough to see that past, present and future have ultimately nothing to offer.

11. A LIVING CULTURE?

China's many pasts have burdened the present with some unbearable loads: the constant *presence* of history; the traditions of autocracy that are still, in their zombie-like way, alive; economic and social forms that appear to offer no way out of the inherited problems that they can only perpetuate and exacerbate. All these problems are linked by a unified high culture that has had great successes in imposing and perpetuating itself and has also produced and sustained a great civilization. But are this high culture and this civilization still alive?

Civilizations can end, and many have done so already since they first emerged some 5,000 to 7,000 years ago, as did Sumer, Pharaonic Egypt, Byzantium, Islamic Spain, the pre-Columbian civilizations of the Americas and pre-Islamic civilizations from the Mediterranean to South-East Asia. I take civilization to mean a fairly *civilization* complete cultural system using a written script or scripts, connected with (though not necessarily coterminous with) a state or states, almost certainly urban-centred and having an identity recognized both by its own members and by outsiders. This loose definition takes civilization to be a much narrower category than culture. Indeed, the word civilization itself has an archaic ring. Civilizations, one instinctively feels, belong to the past. We live in a world of fluid, blurred, overlapping cultural identities. Talk about eighteenth-century French civilization raises few eyebrows, but reference to French civilization in the twenty-first century would make one suspect that the writer was using racist code.

The end of a civilization can be a gradual process, and it means not the end of the elements that made it up but rather the decay or collapse of a dominant high culture, often as a consequence of the fall of a system of political dominance.

The distinctive civilization that emerged in north China by around 1500 BC, a late development compared with those of northeast Africa and western and southern Asia, was from its very beginning intimately associated with a strong central state power having pretensions to universal supremacy. Though a late starter, Chinese civilization has outlasted all those that were established when it began. Even if we regard the profound and all-pervasive changes that took place between about 500 and 200 BC as amounting to the end of an archaic civilization and the beginning of an imperial one, that still gives over two thousand years of continuity till the beginning of this century.

The age and continuity of the high culture and of its political structures have often been a source of pride and comfort in the last century and a half, as the Chinese world has undergone so many batterings. Such comfort is not necessarily a bad thing, as long as it does not mask awkward realities and too high a price is not exacted for psychological security in an era of crisis.

China's present general crisis goes much deeper than the usual power struggle within the ruling group and is intimately linked with the crisis of the culture, more particularly the dominant high culture. By dominant high culture I refer not to very élitist activities but, in a broad way, to the culture of the classroom, of the broadcasting and print media, of the state and party bureaucracies, of what we associate with the concept 'China' as opposed to what is local, oral, unofficial and only grudgingly recognized, in certain approved forms, by the state.

My argument is that the present high culture is in its essentials the continuation of the high culture – the civilization – of imperial China; that while there are many elements of it that present and future cultures in what is now China will draw on with profit, this cultural formation has outstayed its usefulness and does not really work any longer; that while it is not dead yet, it is dying and, in the process, blocking the emergence of cultures with life in them;

that its end will have profound and all-pervasive effects in every aspect of Chinese life; and that only fundamental and, in historical terms, rapid reordering of the inherited tradition can liberate the peoples of China from its crushing weight.

There is nothing very new in any of these propositions. The previous paragraph is very much in the style of many a pronouncement of the May Fourth era some seventy years ago and of much rhetoric among Chinese intellectuals today. What makes raising these questions about the high culture, the civilization, so difficult for an outsider and in particular a Westerner, is the history of Sino-Western contact in the last century and a half. To discuss the possible end of the high culture and, in particular, the damage done by a writing system that is one of the main supports of China's unity is to lay oneself open to suspicions of being anti-Chinese and to risk giving offence. But the problem must be tackled, and the writing system is as good a place as any to get a hold on it.

The Chinese script is a wonderful one. It has a beauty and a *calligraphy* subtlety that cannot be matched by any other. Where calligraphy in European scripts rates only as an elegant skill or accomplishment, not taken seriously in the wider culture, in China it is the supreme art, calling for years of self-discipline and for a sense of abstract form. Good calligraphy in one of the more cursive styles has the exhilarating, controlled freedom of a solo by Lester Young or Charlie Parker. Handwriting in China plays something of the role of marking people socially that speech does in England. It is, to Chinese minds, a mark of the ignorance and barbarism of Westerners that they do not realize that Chinese painting is but down-market calligraphy. While some Westerners can learn to speak Chinese passably well, very few ever master an acceptable hand.

Written Chinese is a code that demands a lifetime's apprenticeship. So much has been recorded and – thanks to the Chinese inventions of paper and printing – preserved in it; allusion has played so large a part in the educated writing of the last 1,700 years at least; and there are so many separate symbols that can be used in so many different combinations, each with its own associations and reverberations. The demands it makes on those who would use it are far greater than those of a phonetic writing system. Written English words are more or less limited to the number of available sounds (despite a few homophones such as 'great' and 'grate'), and although we do not write as we speak or speak as we write, written words cannot stray too far from the spoken language. Speakers of phonetically written languages feel written words to be essentially representations of spoken or speakable words. Primacy goes to the spoken: 'In the beginning was the word.' Not so in Chinese, where primacy is felt to belong to the character, which has an existence and meaning independent of mere speech. Written Chinese permits those capable of using it well to write with a concentrated expressiveness that alphabets and syllabaries cannot hope to match. It does not need to make sense when spoken. Any character or combination of characters can carry a weight of association accumulated over thousands of years. Living languages that are phonetically written can normally keep words and their associations generally recognizable only for centuries. In Chinese, speech acts that cannot be represented with characters are not recognized in writing. New words cannot be represented in ways that are purely phonetic.

Because of its comparative independence from speech and its timeless quality, because it is so demanding and also because of the authoritarian and uncritical way in which literacy is imparted through rote learning, the script encourages copying and repeating what has been written before. Written Chinese faces and emulates the past. There is something very Chinese about the dictionary of clichés, often in four character expressions, that writers are encouraged to use. The influence of learning to write by memorizing long passages to be regurgitated later is one that is hard to shake off. Especially in recent centuries, the code has resisted innovation and originality.

Written Chinese, especially the so-called classical forms that have been left ever further behind the many spoken Chinese languages for some 1,800 years, is a code that prefers implied to spelled-out meanings. Grammatical relationships between words are often left to the reader's intuition instead of being made explicit, as they generally have to be in inflected languages. Writing, especially the more concise and elegant styles, is thus intended to be read by readers who are in tune with the writer, who share enough experience and assumptions to be able to understand the author's meaning without needing clues. Within a world of shared beliefs, assumptions and educational background, written Chinese can be vivid, rich, concise and forceful in ways that no phonetically written language can match. Good classical Chinese gives a pleasure that cannot possibly find an equivalent in any other script. However well done, a translation of it will be sloppy and full of verbosity by comparison with the original. On the other hand, a translation will often have to choose between different possible meanings in vague and ambiguous originals. Written Chinese can be as precise and specific as its user wishes it to be, provided one is prepared to be inelegant, but it will admit, and even encourage, a degree of imprecision and unspecificity that is structurally impossible in a European language. It can juxtapose powerful images, rich in association without having to state their grammatical connections, which has made possible wonderfully concise and ambiguous classical poetry. It does less to help the formulation of clear arguments than do written languages that do not allow the same degree of vagueness.

Although modern written Chinese is not quite as vague as the classical forms from which it has evolved, it still inhibits analytical, logical thinking and sharp definitions, encouraging instead the juxtaposition of powerful but fuzzy images. It impedes, but does not prevent, the linear development of an argument or a narrative in strong, simple, uncluttered language. The ability of Mao Zedong to achieve this was one of the exceptional qualities that took him to the top. Let me state clearly that I am not saying that Chinese people have any greater difficulties in thinking logically than other nationalities: far from it. If this needs to be demonstrated, one has only to look at the successes of Chinese mathematicians and scientists, especially in fields where communication depends essentially on non-verbal codes such as mathematical formulae. Nor is there any reason to believe that spoken Chinese is inherently resistant to clear thought and argument. In no other culture I know are people better at razor-edged spoken analysis of complicated social or political situations. The problem lies in the writing system.

The Chinese writing system is so marvellously self-contained, intellectually absorbing and aesthetically captivating that it does not have to refer to anything outside itself. Despite the onslaughts of Indian culture through Buddhism, of inner Asian cultures through repeated conquests, and of Western, Russian and Japanese invasions and influences in the last 150 years, it has kept itself remarkably pure of the sort of direct borrowings that phonetic scripts encourage – not totally pure but pure enough for Sanskrit words borrowed (as opposed to translated) from Buddhist texts to stand out as much odder than Hebrew, Greek and Latin ones in the English of Christianity. The main exception, of course, is the importation of a huge vocabulary of words for modern Western concepts built from Chinese characters in Japan that the great majority of Chinese readers do not perceive as foreign. Now, it can be argued that the capacity of the writing system to make up the new vocabulary from its existing stock of graphs, and even to be able to invent new graphs, such as those for chemical elements, is a mark of superiority. But is it really such a good thing to insulate a writing system from the rest of the world? In addition, a writing system that reflects changing speech in all its regional varieties as ineffectively as the Chinese one does is cut off from the constant and invigorating renewal to which a phonetic writing system is subject.

The case against the Chinese system that is most disturbing is not the time needed to learn a reasonable competence in it but its very obtrusiveness, its demands that outweigh those of the messages it carries. It looks backwards and inwards, drawing the eye to each graph rather than to the linear flow of thought. Its infinite subtleties are those of an archaic world view that sees everything as unique. It is, after all, a highly developed form of a primitive way of writing, characteristic of a much earlier stage than that of an alphabet, let alone a binary code. By primitive I mean early, not crude. Languages, especially ones that spread widely beyond the original speakers, tend to get simpler with time. English has simplified its verbs and lost its primitive gender distinctions almost completely; and the sounds of the spoken languages of north China have been rubbed smooth in the last two thousand years. But while the many spoken languages of the Chinese family have changed enormously over the last two thousand years and more, the script has changed very little, especially since the use of paper became widespread over 1,600 years ago. Even the modest efforts of the 1950s and early 1960s to simplify some characters were carried out within traditional principles of abbreviation used in handwriting. They did not open the way for any more drastic alterations. A third batch of simplified characters introduced in the 1970s was suppressed soon afterwards. The written code hinders the endless process of self-renewal that a living language, like a living organism, needs.

Which brings us back to an awkward question: do the structures of the Chinese written language inhibit clarity of expression and thought, especially of logically rigorous argument? Or do they encourage acceptance of what is written in assertive rather than analytical ways? I wonder whether the almost complete absence of awkward questions about what many terms in the political vocabulary really mean is connected with the writing system as well as with broader problems in the culture. In the early 1960s Mao announced that the central contradiction in China was between the proletariat and the bourgeoisie. He then went on to turn the cities upside down with bloodshed and chaos as countless millions fought out this struggle over imaginary notions. Why were there no voices asking if the terms had any meaning in a country which had few proletarians and no bourgeois who had not been dispossessed many years earlier? The authority of the written character overrode doubt and reason. Once the formula was established by Mao, it could only be copied; and the relationship between the formula and messy reality became irrelevant.

Some twenty years ago circumstances had me reading, or rather skimming through, reels and reels of microfilmed Red Guard and other unofficial publications of the late 1960s. The concentrated, fast-forward viewing of so much polemical text brought out features of it that had not been so obvious when taken in small doses over a long time. Before then I had believed that there were principles at stake in the Cultural Revolution and that, although the verbal formulae could not be taken literally, there was some substance behind them that, if expressed in more reasonable language, would not be complete nonsense.

The lesson of overdosing on concentrated Cultural Revolution rhetoric was a striking and a simple one: despite all the fortissimo screaming, nobody had anything to say about politics. There was no end of personal abuse, in highly standardized forms, of the officials who were the targets of the day at national or local level. They were renegades, revisionists, bourgeois restorationists, capitalist-roaders, reactionaries, counter-revolutionaries and the rest of it – and all the labels were meaningless, tied as they were on Party bureaucrats who all had their share of responsibility for carrying out ultra-socialism. Ideologically indistinguishable rival factions often used the same terminology against each other. Everyone declared boundless loyalty to Chairman Mao and his revolutionary line and swore to defend it to the death against others who were claiming to do exactly the same. All sides justified their positions from the Little Red Book of Mao quotes for the semi-literate that the army's General Political Department had compiled in the early 1960s.

Yet none of this amounted to any discussion of political issues. For all the abuse of individuals and rival factions, nobody wrote about how China, or even a particular school or work unit, might be differently run. There was no analysis, Marxist or other, of the economy, social structure or politics of China, no proposals for reform or revolutionary change.

The exceptions were very few indeed, and even they could not escape from the web of Maoist language. There was a group in Hunan that applied Maoist analysis to China's political order and called for even more violence and destruction than Mao had sanctioned. Others who raised doubts about how the issues were defined became widely known only long after their wallposters or letters to the Central Committee taking issue with Cultural Revolution policies in orthodox language had led to the executioner's bullet.

In all of the endless verbiage of those years the Chinese written language demonstrated to the highest degree its capacity to be divorced from anything outside itself. The spoken languages followed the written word, so that the same empty but lethal rhetoric was heard right across the empire, inciting countless local wars. No language has necessarily anything to do with anything outside itself, and the Cultural Revolution was no worse than many other follies committed for verbal constructs in human history. But where other conflicts over verbal labels – French versus English, Christian versus Muslim, Chinese versus Japanese, Athenian versus Lacedaemonian and so on – have borne some relationship to the subjective sense of identity that both sides have, the authoritarian language of the Cultural Revolution imposed a completely fictional identity on the enemies of both sides in the conflicts of those years.

It was simply not possible to analyse the terminology imposed by imperial authority or to ask what it actually meant. What appeared to be a mass revolutionary upheaval was, in fact, scripted from on high. Just as the productions all over China of the model 'revolutionary' Peking operas of the early 1970s had to follow the Centre's written instructions, down to the last stage direction and prop, so the real-life dramas could not deviate from the authoritative words that had come from the Centre, which was divided against itself.

Although there has been some relaxation of the control over language since the death of Mao, it remains very hard to use written Chinese as a neutral medium for debate and discussion in which rival views on fundamental issues can be argued out reasonably and calmly on a basis of equality. Down the millennia written Chinese has been a code in which authority asserts, not one in which equals argue.

The script is a good illustration of the principle that the price of being ahead in one stage of development is to be stuck in it. No doubt the Chinese script is infinitely more flexible, subtle and expressive than Egyptian or Mayan pictographs. But whereas the others gave way to phonetic scripts, the Chinese method of writing survived and perpetuated a mental world of its own.

It might have been expected that the somewhat less distant

relationship with spoken Chinese in a few low-prestige genres such as fiction in recent centuries, leading to the wholesale adoption of a written style influenced by northern speech from the 1920s and 1930s onwards, would have brought speech and writing closer together and revived the written culture. For a time it looked as though it might, especially in the hands of writers who had mastered the old code and, in some cases, a foreign language or two. But as time has gone by the modern written culture that China ought to have has not emerged, on the mainland or anywhere else.

It is a sweeping generalization to assert that the whole of Chinese written culture in the last few centuries has, with a few wonderful exceptions, been weaker than what went before. Yet I must make it. A country as populous as the Chinese empire, with so long a tradition of written culture, which in the past was as advanced as any of its contemporaries in the world, if such things can be measured, ought to have produced such cultural riches in recent centuries that it would be impossible to discuss almost any aspect of human intellectual and creative activity without devoting a substantial part of one's attention to modern Chinese developments. Any history of world literature and recorded thought between 500 BC and AD 1500 would need to give a lot of space to China. Not much would be taken up by the five hundred years after that.

Even in these centuries of decline greatness has sometimes been achieved. Cao Xueqin devoted the last ten years of his life to the uncompleted writing and rewriting of *Hong Lou Meng*, his re-invention of the morbidly fascinating world of a very rich family in early eighteenth-century Peking and Nanjing that is variously known in English as *The Dream of the Red Chamber* and *The Story of the Stone*. Lu Xun (1881–1936), is one of those writers, very rare in any culture, whose honesty, intelligence, perception and ability to handle written language make almost any page he wrote a pleasure to read. Lu Xun's language is dense, sometimes hard to unravel, closer to classical than to the standard, Peking-influenced vernacular style, and all that is part of the delight of it. He overcomes the normally irresistible tendency in the culture to write dishonestly and to strike poses, and he refuses to play nearly all the games to which so many of his talented contemporaries and successors succumbed.

Cao Xueqin and Lu Xun are among those few writers in all of literature who grow with repeated reading. They use the infinite resources of written Chinese, at all its levels, with such mastery that one is convinced while reading them that even in recent centuries it is *the* supreme medium for written expression. But they are such towering exceptions to the run of Chinese writers in the last few hundred years that their achievements only remind us just how difficult it is to write Chinese that is both vigorous and subtle, that draws on the riches of the past without being overwhelmed by them, that is as vague or precise as the writer chooses and that can breathe with the rhythms of speech or cut free from them.

In poetry, to take the most obvious illustration of the problem, writers seem to be faced with a number of choices, none of which leads far. They can write in the manner of the Tang and Song, which results in an archaism that may be clever, ingenious, learned and delightful but feels misplaced, like nineteenth-century Latin poetry. Another approach is to pastiche the folk ballad, and when that is done by people who do not belong to one of the living ballad traditions it has all the authenticity of Mississippi country blues lyrics copied by middle-class white boys. Then there are the twentieth-century imitations of European and American forms of the last couple of centuries, which have yielded perhaps a dozen truly memorable short lyrics and vastly much more that is forgettable. There seems to be no way of making poems in written Chinese that can be the equivalent for our time of what Li Bai and Du Fu created for theirs.

According to reports, the most striking works in an exhibition of new art held shortly before the Peking slaughter were ones that were completely Chinese and completely contemporary, unlike much else in the show: immensely long compilations by Xu Bing of invented Chinese characters that could not be read and were meaningless but looked like real classical texts. The works could be taken as a celebration or as an eloquent critique of a mighty tradition that can now say nothing on paper.

I will not dwell on the state of contemporary writing in Chinese in all parts of the Chinese-speaking world. There is by now an international academic industry devoted to persuading the West of its importance and quality. It certainly is of interest to anyone concerned with contemporary Chinese issues. Much is highly readable, and it is always possible to set standards by which some writing is outstanding. By any criteria, Wang Shuo is a writer of very rare perception and talent; some others are not bad; and there is enough to justify a few volumes of translations a year. This is not much for a fifth of the human race, given the dramatic lives of many people, the essentially literary nature of Chinese high culture, the many intelligent and sharp-eyed writers and the huge number of publications that print literature. I believe that one of the fundamental causes of the disappointing outcome of over a decade in which writers have been less unfree than since the 1930s is the script itself.

Perhaps the Chinese writing code would not have been so limiting in its effects if it had given itself the capacity to combine characters with a purely phonetic system, as those of Japan and Korea did long ago. As it is, no presently available Chinese writing system can win. A switch to the Hanyu pinyin alphabet or any other purely phonetic script would cut all of its readers off from almost all that has been written in characters and make communication difficult for everyone whose spoken Chinese is not standard – the great majority of the population. Within a generation it would lead to the emergence of several distinct phonetically written vernaculars, with all that implies for the unity of Chinese high culture and the maintenance of the Chinese state. The continued use of the graphs will sustain the present problems, and it will remain hard, though not impossible, to express in writing what is local, new, unconventional, or foreign.★ Written culture will remain only half awake, tying its users to a dead past by a code in which very few people are really competent.

It is not just that the civilization and its writing have been on a downward slope for at least five hundred years. During this century the ability of all but the most highly educated to exploit the rich,

---

★ One can see how attractive this incapacity must be to China's dictatorship.

expressive possibilities of the script has been in decline. Few people under sixty can really use the resources of written Chinese. Contemporary written Chinese lacks the density of meaning of good writing in earlier versions of Chinese or in modern phonetically written languages, despite efforts to keep the script alive on the part of several regimes, especially the Communist Party.

Before the Cultural Revolution the Communist Party had stood some traditional values on their heads, but its reversals had nearly all been within the tradition itself. It placed itself firmly in the tradition of Chinese moralistic historiography and of the autocratic state. It had also tried much harder to revive and popularize knowledge of its version of traditional high culture than had its Nationalist predecessors. Great effort and expense were devoted to editing and publishing, at subsidized prices, new and old scholarly editions of the classics, as well as popular readers of all kinds to make the heritage accessible to people who had never had the opportunity to master the classical language. But this effort could provide only limited and passive competence, much as the classical languages of Europe can now be sampled in translation, easy readers and bilingual texts but are in reality cut off from all but a very few. When some of the post-Cultural Revolution intellectuals try to turn to China's past for comfort and strength they are usually frustrated by a code they admire but, with a few exceptions, cannot handle.

There is an extremely close connection between the problems caused by the written language and the long tradition of education by rote learning. Because even everyday literacy requires the ability to recognize and write several thousand characters, there is a long process of learning by copying and copying again for several years before a pupil can read and write independently. There is, and can be, no substitute for years of memory work at the beginning of formal education. Whereas a phonetically written language enables the learner to start playing with the script very early, it takes such a long time to attain freedom in writing Chinese that by then one has probably lost the ability to be original in it.

Education is also deeply influenced by the inherent authoritarianism of the whole culture: a student is expected to accept uncritically what teacher says. Up to the beginning of the twentieth century classical texts had to be learned more or less by heart, as had the approved interpretations of the texts. Education for the sons of the rich encouraged – thanks, in part, to the writing system and thanks to the syllabus for the official examinations – an extremely fragmented, unanalytical view of a world, governed by unquestionable political and moral principles, existing primarily on paper and to be mastered by attention to the finer points of the written code.

Although the imperial examinations were abolished nearly ninety years ago, and such foreign subjects as science and European mathematics were brought into the schools, the rote-learning approach has persisted, right through to university. This may be good for learning skills and accumulating data, but it does little for the ability to think independently and analytically or to question received wisdom. It is a commonplace, when the problems of Chinese students studying in Western universities are discussed, to consider how best to help people who are often very intelligent and well informed to start expressing their own views and challenging their teachers. All their training up till then has taught students to conform with the views of authority when speaking in class or writing formally. Doubts and explorations are for private thoughts and conversations. It can be extremely uncomfortable for a Chinese student to be asked to question a teacher's interpretation. That is not what the teacher–student relationship is supposed to be about, whether in mainland China or elsewhere in the Chinese world.

Chinese education does not encourage the asking of questions, such as ones about what words actually mean or whether an authoritative statement could possibly be incorrect. There is little awareness of the sorts of doubt about language itself that have characterized so much twentieth-century thinking elsewhere in the world. Except at the very highest levels, Chinese education cannot accommodate originality or unorthodox approaches. It rewards those who perpetuate existing orthodoxies, which is good for continuity and bad for innovation. At a time when innovation is very badly needed this is not a desirable tradition.

The high culture of the past is now dead, but it has taken a long time to lie down since its vital link with an official career was broken by the end of the imperial examinations system. If that was the death, the decline started long before then. Chinese high culture never really recovered from the shock of the Mongol conquest. To take an obvious example, while Song painters produced works of uncanny realism or breathtaking calligraphic magic, from the Yuan dynasty onwards nearly all painters were either artisans producing intricate but dead displays of skill or gentlemen concerned more with displaying their cultural knowledge and appreciation of the ancients than with looking at the world. (There were to be a few wonderful exceptions, but they were treated as oddities, freaks.)

Of course, there is much that is delightful in Ming and Qing high culture – marvellous gossipy little essays, informal eighteenth-century paintings of cabbages and mushrooms and so on. There was room for some very remarkable and original talents to develop quirky and unorthodox views of the world. Popular cultures flourished and sometimes interacted with high culture to yield such interfused forms as the commercially printed story and novel and even the unfinishable masterpiece *Hong lou meng*. But there has been little in the high culture to compare with the explosive changes in Europe in the last few centuries. While Europe was inventing modern science, and thus transforming the relationship between mankind and nature, the highest intellectual achievements of Qing China were in textual criticism and historical philology. The successes of Qing scholars in these fields were formidable, but they were hardly equipping China's best and brightest to respond to the challenges of a dangerous outside world. Yet such was the seduction of the written character that its study remained the highest of all intellectual pursuits. The fragmenting of nearly all educated minds paralleled the fragmenting of economic activity and of potential political challenges to the state's authority.

It would be vain to hope for a successful revival of the high culture of the past and its writing system. Few high civilizations have ever imposed on themselves from within as clean a break in the transmission of tradition as the one that afflicted China between 1966 and the early 1970s. The ending of the education of a whole generation was a big enough disruption in itself. The urban young who a few years earlier or a few years later would have been undergoing education to prepare them for top jobs were instead first drawn into the excitements and horrors of the so-called Great Proletarian Cultural Revolution, then sent to live in the country-side – in many cases the most backward parts of the countryside – expecting that it was to be for life.

By exposing what would otherwise have been a privileged urban minority to the anarchy of the Cultural Revolution and then to the realities of rural socialism, and by sparing it some of the mind-numbing experience of most Chinese education, Mao created something that had never before existed in China: a generation of intellectuals or potential intellectuals who had seen through the whole system, had been willing to talk to each other with unprecedented freedom during rural exile – what had they to fear when they were already living in circumstances virtually the same as those of labour camps? – and were not necessarily in search of an alternative pre-packaged ideological thought kit. They had made their journeys to the end of the night, and most had survived. They could not be fully reintegrated into the unitary high culture.

The millions of half-educated, no longer young ex-urbanites returning to the cities from their rural exile in the late 1970s were a more subversive force in the history of Chinese culture than any previous generation. With a few exceptions the best of them believed in no ideological system and felt no need for a belief package. Earlier generations had attacked tradition but only to try to replace or modify it with something else – Buddhism, new varieties of Con-fucianism, Christianity and sinified versions of scientism, Marxism, militarism, fascism and other sets of ideas. If you have beaten up, possibly even killed, an official and a school teacher or two in your teens and rebelled against your parents and the local Party bosses, you can never quite be reabsorbed by a value system that depends on unquestioning acceptance of the authority of such people. And when you have then been cruelly deceived by the alternative 'revolutionary' value system, there is not much room left for illusion, except perhaps about the outside world. This generation and its successors have been unable to put together what was broken, even when some of them try to find strength and meaning in the traditions they rejected in their youth. They do not feel the need to share a common ideology; and because they grew up in a China that for all its internal problems has been strong enough to deter foreign attacks, they have been less passionately xenophobic than earlier generations. They are, however, vulnerable to fashionable trends and eager to find quick-fix solutions to fundamental ills.

This historic disruption poses a great challenge to one of the most basic values of Chinese civilization: that uniformity is inherently desirable, that conflict is bad, that there should be only one empire, one culture, one script (as opposed to a Babel of mere speech), one tradition. While a huge variety of local low cultures, mainly Han but also non-Han, could continue to exist, they were not 'civilization'. This centralizing, authoritarian tradition has since the Qin tyranny abolished local variations in script and used uniform characters as the medium of imposing its view of the world; and when the Communist Party in the 1950s was able to exclude first Western, then Soviet influence this was to many Chinese a good thing. The script, identical through space and time, permanent and absolute, inhibits the development of local linguistically defined loyalties because they cannot be written down. Imagine how China might have developed if Indian or Central Asian Buddhist missionaries in the fourth and fifth centuries AD had persuaded their less-educated converts to use an Indian-derived phonetic script. This might have spread through the Chinese world as an alternative to the characters till different written vernacular languages emerged that existed beside a high culture written in characters, like the European vernaculars alongside Latin. Would local nationalisms and local nation-states have emerged, acknowledging a common heritage but each going its own way? Would things have been worse if a multi-state Chinese world had developed with different local high cultures, harbouring each other's dissidents and having to earn the loyalty of their subjects through constitutional compacts? These are, of course, improper questions and, like all historical what-ifs, not really answerable.

The homogenizing effect of historical records kept in a single, unifying script that has only a marginal relationship with spoken languages limits perceptions of past ethnicities. They make most non-Han personal names they record appear to be Chinese or very nearly Chinese. The script and those who keep records in it would comfortably accept only names in the standard Chinese form. When this could be done the name was essentially fixed by characters, not its sound. To this day it is striking that foreign names from other cultures that use or have used Chinese script can be pronounced in Chinese only in accordance with the standard or local readings for the characters.

I have dwelt at some length on the problem of the writing system and what was expressed in it, and I have probably argued one side of the case too strongly. There are plenty of countries around the world in trouble as deep as China's that use phonetic scripts. In other parts of the Chinese world the writing system has not prevented prosperity, even though it has been no better at producing literature of the greatest intellectual or aesthetic value than has the mainland.

12. WAYS OUT?

═══

This book has been a set of mainly gloomy reflections. It has not tried to present a balanced argument or to dwell on all the things that are good and attractive in Chinese cultures. I have looked briefly at some of the deep and apparently daunting problems that a tyrannical past has forced on the present and at ways in which the past influences people's minds by restricting and distorting perceptions of the world, patterns of thinking and value systems. This in turn would seem to make solutions all the harder to find.

My treatment of huge issues has been brief, impressionistic and highly generalized, with all the concomitant drawbacks that go with sketchy and schematized analysis. Because my main aim has been to point to the structural problems, with roots deep in the past, to be found in virtually every aspect of China as a cultural invention and also of China as a group of actually existing human societies, I have no doubt erred on the side of pessimism about the prospects for China; I have argued that the general crisis that is the sum of all the problems is so grave that the political survival of China as a unitary state, the physical survival of those who live in the poorest and most remote parts of the countryside, the moral survival of value systems inherited from the past or adapted from abroad that might be adequate to today's and tomorrow's needs, and the intellectual survival of the written code and the traditions and thought patterns it carries are all at stake. These have been grim propositions to argue, and I have consciously tried to avoid softening their impact with too many ifs and buts. The arguments are ones that have to be considered. And if the message that gets over, in however oversimplified a form, is that the crisis is profound, general, and insoluble within the present conventions, that is a less misleading impression to be left with than that all is basically well despite a few temporary difficulties, or that it only needs the Communist dictatorship to collapse for China to become a land of sweetness and light.

Looking for ways out might then seem to be pointless. Not so. Without retracting any of the arguments in this book, there are plenty of ways in which the effects of the crises can be mitigated for some; and some of the problems may, by their very insolubility within prevailing assumptions, lead to unexpected breakthroughs by forcing the questioning of conventional wisdom.

To borrow a familiar observation that is as true as it is hackneyed, Chinese people have an amazing ability to accept, adapt to, and make the best of every kind of hardship and difficulty. Many centuries of living under bureaucratic autocracies have taught people how to cope with governments and to minimize the effects of unwanted interference by the state. During the twentieth century people and communities have adapted to weak governments, to the existence of rival regimes and to overpowerful governments that went further than any other over the last two thousand years in controlling and intervening in everyone's life. (The plural in the last category includes both the Taipei and the Peking regimes.)

The countless local cultures on which the unified high culture has been imposed still exist. From as far back as records go the state was applying its power to groups that it saw as different and referred to by various ethnic labels. Even though there was a process of assimilation over the next 3,000 years the multitude of local cultures have not disappeared completely. It seems more than likely that the huge variety of spoken tongues regarded *politically* as dialects of a notional single Chinese language represents an almost infinite number of local hybridizations. Just as the English of the west of Ireland has preserved phonetic and grammatical features of Gaelic, so an analysis of the more obviously creolized languages of the Chinese family would bring out the ethnic diversity that lies underneath the myth of the oneness of the Han nation.

For this myth is a powerful one that cannot really be discussed without challenging the ideological basis of the Chinese state. The state needs to insist that the inhabitants of Harbin and Canton speak different dialects of the same language, even though it is immediately obvious to anyone hearing the two tongues spoken that they are different languages. Because they are ruled by Peking the Cantonese will have to understand northerners' speech, but northerners will usually be completely flummoxed by spoken Cantonese. What applies to language also applies to many other aspects of life in smaller towns and villages across the length and breadth of China, where what is local and different is treated by the high culture as deviant.

Does China have to continue to insist on uniformity? A played-out high culture based on uniformity could give way to a much more diverse and interesting country, in which all sorts of things now suppressed, unrecognized or undervalued were given some recognition and allowed to develop. Let us imagine emerging from the present crisis some rather different values. A political culture might develop that stopped using the rhetoric of absolute certainty, stopped talking about political parties as 'great, glorious and correct' and as having a historical mission to impose their dictatorship. How delightful it would be to read in the Chinese press articles uncertain as to the best policies to follow and making their recommendations in provisional, guarded ways.

Given the seriousness of the crisis and the failure of traditional state-centred high culture to solve it, it may be that the low cultures should be given more of a chance. Perhaps smaller, more manageable areas should be allowed to develop the local identities whose full emergence the high culture has thwarted. Perhaps Chinese identity could be redefined as something much looser.

Back in the 1920s and 1930s Lu Xun frequently expressed despair over what he saw as the ineffectual national character that the culture had created. There were many aspects of this. Among them were self-deception, a lack of awareness of how the world really was, the inability to do things properly and the numb indifference of people who were mere spectators of life and politics, unwilling to make their own histories for themselves. Although all these charges could be laid against many other nations, they are uncomfortably close to the mark in China.

We can add to Lu Xun's charges the problem of the weak sense of individual identity, of an isolated self who ultimately has to bear responsibility for actions. The Japanese social scientist Maruyama Masao commented a generation ago on the lack of a sense of personal responsibility among Japan's leaders for their actions in the Second World War, contrasting this with German attitudes. Perhaps similar comments could be made about individual responsibility in China, where it does seem to be easy for officials who implemented the murderous policies of the Great Leap Forward and the Cultural Revolution to come back into public life condemning the very crimes (or 'mistakes') of which they were themselves guilty. On the other hand, intellectuals were willing to accept guilt by category, such as class origin, in the 1950s irrespective of their individual actions.

This underdeveloped sense of independent personal identity may be connected with the absence from all Chinese religions, except the minority ones of Islam and the two Christianities, of a strong relationship between an individual soul and an omnipotent and judging deity. Another factor may be the way in which, from early childhood, one's identity is defined within the family in relative terms, making a name of one's own not very important.

If there is no salvation to be hoped for in the unitary culture, which is so hostile to diversity, where can the variety come from? Foreign influences are likely to be counter-productive unless they coincide with Chinese forces for change. Perhaps the popular cultures, the little traditions, have something to offer when the high culture seems to be at a dead end. Many features of the high culture are there essentially only to distinguish it from the tastes of common people. When they are allowed to show it, there are in popular cultures strength and vigour that have long gone out of high culture. This is why much better pottery can often be bought in a hardware shop or at a market stall than in the arts and crafts shops or tourist trap selling technically superior but aesthetically dead ceramics.

In the graphic arts the brightly, garishly coloured woodblock

New Year prints and real peasant papercuts, all in countless local styles, have a life to them that is almost impossible to find in the chocolate-box productions and imitation modernisms of superior artists. The living performance traditions of storytellers, balladeers and low-class local opera forms have a lot more energy and vigour than such superior genres as Peking opera, which offers – through no fault of its own – a good illustration of the deadly snobbery of high culture. In the 1960s Jiang Qing, who posed as the cultural commissar of the proletariat in its battle with the bourgeoisie, launched her programme of 'revolutionized' dramas. Characteristically she focused her efforts on forms that were foreign, such as ballet, or high-class, such as Peking opera. She even tried to marry the foreign and the high-class traditions by having Peking opera set to piano or European orchestral accompaniment. What she could not or would not do was to conscript the rough, low, local forms, which are a lot more alive than Peking opera.

In their years of success the Communists were able to tap the strengths of local cultures, just as they were able to attune themselves to village society, make themselves part of it and use the peasants of north China to bring them to power. Just because the Communists have lost their common touch, that does not mean that the rough strengths have disappeared. As the component parts of the Chinese empire begin to find their post-imperial identity, those strengths will be needed in whatever new cultural formations appear.

Popular local cultures, far more complex and diverse in their totality than the homogenizing high culture of written tradition, have a formidable capacity for softening the impact of normative central power. Even when, in recent times, it seemed on the outside as though the whole country really had turned into a school of Mao Zedong thought (in the words of the propaganda cliché of the late 1960s) and that bad old traditional values had been swept away by the bright-eyed revolutionary masses, it turned out that nothing much had changed underneath, as was shown by the re-emergence in the 1980s of virtually everything that had supposedly been suppressed. These powerful conservative tendencies block changes that we might think well worth encouraging, but they also will resist future would-be centralizers and imposers of compulsory correct thinking.

Localism may also help people to cope with whatever disruption and chaos follow the collapse or slow disintegration of Communist Party rule. It helped village communities to moderate the impact of such breakdowns of national order as the collapse of dynasties in the more distant past and the endemic civil strife of the warlord era, the divisions imposed by Japanese aggression and the lethal struggles of the Cultural Revolution. Where local leaders were strong and clever enough to do so, they spared their communities the worst of the post-Great Leap famine and the Cultural Revolution, just as their predecessors had often been able to placate rival regimes competing for control of their territory. Localism can also help keep petty tyrants in place, as most recently when Party rule in the countryside has often meant domination by local bosses who hold all power in their hands, whether through the structures of collectivism or through control of key resources in the decommunized rural economy. Localism helps some parts of China to look after themselves economically as the central government's ability to allocate resources is weakened, just as it did when China was divided by wars and warlords throughout the second quarter of the twentieth century. It now enables communities lucky enough to have relatives overseas to bring in investment capital that could be had no other way.

Community loyalties, with their closed little circles of obligations and untidy particularisms, have been the despair of all those who down the ages have tried to remake China's societies from the top downwards, so as to force them to conform to some schema of what human society ought to be. We find the Qin governor of the newly conquered Southern Command inveighing against the pigheadedness of Qin's new subjects, who stayed with their own old ways and resisted the new totalitarian uniformity, and threatening to impose the new order with all the harshness of the Qin penal code. Nearly 2,200 years later the Red Guards were still trying to crush the values underlying localism through their attacks on the 'four olds' – old thinking, culture, customs and habits. Both attempts, like countless others between them failed. Whether any future efforts to remake China from the top down will do better is doubtful.

It is at levels below those China's bureaucratic historians usually condescend to notice that the great transformations of the turn of the twentieth and twenty-first centuries can be expected. Already the economy of the coastal regions is being remade as a result of countless community initiatives led by local officials, entrepreneurs and local officials turned entrepreneurs. Even in the absence of a high culture that openly accepts and legitimates horse-trading between interest groups as a proper form of political activity, the centralized command economy that is the material basis of the centralized dictatorship is rapidly being undermined by the growth of new patterns of making and trading.

The uncontrollable highway is replacing the government railway as the main transport medium. If they are to survive and prosper, enterprises have to cut through the boundaries of the vertically integrated systems that make up the unified empire and to fix an endless number of deals to keep themselves in business. What the ministries in Peking and the Communist Party decree no longer matters as much as the demands of the market, and for coastal China at least that market is increasingly an international one. Eyes look outwards, and across to potential partners in other localities, rather than up to the political bosses whose word was all that really mattered not so very long ago.

The assertiveness of provincial and of even more local interests that have been coming out into the open in the last few years, and especially since the Centre's spectacular demonstration in 1989 of its unfitness to rule, is not only ominous for Peking's hopes of keeping control. It also points to ways out. People in positions of power, however minor, used before the Cultural Revolution to bombard the foreigner with much talk of China, with which their identi-fication seemed very strong The emphasis now tends to be on what is local or sectional: our town, our company, our institute. A striking rhetorical change can be seen after the historic year 1989. The Party itself at the provincial level has become careless about observing the forms of its own national unity. One wonders how much of a force for holding the empire together it will be in the coming years. Local Party organizations may evolve quite rapidly into the guardians of local interests, able to negotiate with their counterparts elsewhere and to prevent destructive disorder following the decline of central power.

How long local Party structures might be able to play this role, which should have Mao turning violently enough to break the sides of his display case, is another question. In other countries one might doubt whether a highly centralized totalitarian party that, from its early years, has been all about a strong, unified state could really, like the Monkey King in the *Journey to the West*, pull a few hairs out of the back of its head, chew on them, blow a magic breath and change them into anything it pleases. But just as Monkey could turn himself into whatever he liked, single or multiplied, but could never get rid of his tail, so the Great, Glorious and Correct Communist Party of China can and will do anything to keep power locally and nationally except lose its authoritarianism. So while it remains hard to imagine that the Communist Party might become democratic, in whole or in part, we may yet see local Party structures as transitional centres of authority while something new – or else the old repackaged – emerges from a period of confusion.

To indulge in a little imagination, it may be that a kind of development has already started by which local wheeling and dealing, networking, the trading of favours and the formation of new patterns of economic and political power are creating new realities from the ground up. They could perhaps make it possible for the centralized Communist Party dictatorship to fade away as an effective institution without leaving the way open for chaos.

This is an optimistic hypothesis. It would require much political judgement and restraint to be shown by very many people. Somehow or other the military would have to be cut into the action locally, while also being assured of enough of the resources of the present Chinese empire to keep them in the style to which they aspire and to provide the expensive toys that armed forces expect. This is a lot to hope for. The alternative of strife between the military protectors of local interests as have-not regions struggle with the richer ones for their share of coastal wealth seems rather more likely. But compared with the very small chances of representative governments elected through universal suffrage ever gaining and keeping power over the whole empire, or of the present dictatorship managing to hold the show together for more than a decade or two, the prospects of grubby, unidealistic but practical arrangements getting China into the post-imperial era are rather less bleak.

If imperial absolutism gave way to a world of relative values, local deals, diversity, corruption, fragmented power and the death of a unified and uniting ideology, that would not be such a bad outcome, provided major civil wars could be avoided. At the very least it would make possible the emergence and consolidation of areas of *de facto* autonomy as the unitary Chinese state changes from a fairly solid reality to a hollow shell. The issue is not yet – except in Taiwan – whether provinces or other localities should become sovereign and independent states but whether they can be allowed actual control of their own destinies.

A lowering of the insistence on uniformity could also leave more room for the hitherto stunted growth of local linguistic and cultural autonomy. More and more radio and television broadcasts could be switched from the imperial lingua franca to the tongues that people actually speak in their daily lives, thus strengthening local identities and loyalties and preparing the way for the growth of the sorts of linguistically defined nationalisms that have given Europe its diversity and vigour in recent centuries. A Chinese federation or confederation in which no central authority could impose its will on broadcasting, print and recording could be a lively and creative part of the world. With all its limitations, the written code may yet carry some surprising and interesting messages; and if the heavy hand of the centre comes off radio, television and recording studios an amazing diversity of new oral and visual cultures could very quickly develop from the many local types of vernacular theatre, song and story. Even if new standardizations emerge, they will be produced by market forces rather than by political power.

Popular cultures still have a lot going for them that high culture has long been without. The interaction of these vernacular performance cultures with each other, with the high traditions associated with the state and with everything from the outside world that can make itself felt in China promises to be a creative and stimulating kind of chaos, provided that it is allowed to happen. Even under the Peking dictatorship some interesting things have been happening in film and popular music; and as the central tyranny gives ground to local despotisms some of the new bosses may see advantages for themselves in easing the boredom that goes with too much centrally determined, ideologically correct culture. It is unlikely that any of these local cultures will be free, but they could be in competition with each other, subject to different restrictions and alive. Even under the centralized dictatorship the different attitudes and interests of provincial Party secretaries have made for much greater diversity and openness since the late 1970s than was ever possible while Mao ruled: the centre no longer has enough hands to close all of the shutters all of the time or enough money to persuade outfits such as publishing houses fighting for economic survival to give the public what it ought to have instead of what it is willing to pay for.

It is not too fanciful to imagine Shanghai re-emerging as a great centre of print and electronic culture for the Chinese world or a politically weakened Peking becoming a hive of intellectual activity – a return under transformed conditions to the liveliness of the two cities in the 1920s and 1930s, when they made good use of the inability of any government to control the whole of China. The differences between local warlords in the south-west and the Nationalist government during the Japanese war allowed for some intellectual excitement even under primitive conditions in such remote cities as Kunming and Guilin. The most unpromising of provincial cities could turn out to be centres of excitement and new life. The infrastructure of broadcasting and recording studios, printing and publishing is all in place in dozens of provincial centres, ready for it to happen.

It won't be easy. All the obstacles to the emergence of new Chinese cultures from the ruins of the old that were mentioned in the previous chapter will still be there, as will the difficulty of turning potential into achievement. China has plenty of very talented people who in circumstances that provided the right mixture of stimulus, education, opportunity, freedom and competition could be doing memorable things. Meanwhile, as has been the common regret of foreigners who have spent more than a few weeks in China, remarkable abilities continue to be wasted and talents frittered away. Perhaps the lead will have to be taken by the rough and tough younger men and women who have somehow avoided being tamed by the cultural establishment, the dangerous characters who can still make it new. The Hunanese composer Tan Dun, reinventing ancient Chinese musical traditions in ways only possible after the changes in European music since the Second World War, and the stimulus-starved writers producing their instant reactions to whatever new foreign fad comes their way for their irreverent readers in China may point to possible growth points. So too may the inchoate rock-music business.

As long as art can be a threat to the dying order it is still alive. So too is the very necessary nihilism of the critic Liu Xiaobo's onslaughts on virtually everything that catches his eye, from Chinese high culture in its ancient and modern forms to the ignorance and silliness of any Westerner foolish enough to try to pat him on the head. If the dictatorship that arrested him in June 1989 could not suppress him despite his open attacks on all it stood for and had to release him a year and a half later, this suggests that the system itself is going soft – or else that it is incapable of managing a sustained, thorough repression. It can organize a bloodbath but has lost the degree of general acquiescence that once enabled it to turn the whole of society against even mildly heretical thinking. Its own officials no longer believe in it.

What is neither alive nor capable of resuscitation is the dreary official culture: the work of painters producing feeble imitations of a once great tradition or else dabbling in cautious 'modernism', like the output of nearly all the semi-liberal or frankly conservative middle-aged and older writers whose collected works gather dust on bookshop shelves because nobody reads them any longer. Nor is it likely that salvation will come from Taiwan, Hong Kong or Singapore – except that as Hong Kong people are drawn ever more closely into Chinese affairs their culture is becoming more tough-minded.

There is much more to hope for in the disaffected youth cultures of Peking – breakdancing through the end of an empire – in the film-makers who go on trying to make films that give their generation voices and images despite official stupidity and censorship, in the popular musicians who hit back with loud, aggressive noise and with words that (echoes of the sixties in other parts of the world) the elders can't understand because they can't hear them, and in the writers who do not care whose toes they tread on.

It is not because the nihilist phase promises great art that it is to be welcomed. Rather it is because only a far more thorough rejection of the tyranny of traditions than has yet happened in the twentieth century can clear enough empty space for future post-imperial Chinese cultures – or post-Chinese cultures, as they might be called – to find their own confused identities in global culture, in the Chinese world and in their own particular time and place. The limitations of the written character will remain: it will continue both to resist innovation and fail to convey the sound of living speech in all its variety.

Yet the character will be the only possible writing system through which anyone in the Chinese world will be able to communicate with all other literates within it. Much would be lost if standard Chinese were written only phonetically. It is, besides, inconceivable that any part of the Chinese world would replace characters with a phonetic script as the standard way of writing standard Chinese. Despite all the limitations of the script, and especially its inability to convey the flavours of the many different local Chinese languages, the cost of replacing it with each local language written phonetically would be far too high. Those already literate have a strong interest in perpetuating the writing system they know and love. They will never accept its replacement with mere letters, be they those of the Latin alphabet or of a Chinese one such as the syllabary used to teach children to read in Taiwan. Their resistance would be a thousand times stronger than the ferocity with which writers of English and French defend the archaisms in spelling that we feel, quite irrationally, to be part of the languages' very soul. Emotional considerations aside, much would go with it if the Chinese world's universal medium of written communication were to disappear, to be replaced by a Babel of mutually incomprehensible phonetic systems. But other gains would offset some of the cost of adopting phonetic scripts, especially if it were possible to keep characters as an inter-regional medium while writing local languages phonetically.

If, as seems inevitable, the characters stay, this could have some surprising consequences. As they become more and more restricted to being a vehicle for formal writing and the key to the shared high traditions of the past, their inadequacies for expressing the personal, informal, new, local and particular will further limit the possibilities of written expression. This apparent disaster, happening at the same time as the facilities for broadcasting and recording sounds and images become more widely available, could prompt a multiple flourishing of local and visual cultures. There has long been a great variety of local performing arts using local languages – ballad-singing, opera, storytelling, puppet theatre, comic arts and so on – from which new developments could come. Although written poetry is in a sorry state from one end of the Chinese world to the other, the possibilities of contemporary spoken poetry or rap in many vernaculars have hardly begun to be explored. The principal Chinese languages are all spoken by enough people to make local-language television and radio as practicable as in a medium-sized European country.

Letting the imagination run a little wild, it is within the bounds of the possible that as local loyalty leads to local linguistic self-assertion a multitude of invigorated bilingual oral cultures will develop – that is, cultures made by people who, as now, speak both a local language and an approximation to standard Chinese, which no more needs to be enforced by a single political authority than does world English. Even within the cramping restrictions of the written code there is room for some adaptation to hint at local languages, as has been done for Cantonese, with its own characters invented to represent, in such informal situations as comics, some of the features of the language that cannot be conveyed with conventional characters. Hong Kong writers thus already have the option of using a somewhat standard written Chinese (by Peking standards odd but comprehensible) or of being low and vulgar by resorting to characters, vocabulary and grammatical structures that evoke Cantonese speech for Cantonese speakers but look all wrong to northerners. The unwillingness of most Hong Kong writers who want to be taken seriously to write Cantonese characters indicates that there is still a powerful resistance to using local variants even when there are no political pressures forcing writers to write in standard written Chinese.

If the experience of medieval Europe is any guide to possible Chinese futures, we could see at the same time stronger local cultural identities, in which artists address their own people in their own tongue, and a continuing but reduced role for standardized written and spoken Chinese as a second language with which to communicate with the rest of the Chinese world. Here we need not be too discouraged by the neat, bloodless standard Chinese of Singapore. There is no danger whatsoever that mainland standard Chinese will ever become that boring and lifeless.

The best to be said about prospects for the visual arts is that the only way from here is up. The high tradition of painting that has been dying slowly since the fourteenth century and has resisted efforts to bring it back to life in recent times needs to be put at a certain distance if it is not to stifle living talent. The various attempts to respond to Western high art over the last century have yielded nothing really memorable and a surplus of imitation and pastiche. Late-twentieth-century professionally designed architecture has been a disaster, with very few exceptions, such as the wonderful soaring Bank of China tower in Hong Kong, that marvellously light, free and inappropriate assertion of the Chinese state's power over the territory – and I. M. Pei had to spend many years in the United States before he could create it. Yet vernacular architecture has dignity and style in many parts of China and can inspire the exceptions to the awfulness of new Chinese buildings. While the monuments of the People's Republic in Peking include some monsters from thirty years ago, as well as the standard international hotels and office blocks that every tawdry Third World capital has to have, the best of the city's new constructions are the public lavatories of the 1980s, which play traditional games with doorways and are broadly traditional in style as well as scent.

The look and quality of manufactured objects is another area where things can only get better. Bicycles do not have to go on being cheap copies of 1940s Raleighs for ever; nor do cassette radios have to look as cheap and nasty as they nearly all are. Time will no doubt help as manufacturers are more exposed to the outside world and the demands of overseas markets, and state monopoly industries lose their protection from competitors. Traditional handicrafts, especially cheap and everyday objects, are often very pleasing. 'Made in China' will not always be synonymous with shoddy. Sixty years ago, after all, Japanese goods were only for those who could afford nothing better, and in recent years some Taiwan and Hong Kong products have moved a long way upmarket. One area in which there have been some signs of life recently has been book covers. The partial opening up of publishing to market forces has resulted in plenty of trashy covers for trashy books, but it has also allowed some escape from the quiet good taste and discreet calligraphy that characterized most books before the mid-1980s. Hong Kong, and especially Taiwan, show something of the liveliness of Peking and Shanghai in the 1920s returning to the appearance of books. As in so many other areas, it is vigour that is needed now.

To borrow Roy Campbell's image, China needs some horses that are alive before worrying about snaffles and bits. The vigour is there, if only it can be allowed enough freedom in which to grow and to find its own discipline. This is unlikely to happen if the centre can reassert effective control. Market forces in coastal China could, however, permit local youth cultures to emerge that have the spirit of rebellion that was shown by the Red Guard generation but will not be put to the service of political violence. In some coastal cities this is already beginning to happen. It all promises rather more than do the self-regarding metropolitan intellectuals waiting to be discovered and taken up either by foreign scholars (in a useful symbiotic relationship: I discover you and make my name by making yours, while you get your visiting fellowship in the USA) or else by senior officials who might lift them into the world of the palace. There is more hope in a few rough, uncouth youngsters who don't give a damn and are not trying to please anyone.

Aesthetic problems are only a minor concern when we consider that the present deep crisis of the whole political and cultural structure could, if handled badly, lead to a tangle of civil wars, with regular army units involved and losses much worse than those of the Cultural Revolution. The fear of chaos and famine that the Peking authorities use to back up the case that their rule is the only alternative to catastrophe for all is a powerful argument against any challenge to the dictatorship. But are deadly chaos and stupefying tyranny the only options?

Of all the arguments for being hopeful none is stronger than the feeling that people with such admirable and likeable qualities and talents deserve a future that is better than the last two hundred years. Where they have been given a little freedom, as in the rural economy this last ten years, they have shown the ability to make good use of it. However bleak the prospects, there have to be ways of avoiding or limiting the disasters that appear to be ahead. It cannot be that the only escape from decrepit political traditions and the high culture associated with them will be into horrors at least as bad as those of the Great Leap and the Cultural Revolution. The future must offer something better than the choice between mental death, as minds are crushed by ageing traditionalists struggling to maintain their imperial monarchy, and liveliness to be bought at an incalculable price in physical losses if the empire breaks up through violence and the civil wars for which some are already preparing themselves in their thinking. There must be some alternative that is less grim.

Although representative democracy seems a very long way off, the evidence of how people coped with weak central authority in the Republican era suggests that a further weakening of Peking's power will not necessarily make life impossible. After all, it has been under strong central rule that such catastrophes as the all-controlling

Qin tyranny, the wars of the emperors Han Wu Di and Sui Yang
Di and the Great Leap Forward have been possible. It was political
division that brought about the polycentrism, variety and intellectual vigour of the Warring States, the Southern Song and the
Republic. In the twentieth century the internal cost of division has
been much lower than the toll exacted by a powerful and at times
deranged state. Only the remembered horrors of Japanese aggression
from 1931 to 1945 remain as a warning of the external costs of not
having a government strong enough to keep foreign armies off
Chinese soil. At a time when the main job of the centre's armed
forces seems to be crushing challenges from within the empire, and
there is no apparent foreign military threat, the need for a powerful
centralizing state is no longer self-evident. This could do a lot to
weaken inhibitions about loosening the bonds that tie provinces to
centre.

With weakened central control will develop both the necessity
and the means for different parts of the empire to make deals without
bothering to involve Peking and its officialdom. Chinese merchants
have had many centuries of experience in fixing and enforcing deals
without recourse to officials and courts and of using networks of
brokers, guarantors and other go-betweens to enable strangers to
do business with each other with confidence. In country towns and
villages local bosses have always emerged to impose a local tyranny
when the big tyranny of the state is weak, and such people have the
networks of contacts and the diplomatic skills to enable them to
achieve reasonably harmonious relationships with the other communities with which they have to deal. This is not the beginning
of local democracy, but it does show that Chinese cultures have
encoded in them patterns of social organization that might, if
allowed to do so, hold things together.

It seems to be a general problem in human history that the longer
a society is able to make any form of social organization work, the
harder it is to get out of it when it ceases to serve the general good.
A society can be locked into a self-perpetuating structure that, with
the passage of time, cares only for its own interests but has developed
such effective mechanisms for ensuring its own survival that it

becomes virtually impossible to be rid of it even when its deficiencies are obvious.

Profound change needs more than one drastic upheaval before it can happen; and successful change that actually makes most people's lives better is also inseparable from such unglamorous, expensive and long-term investments as an educational system that turns out large numbers of people who can read, think analytically and handle the discipline and technology of more advanced modes of production. England's success in developing a rather early form of industrial society gave it a dominating position in the eighteenth century and the first half of the nineteenth, but it lost the race with Germany in the twentieth. There was no follow-up to England's seventeenth-century upheavals, and education for the majority was never taken seriously. The catastrophic discontinuities in German development have both forced and enabled Germany to renew itself again and again, though German education did not prevent the rise of the Nazi regime. A revolution from above in the 1860s, followed by a revolution imposed from outside in 1945, enabled Japan to make the two fresh starts – once again, based on an educated people – that have turned it from a quaint archaism to a model for other nations' material futures in not much more than a century.

Both Germany's and Japan's transformations went much deeper than mere changes of government, as did those of Taiwan and South Korea, where first the imposition then, half a century later, the end of colonial rule (to be followed in Taiwan by a new quasi-colonial regime of mainland exiles) wreaked enough damage on traditional institutions larger than the family to clear the way for the two countries' quite untraditional economic performance of recent decades.

I have argued repeatedly in these pages that China has not yet had a clean enough break with the past to be able to escape from its tyranny. By the time the Qing began, in its last eight years, to dump ancient institutions and start on its version of a Meiji reform programme the dynasty was itself on the way down; and none of the governments of the Republic was ever able to control enough territory for enough time to push through thoroughgoing, nationwide changes. The Communists took over a countryside that was still being run much as it had been for centuries. Although the big industrialized cities and the main railway lines that connected them were a network of a kind of modernization, they could not dominate or transform most of the countryside. The urban bourgeoisie was too weak ever to become an effective independent political force. The highly educated few who had found out about how more successful societies were organized had but limited influence under the Republic. Although the Communists have made basic education much more widely available than ever before and have trained an army of petty officials, workers, technicians and other lower-level specialists to run their huge but archaic state and its outdated industry, most of China is still generations away from having a population well enough educated to cope with the continuous technological change of the future. The education system will need a very long time before it can nurture independent, critical thinking.

To continue the comparison with Japan, China did not push through a successful reform programme that went as far as the Meiji remaking of Japanese society till the 1950s, and it has yet to have the second shock. Nor has the educational gap between the two countries that was so apparent to Chinese students in Japan at the beginning of the twentieth century closed over the last ninety years. Lu Xun's longing for Chinese to be able to do things properly, as the Japanese did, is still largely unrealized. Although China's élite in any field can match the world's best, they are few in a vast population.

China, taken as a whole, seems ill-prepared for the challenges of the twenty-first century. But let us imagine coastal and big-city China, or parts of coastal China, trying to make a go of it without being dragged down by inland China. It becomes conceivable that these regions, some of which have much higher proportions of high-school and tertiary graduates than the national average, could pull themselves out of the mire and come through a second reform shock. Even here, however, educational standards outside the big cities are woefully low. In apparently promising provinces such as Guangdong, Fujian, Zhejiang and Jiangsu only about a quarter of the people had more than a primary education, according to the census of 1982. This suggests that going beyond the cheap-labour, low-tech capitalism of the 1980s is going to be a very hard job even where the conditions are best. This certainly applies to China considered as a whole, especially when we remember the drastic contraction of secondary schooling since the death of Mao. According to official statistics, the number of secondary students fell from 58 million in 1977 to under 39 million in 1990, though the age group was half again bigger by then. It also reflects the state's decision to concentrate secondary education in the cities and more or less abandon the attempt to give village children anything more than basic literacy, as Marianne Bastid has pointed out.

Should the big cities on or near the coast decide to look after their own interests, they are well placed to commit themselves further to the broken rim of prosperity around the Pacific. To some extent Canton, Amoy and other southern cities have begun to do so, but their achievements in the past decade have been less than they would have been if they had not been kept on a leash by Peking.

If whatever central regimes emerge in the next few decades are wise or weak enough to allow the big cities the latitude to rebuild their institutions and make better use of the wasted talents of their citizens, these cities could be islands of enlightenment. The ancient pattern of cities as strongholds of central state power through which the countryside is kept under control could conceivably give way to cities with the economic strength to buy themselves a measure of autonomy and the chance to invest in the education of their young. Such cities might even develop the reliable legal institutions without which modern urban economies cannot flourish.

The cities will have to be selfish and strong enough to avoid being swamped by tens or even hundreds of millions of displaced peasants who will pour into them to escape rural poverty. But it is in the long-term interests of the whole Chinese world that parts of it be allowed to get out from under the weight of the imperial bureaucracy and of rural backwardness, squalor and ignorance. In the short term the cities will not be able to do much to ease the sufferings of the most wretched parts of the interior. Only if they are able to flourish will they be able to start spreading prosperity and enlightenment along the highways and waterways into parts of the countryside. If, on the other hand, the imperial state is able to hold the cities down indefinitely, the prospects of interior, upland China ever breaking out of its secular poverty and backwardness are bleak.

Optimism would see ways by which cities could win autonomy without having to fight civil wars. The centre is not always going to be able to send in the troops when it is provoked by city dwellers. We have to hope against experience that the empire's central power will decline gracefully and that the assertion of local claims to autonomy will be so discreet that the reality of it will be achieved while everyone pretends nothing has happened, thus avoiding the necessity for blood in the gutters. Peking's continuing threats to crush Taiwan's possible self-determination do not give grounds for much hope that formal secession may be peacfully won.

Even though the empire seems more likely to end with a lot of bangs than with a quiet whimper, it is just possible that the horrifying costs of unlimited civil war between nuclear-armed rivals will be a strong enough deterrent to prevent any grouping from taking up a position that compels others to use force. Understandings are more likely to be reached between Han Chinese regions and the centre than between the subject nations that do not think of themselves as Chinese and any imaginable Chinese central government. A Peking regime wise enough to make a deal with the present Dalai Lama that would spare Tibet and China more bloodshed is one that is hard to foresee, as is one that agreed to allow Uighurs self-determination. But if renewed colonial wars seem likely to afflict the western half of the empire before many more years have passed, they could also be an argument for the peaceful reordering of the Han Chinese provinces. A state with its military resources stretched in Tibet and Turkestan will probably be reluctant to use force in the coastal provinces, provided that the challenges to its authority are not too blatant and the outward forms of national sovereignty are observed.

Tanks in the streets are bad for foreign investment and only deepen local hostility to the centre even if they succeed in crushing opposition in the short term, as can be seen from the profound alienation of the citizens of Peking. Although the danger of civil war will remain a very serious one, the chances of some cities and their surroundings getting away with ever more *de facto* autonomy and using it to bring about change are not hopelessly bad. Untidy compromises with the centre, by which the cities agree to hand over a certain amount of revenue in exchange for being left to their own devices, do not seem entirely improbable. Open demands for local representative government seem less likely to be met.

Whether or not future central governments label themselves communist is not all that important to the prospects for coastal China. What seems reasonably certain is that they will represent parts of the military and other national power systems discussed in chapter 3. The unpredictable and vital question is whether these future regimes will see themselves as having more to gain from preventing the coastal provinces from getting too far ahead of the backward interior than from allowing them to go their own way.

It is only by looking at possible outcomes for coastal China that one can see some grounds for optimism. For the rest of the Chinese empire it is hard to see solutions under the present dictatorship or under any conceivable alternative arrangements. China is so littered with nuclear explosives, both literal and metaphorical, that the country is at any time only a short time away from going up. Nobody can deal with the underlying problems of inner China, and it may only be a matter of time before the primitive rebellion that on a small scale is endemic in some regions gets out of control, setting off all sorts of other explosions.

History's tyranny is not dead yet; and the history of tyranny still has many more chapters to be written. The unravelling of the Chinese empire may be quick or slow. It will certainly involve much suffering, will liberate both constructive and destructive forces and will change the world. The world might do well to start thinking about how it will cope with the end of yet another apparent certainty.

INDEX